this life at play

'A sparkling, unputdownable memoir by a towering literary and theatrical genius.'

– AMITAV GHOSH

'This is an absolutely fascinating memoir about a boy from a small town who sets out to make the world his oyster. Ambition, hard work, an insatiable hunger for knowledge and experience all come together and create an auspicious constellation in this eager life, but what truly propels the young man to eminence as the playwright of our century is his prodigious talent. With his customary candour, Girish Karnad tells the story of his remarkable life, a life lived so richly and so well. But this is also the story of how a young generation in a newly independent nation forged a language in the arts that challenged tradition and the status quo, that sought to understand and inhabit modernity in their terms. Read this book not just for the story of an exceptional writer but as a manifesto for the roots of our contemporary culture.'

– ARSHIA SATTAR

'An autobiography as vividly theatrical as any of this titan's works, seemingly unfolding not on paper but within the confines of a proscenium arch.'

– BARADWAJ RANGAN

'It reads like he is talking to you. No scores being settled, no "points" being made. Just recalling, with laughter behind every line, reflection behind every other and, between passages, some sadness. Karnad at his captivating best.'

– GOPALKRISHNA GANDHI

'*This Life at Play* is, among many things, a mesmerizing and magical account of a childhood in Sirsi that decisively shaped Girish Karnad – the man and the writer. Read with delight his uninhibited enjoyment of a multicultural world, its theatrical traditions, and understand how these nurtured his extraordinary talent. I was stunned by the vividness and intimacy of the account of his student years in Dharwad. It was exposure to ideas and ideals during this time that gave him the sense of direction, principled and unflinching, which marked his leadership in every sphere of our cultural life and as a public intellectual.'

– MARIA AURORA COUTO

'What an extraordinary man. What an extraordinary life. A reminder of a bygone era, when being a good human being meant as much as being a public figure.'

– NAGESH KUKUNOOR

'As writer, actor, director, and administrator, Girish Karnad made indelible contributions to the cultural history of modern India. Now in this warm, witty, and deeply insightful memoir, so deftly translated into English by Srinath Perur, he has given us a posthumous parting gift to cherish. I read it at one sitting, enchanted and educated by its contents.'

– RAMACHANDRA GUHA

'A life story is only as rich as the life it records. This life, says the title, is at play. But don't let the implied lightness of that mislead you. In reality, Girish Karnad's memoirs are dense with people, places, events, enquiry, insight, observation and, above all, creative expression that progresses from poetry to film-making to acting, with theatre as the supreme constant. The only lightness here is in the telling, in Karnad's candid, irony-tinged observation of himself as he moves from the village of Sirsi to Dharwad to Bombay to Oxford and back.'

– SHANTA GOKHALE

'A candid and intimate account of a life rich in achievements and friendships, with fascinating glimpses of the making of a writer.'

– SHASHI DESHPANDE

'The late Girish Karnad was a towering figure, a singularly original creative spirit, powerful in his ideas, mesmerizing in his presence, who left a huge mark on Indian cinema and theatre. By turns humorous and moving, and always insightful, *This Life at Play* reminds us of the life and times of one of our greatest national treasures, and complements his formidable artistic oeuvre.'

– SHASHI THAROOR

this life at play

MEMOIRS

girish karnad

Translated from the Kannada by
GIRISH KARNAD and SRINATH PERUR

FOURTH ESTATE • *New Delhi*

First published in hardback by Fourth Estate 2021
An imprint of HarperCollins *Publishers*
4th Floor, Tower A, Building No. 10, Phase II, DLF Cyber City,
Gurugram, Haryana – 122002
www.harpercollins.co.in

This edition published in India by Fourth Estate 2022

2 4 6 8 10 9 7 5 3 1

P-ISBN: 978-93-5489-584-5
E-ISBN: 978-93-9032-781-2

Typeset in 11.5/15.2 Arno Pro at
Manipal Technologies Limited, Manipal

Printed and bound at
Thomson Press (India) Ltd

MIX
Paper
FSC FSC® C010615

This book is produced from independently certified FSC® paper
to ensure responsible forest management.

Contents

Dharwad, 1973

Aayi (my mother), Bappa (my father) and I were having lunch. My first film *Samskara* had won the President's Gold Medal. My second, *Vamsha Vriksha,* had had a successful run and won the National Award for best direction. My latest film *Kaadu* was in the final stages of production. I was a Sangeet Natak Akademi awardee. And I had just been named the director of the Film and Television Institute of India. The air at home was thick with self-congratulation.

Then Aayi looked at Bappa and said, 'And we had thought of not having him.'

Bappa went red in the face. After some stammering, he managed to say, 'That was all your idea, not mine. Why bring this up now?' and hid his face in the plate in front of him.

I had to know more. I asked Aayi, and she explained: 'I had three children already when I became pregnant with you. I thought that was enough, so we went to a doctor in Poona named Madhumalati Gune.'

'And?'

'She had said she would be at the clinic, but she wasn't. We waited an hour and returned.'

'And then?'

'And then, nothing. We never went back.'

I was stunned. I was then thirty-five years old. Still, I grew faint at the possibility that the world could have gone on without me in it. For a while, I sat there unaware of my surroundings, considering the idea of my non-existence. A thought struck me. With some bewilderment, I asked about my younger sister: 'Then, what about Leena ... ?'

Aayi said, somewhat coyly, 'Oh, we had stopped thinking of all that by then.' She burst out laughing. Bappa remained engrossed in the contents of his plate.

Had the doctor arrived at the clinic as promised, these memoirs and their narrator would not have existed. So, I dedicate this autobiography to the memory of the person who made all this possible: Dr Madhumalati Gune.

Girish Karnad
Bangalore, 19 May 2011

1

PRAK

Prelude

My mother's name was Krishnabai. Krishnabai Mankikar. But she was 'Kuttabai' to the elders in the family and became 'Kuttakka' to those younger than her. In 1984, when she was eighty-two, my sister-in-law, Sunanda, persuaded her to write her autobiography. It is about thirty pages long, written in Konkani, jotted down in an old diary of my father's, in spaces left blank after he had scribbled his daily accounts. Until we read that narrative, my siblings and I had struggled to come to terms with the many anxieties and nightmares that had disturbed our childhood nights. Her autobiography helped resolve these fears by bringing them out into the open.

Kuttabai was born in Hubli in 1902, but while still a child, moved to Poona with her father, who worked for the Madras & Southern Maratha Railway. At the time, Poona sizzled with social and artistic ferment. The Marathi language was confronting the challenges of modernity with a literature that explored new areas of social experience and an energetic journalism that demanded that Maharashtrian society prepare itself for independence. Then there was Marathi theatre, at its peak commercially, with actors like Bal Gandharva and Keshavrao Bhosale, but also being hailed by the elite as representing the essence of Marathi culture. Kuttabai was a voracious reader, and these years in Poona were some of the happiest in her life. What excited her most were the opportunities the city held out for education. Maharashtra had a vigorous movement for women's education, led by missionaries, social reformers and the government, and the opportunities opening up were unthinkable a generation ago. 'One Sarlabai Nayak had even got an MA,' she remembers seventy-five years later.

But when she was nine, and in the third Marathi standard, her father was suddenly transferred to a small town named Gadag, where Kuttabai faced the first of many disappointments that were to confront her over the next few years. The language of instruction in Gadag was Kannada, which she had to start learning from scratch, and its literature had not yet begun to emerge from its medieval moorings. In fact, those enamoured with the Marathi milieu openly sneered at Kannada culture as backward. Gadag was socially conservative and there were no facilities for educating girls.

She writes: 'I went to my headmistress and wept. "I don't want to go to Gadag," I said. "I want to learn a lot and become a BA. There is apparently nothing there except Kannada." The headmistress and her sister, who taught in Huzurpaga [a well-known school for girls], came to our house together and pleaded with my father: "Krishni is hungry for education. Leave her behind. She can stay at the Huzurpaga hostel. You don't have to spend anything on her education. The government will bear all the expenses of her boarding and lodging." But my parents would not agree.'

The fear was that, if left behind on her own, she would be converted to Christianity. So Kuttabai had to move to Gadag and join a Kannada school in which she was the only girl in class. Nearly half a century later, tears welled up in her eyes as she recounted the event to me.

When she came of age, Kuttabai was still unmarried. And the family, after desperate attempts at concealing this shameful fact from relatives and neighbours, and pretending from month to month that everything was normal, ultimately found a boy for her from the Gokarn family.

She was married. A son was born to her: Bhalchandra. And within a couple of years, her husband died of anaemia and malaria. Her parents-in-law did not bother to visit her. She writes: 'Except for the jewellery given to me by my father, I did not possess a penny. There was a life insurance policy, but that too had lapsed, as no one had bothered to pay the instalments.'

Aayi

Thus, Krishnabai and her infant son came back to Gadag to live with her parents. She had no future to look forward to.

All this was – and continues to be – the common fate of widows from the more deprived sections of the middle class in India. Fortunately, by the 1920s, the Chitrapur Saraswat Brahmin community had abandoned the custom of shaving their widows' heads, so Kuttabai's long hair, which when loosened tumbled down to her knees, was spared the barber's scissors.

Even in this desperate situation, Kuttabai was determined to educate herself. She wanted to achieve something of significance in her life and, if possible, even become a doctor. Though Gadag was in the backwoods of the Bombay state, Poona and Bombay were no more than a day's journey away by train. But no one in her family had the inclination or the time to accompany her to either of these cities and enrol her in an educational institution.

The one person who came to her help at this moment was Mangesh Rao Sashittal, her elder sister Shanta's husband, who was a mamlatdar – a revenue official in government service. First in Haveri and then in Dharwad, his house was like a huge orphanage. Apart from his own seven offspring, he and his wife sheltered several orphaned children, often only distantly related.

Mangesh Rao was obsessed with ensuring that this entire brood was properly educated and cultured. A teacher would arrive early in the morning to provide tuition in Sanskrit. Then again, even as the children reached home from school in the evening, another teacher would present himself at the doorstep. Besides, Mangesh Rao himself was a keen and enthusiastic teacher who loved to spend his hours at home revising their lessons. This hectic training schedule helped Kuttabai educate herself. She writes: 'I sat down to study with the children. Since I loved studying, I reached the English class-four level within five or six months. Algebra, fractions, time-work-and-speed, etc. There was a subject called Sanskrit translation, which I mastered. And I decided to appear for matriculation from home. In those days, it was enough to be a matriculate to get admission to the medical college and I was desperate to become a doctor.'

But Mangesh Rao was transferred to Bailhongal, virtually a large village with no educational facilities whatsoever. Again, Kuttabai had to move with some of the youngsters to a temporary arrangement in Dharwad.

Kuttabai narrates: 'My brother-in-law often needed to visit Belgaum for his work in the courts. On those visits, he would stay with a relative of ours, Dr [Raghunath] Karnad. While there, he saw the nurses working in the hospital and had the brainwave of sending me there to train as one. He asked the doctor whether I could be admitted to the nursing course. The doctor agreed. I protested that I wanted to study medicine and become a doctor. But my brother-in-law insisted. He argued that I could continue my studies while training to be a nurse and appear for the exams. He even said he would find someone to tutor me.

'He got me admitted to a year's midwifery course and went away. In our entire family, he was the only person willing to help me, so I had no choice but to listen to him. I had neither money nor jewellery. Mother had given a bori necklace, a gold bandi, and todas for my wrists weighing four or five tolas. Except for the bori necklace, I have no idea where the rest of the jewellery disappeared. At the time of my wedding, my mother-in-law had given me her traditional putali necklace, which reached down to the stomach. But she took it back with her when she returned home. I paid no attention to all that at the time.

'When I joined the nursing course in Belgaum, the problem of accommodation came up. I used to get a scholarship of twenty rupees per month. The hospital had quarters only for the head nurse. The doctor said I could stay in his house. I had no alternative but to accept his offer. The doctor's wife suffered from some disease and was chronically bedridden. No bathing. No getting up or moving about. Next to her was a stool on which food was served. They had a cook and a nurse to look after her.

'The doctor was handsome. Nearly six feet tall. Curly hair. Fair-complexioned. With a gait that would attract anyone. A figure that was neither fat nor thin. He wore a hat to the hospital, as a result of which people often mistook him for an Anglo-Indian. He was thirty-four or thirty-five then. The doctor asked me if I had considered "remarriage" and the thought started burrowing into my brain. I was all of twenty-two then.'

Thus began Kuttabai's five years in the doctor's house, the 'five years' that lacerated me and my siblings during our teenage years. It is true they ultimately got married. But what was the nature of their relationship during these five years? Could it have been sexual? The very thought that our mother might have lived in sin with a married man – never mind that it was our father – was painful in the extreme. When we were in our teens, if I even remotely suggested that they may have occasionally slept together, my sisters would fly into a rage or burst into tears. Kuttabai's autobiography gave forthright answers to our obsessive worries and did much to calm our anxieties, although by then we had decided it was more mature to pretend that history did not matter.

What continues to intrigue and amaze me, however, is the reasoning by which Mangesh Rao casually dumped a beautiful young widow into the arms of a thirty-five-year-old married man and disappeared. What norms of Hindu society back then could have provided this pillar of the community with a justification for this most unusual action? He could not have assumed that the situation would automatically lead to marriage, as indeed it didn't. Could he have assumed that the sense of propriety and restraint expected of members of the Saraswat Brahmin society would keep these two young people on the straight and narrow path? Or did he just decide that he had a hopeless situation on his hands, that the widow had no future and he couldn't go on wasting his time supporting her? Whatever the case, Mangesh Rao turned out to be the purana purusha – the ancient sage – of our family.

For five years, the doctor did nothing to follow up on his proposal. 'Bigamy was not illegal in those days. There were several men in Maharashtra who had four or five wives. But the doctor was scared of public opinion,' says Kuttabai, without explaining what his fears were. It is evident, however, that whatever held him back was not so much the thought of bigamy as the fear of precipitating a scandal by marrying a widow.

She finished her nursing course in three years and began hunting for a job. The civil surgeon in Belgaum offered to have her sent to London if she would, in the meantime, stay in his house and look after his ill wife. She did not dare refuse directly, but said her family didn't approve. She travelled alone to distant Bangalore to seek employment at a large hospital, but was rejected because her English was not up to the standards required by the Anglo-Indian staff there. This going out in search of a job only to return empty-handed to Belgaum, back to the shelter provided by the doctor, became the recurrent motif of her life.

'Our intimacy had grown. But I had begun to find the public sniping impossible to bear. Then in 1928, the doctor was transferred to the civil hospital in Dharwad. He told me that the position of a staff nurse was vacant there, and that I should apply for it. I thus joined the Dharwad civil hospital. Another year passed and he still showed no inclination to proceed any further. It was then that I decided to take the lead.

'I confronted him with the fact that I had suffered enough poisonous gossip for his sake and demanded to know if he was now going to let me down halfway down the road. I insisted that he should get himself transferred to another posting [presumably so remote that the scandal of widow remarriage would not catch up with them], where we could move after our marriage.'

The doctor's reluctance was hardly to be wondered at. Saraswat Brahmin society is not known for encouraging its children to be adventurous, the emphasis in their upbringing being always on playing safe. The doctor was born in a large, not very well-to-do family, and in his childhood, had been shunted from one cousin's home to another. He shrank from the very idea of a risky move. All he had aspired to in his life was stability – not tranquillity, but simply distance from any possibility of disturbance. He had loved history as a subject, but had gone into medicine because there were special scholarships to encourage Indian students to enter that discipline. And even there, he had entered government service at the earliest opportunity because of the security of a regular salary. He took up autopsy as his specialization, since that brought in further emoluments, and was good enough at it to be awarded the title of 'Rao Saheb' by the government. But while he admired and gave us glowing accounts of his more 'brilliant' colleagues who went abroad and made a name for themselves, it never occurred to him to exploit the new opportunities to better his own position. The principle he drummed into us, his children, emphasized the necessity for caution at every step and the advantages of not being too ambitious. 'Present pleasures,' he repeatedly cautioned us, in English, 'need to be sacrificed for future comforts.' One should be like everyone else. One should live like everyone else. It was folly to attempt to stand out. The only adventure he risked in his entire life was to marry a widow. And even there, the credit went indubitably to her.

Ultimately, they travelled to Bombay separately, to a Mr Vaidya who used to perform weddings according to Vedic rituals. He had arranged for everything, including the mangalsutra. 'There,' she writes with an almost audible sigh, 'at long last, we got married with the fire as the witness. Only I know the mental torture I had endured during those five or six years.'

Within a page of recording this event, Krishnabai's autobiography comes to an abrupt end. When questioned, she would laugh and say, 'What more was there to say? You all arrived one after another. Samsar!'

Later on, Aayi would often say that, except for these difficult years, she had a remarkably happy life. She was surrounded by her children, grandchildren, dependents, and servants who soon turned into members of the family. She lived zestfully, travelling around the world, making friends, writing Konkani programmes for All India Radio, Dharwad. She egged her children on to spurn her husband's philosophy of playing it safe, and never quite forgave her daughters for becoming housewives when every opportunity to strike out was offered to them on a platter. She was past ninety when she sat on the pavement in the hot sun holding a placard as part of a public demonstration in support of the Narmada Bachao Andolan.

When I was director of the Film and Television Institute of India (FTII) in Poona, and used the office jeep for moving around in the city, she declared that, as the mother of the institute's director, she didn't like being seen in a jeep and insisted on using only the imported limousine. And I was always aware that she probably felt she would have made a better director.

But she never stopped ruing that as herself, rather than as my father's wife or as our mother, she had nothing she could claim as her own achievement. She was not an unhappy person, but she remained discontented. One of the several drafts of her autobiography starts with the paragraph: 'Sometimes one gets tired of this lonely life. I have reached this age now, but have been of no particular use to anyone. Standing here on the brink of my seventy-ninth year and looking back, I see nothing but the mistakes I have made. I have been unsuccessful since my childhood [in everything]. Nothing that I desired has been achieved.' And elsewhere: 'Often, when anger or immense sadness overwhelms my mind, I feel I should write down my thoughts. I could not fulfil any desire of mine in my life. I wanted to study a lot and become a BA or an MA, to learn to sing and to play the harmonium, to read a lot and so on. Except for the occupation of reading, nothing was achieved.'

When I was discussing my play *Naga-Mandala* with the sociologist Veena Das, I summed up the denouement with the traditional words: 'And then Rani gets back her husband and her child and lives happily ever after.' Veena shot back: 'No, no, she drowns her individuality in her domesticity and becomes a nothing.' I suspect Krishnabai would have agreed.

Krishnabai had a temper, and she told me herself that, while Bhalchandra lived with the Sashittal family in Dharwad, she had an ongoing battle with Mangesh Rao about her son's position in the midst of his family. There were nearly fifteen children living under one roof, and strife must have been a recurrent occurrence. But in her own silent fashion, she remained grateful to them for what they had done for her. When her sister Shanta was bedridden during the last few months of her life, her children were spread all over India and a tenant was refusing to vacate her Dharwad house. My parents took her to their congested house in Sirsi and tended to her. We, the progeny of her husband's incomprehensible gesture, were around Shanta when she died.

A good eighty years after these events, my daughter Shalmali too lived with her boyfriend for five years before marrying him. By then, it had become an accepted part of the lifestyle of educated young women to live with their boyfriends before deciding whether to get married. It is true that when these modern women surrounded my mother to gush, 'You were so courageous! We are so proud of you! You are our heroine!' Aayi accepted the adulation with unconcealed delight.

But from the moment they got married, the doctor and Krishnabai launched on the enterprise of wiping out the smallest sign, the remotest memory, of her history prior to their marriage. I need not mention that 'Krishnabai Gokarn' became 'Krishnabai Karnad', since she would have had to experience that transformation even if she had been 'Krishnabai Mankikar'. Our laws themselves take the initiative in wiping out the premarital life of a young woman. After their wedding, the doctor got himself transferred from Dharwad to the remote town of Bagalkot, where they could start life afresh and be sure that the past was firmly kept out. The nursing certificates of Krishnabai Gokarn remained unframed, and were rolled up and locked in dusty old trunks. Notebooks and the books which carried her name lost their front pages or vanished entirely. Thus these two, who had shown the courage to challenge Hindu orthodoxy and shake contemporary society to its core, acted as if it was they who were the guilty party and attempted to slink away to escape the eyes of the public. In this great plan to wipe out the past, the doctor's first wife naturally vanished without a trace. Neither I nor any of my siblings ever heard our parents mention her.

But in a grateful acknowledgement of the fact that it was the social revolution initiated by the Arya Samaj that had made it possible for my parents to get married at all – Mr Vaidya, who had organized their marriage, was a follower of the Arya Samaj – a photograph of the founder, Swami Dayanand Saraswati, mounted on a black velvet background intricately embroidered by Krishnabai in gold silk threads and decorated with seashells, was installed in our gods' room. It hung there mutely through our childhood, with no explanation as to what it was doing there.

Within three years of their marriage, the children started arriving – Vasant first, then Prema, myself and Leena. By the time I was five or six, my brother Bhalchandra too had given up the surname 'Gokarn' to adopt 'Karnad' and, since officially one had to have a patronymic, 'Bhalchandra Atmaram Gokarn' had transformed himself into 'Bhalchandra Raghunath Karnad', as a result of which we grew up believing him to be our natural brother.

In 1943, when I was just over four, Bappa, who was working in Sassoon Hospital in Poona, retired. But the Second World War was at its height and young doctors were in demand at the front. He was offered an extension of service by the government. Unsurprisingly, despite fierce opposition from Aayi who wanted him to use the immense goodwill he had garnered in Poona to start a private practice, he accepted the extension of half a dozen years and moved to Sirsi, a remote jungle outpost situated in the heart of the Western Ghats. Sirsi had no electricity, was infested with malaria, and was generally known as a punishment posting.

But the history which my parents had hoped to bury safely behind them continued to pursue us children even in those wilds, whispering, winking its eyes, swirling around us in various guises. Since our parents never took us into confidence about their past, our childhoods were made miserable by the nightmare that some mysterious, unbearable happening, something that needed to be concealed from us as well as from the prying eyes of our neighbours, was at the heart of their relationship.

Aayi with Vasant, Prema and me

One day, as I passed a group of women sitting gossiping in a courtyard, a woman asked me, 'Why is your father so much older than your mother?' and those around her suppressed their smirks with such obvious glee that the question sprouted all kinds of imaginary horns and fangs. Prema was informed by a girl her own age, who had been employed to look after my younger sister, that Bhalchandra was not her natural brother but a stepbrother. She apparently cried for days in a corner, hiding her face. A boy in my class gravely informed me, 'My grandmother knows all the facts and she told me herself. When your mother was getting married the first time, the mangalsutra in her hand turned into a live snake. When she dropped it to the floor, it bit the bridegroom and disappeared. He died instantly.' For nights thereafter, I was planning the various tortures I would inflict on him, chopping him into little pieces limb by limb. But who was there to turn to?

In 1948, Bappa finally retired from active practice. In 1952, we moved to Dharwad, where we came to live in Saraswatpur, a residential area occupied exclusively by Saraswat Brahmin families, where everybody knew everyone else's family history. I asked a boy slightly older than me about mine. He gave me the straight facts in five minutes and I heaved a sigh of relief. I was fourteen then!

Instead of making such an effort to blind us to our history, if our parents had told us the plain truth, we children would have had less tortured childhoods.

In the stormy epic of my mother's married life, the person who was relentlessly tossed about but somehow managed to survive was my eldest brother, Bhalchandra. He was a good-looking man. My wife, Saraswathy – then my fiancée – remembers that when he was to meet her in New York, she had asked how she could recognize him, and he had replied, 'I look like Girish – only more handsome.' He was intelligent, had a brilliant academic career, and was artistically gifted – he painted and could play the sitar. He was hungry for affection and eager to return it in equal measure. He was immensely energetic, and you only had to suggest an activity for him to be on his feet ready to embark upon it. When he visited us in Sirsi, this officer of the Indian Railway Service (IRS) was up and ready every morning to draw water from the well in our backyard and fill the huge metal pots in our bathroom. His arrival on these holidays was awaited by us with great anticipation and treated as a kind of celebration. Leena, my younger sister, never tired of declaring that he was her model for an ideal husband.

He was also sensitive. I remember reading a letter he had written to Aayi when he first saw her in Dharwad after she was married. 'On that day, for the first time, I saw you with kumkum on your forehead. You were wearing flowers in your hair and there was a mangalsutra around your neck. Your face glowed with happiness. Do you know how beautiful you looked that day...' and so on. He had a most relaxed relationship with Bappa. They would sit and chat, or even lounge around together in silence, for hours, without any strain. But his relationship with Aayi remained fraught.

One day, sometime in the seventies when he was about fifty-five, I found lying open on the table a letter he had written to Aayi. By then, she had stopped being secretive or even careful about these letters. This one said, 'You have never considered me your son.' I asked her why he should say that, and her explanation provided a clue to the anguish that ran through his life.

When Bappa and Aayi were in Bagalkot immediately after th[illegible] Bhalchandra had come to visit them during his school vacation. One of the nurses asked Aayi who the boy was. Aayi was lost for words. How was she to fit in a boy of eleven into a marriage that was only a few months old? 'My nephew,' she had said, with Bhalchandra listening. She smiled wanly when she recounted this: 'It happened forty years ago. He is over fifty now, and yet he won't forget it. What can I say?'

When I think of Bhalchandra's life, I am amazed at his ability to sustain his ebullience through the tribulations he had to face. He had lost his father in his infancy, and had been brought up by a mother who was no helpless widow, inclined to sit in a corner counting beads, blaming her stars for her misfortunes. She was ambitious and restless, eager to reshape her life, quick to flare up, and given to intemperate responses.

While she was in Belgaum, he lived in the house of the venerable Mangesh Rao Sashittal in Dharwad, along with some fifteen other children, and it is not difficult to imagine the reports he must have received about his mother, the snide remarks and malicious thrusts he would have had to tolerate.

But fortunately for him, around this time a Rao Bahadur Deo Rao Koppikar, one of the respected residents of Saraswatpur, brought to Dharwad as his third wife an almost entirely illiterate girl from the Gokarn family named Tarabai. She was Bhalchandra's aunt. Deo Rao took pains to educate her, even sending her to the medical college in Poona. He also sent for her two younger brothers from Gokarna and settled them in a wing of their house in Saraswatpur. One of them joined the forest service, the other set up shop as a tailor. As a result of this relationship with the Gokarn family, Deo Rao got involved with Bhalchandra as well and paid for his education in the engineering college at Poona. This development allowed Bhalchandra a greater proximity to his father's family.

Sometime in the early 1940s, Bappa called Bhalchandra aside and said, 'I am growing old, and I have become the father of these four children in my advanced years. You are their elder brother. Should anything happen to me, you have to accept the responsibility of looking after them.' More importantly, he suggested that Bhalchandra could give up the surname Gokarn, take on Karnad as his family name and become a part of the family. According to the history we were nurtured on, Bhalchandra acceded to the suggestion without demur and officially became 'Bhalchandra Karnad'.

Bhalchandra's own reaction to the episode is as follows: 'When Bappa asked me, I was deeply shocked. I didn't know how to react and went to Deo Rao for his advice. He consoled me with the words, "How does a change of name really matter? Dr Karnad has asked you in all affection to be one of his own and there is no harm in agreeing. What advantage is there in insisting on your separateness?" So I agreed to the change of nomenclature despite the fact that I was most reluctant. I have never fully accepted that I am a Karnad.' He added: 'Bappa always treated me with immense love and affection, but he did not pay for my education in Poona. That expense was borne by Deo Rao.'

Thinking back, it is hard to see what other advice Deo Rao could have given the young man. Even if he were not personally enthusiastic about the change of surname, he could scarcely have risked offending a prominent member of the tiny Saraswat community, a decorated government servant like Dr Karnad, by recommending open defiance. His advice was the only one possible under the social circumstances of the day.

Nor was it a society that took seriously the notion that a young man of twenty-three may have ideas of his own about his identity. It was imperative that he fit in. And it must be admitted that it was not like Bhalchandra to stand up in defiance. He was not a person to welcome a head-on conflict with anyone, or even cause embarrassment. In that sense, he was more like Bappa than Aayi.

Bhalchandra had by then graduated with distinction from the engineering college. Yet he spurned Aayi's repeated pleas to start a private civil engineering practice of his own and entered the IRS, accepting Bappa's advice that it was better to be safe than sorry. He married Suman, the beautiful daughter of Narayan Rao Koppikar, a prominent lawyer in Dharwad, and went to serve in the North Eastern Railway.

So the family life of the Karnads seemed to have attained the quietude, if not the tranquillity that Bappa had always argued was the prime goal of life.

But when Bhalchandra's children grew up and started visiting Dharwad during their vacations, they spent most of their days, as is the norm in Indian families, with their mother's parents, Lalita and Narayan Rao Koppikar. They were emotionally closer to them than to Aayi and Bappa. And questions began to be raised in low voices: Why had Bhalchandra changed his surname? Had he agreed to it voluntarily or was he in some way compelled by Bappa to do so? This was not a matter of any consequence for us Karnads since we had been brought up to believe that Bhalchandra was our natural brother. There had never been the slightest hint from Bhalchandra that he was conflicted about this issue. But the question continued to be asked, with increasing frequency if never directly, and became a source of annoyance.

The almost traditionally ordained tension which defined the relationship between Aayi and Bhalchandra's mother-in-law Lalita, began to grow with these queries. Aayi was convinced that Lalita had fed her grandchildren lurid accounts of Bhalchandra's deprived childhood. And she had no doubt that the two Gokarn brothers ensconced in the Deo Rao household – uncles of Bhalchandra and her erstwhile brothers-in-law – were active with their own shenanigans. (Bappa was supremely indifferent to these goings-on.)

That Aayi was right to be wary of the Gokarn brothers was confirmed many years later, and in a rather unexpected manner. Sometime in the 1990s, Nileema, Bhalchandra's daughter, decided she needed her birth certificate. Since she was abroad, I applied for a copy on her behalf. The copy I received stunned me. It mentioned the father's name as Bhalchandra

Bhalchandra, his wife Suman, their baby Bharat and his father-in-law Narayan Rao Koppikar photographed with Bappa, Aayi and us children

Atmaram Gokarn rather than Bhalchandra Raghunath Karnad. It took some investigation to unravel the facts. When Suman, Bhalchandra's wife, had come to her parents in Dharwad to deliver her child, she was attended to, naturally, by Bhalchandra's aunt Tarabai, who was the doctor in the family. One of the two Gokarns had gone to register the birth with the municipal corporation and had presumably decided that Bhalchandra's ditching of his family name was unacceptable to him. He had simply ignored the Karnad part of the tale and recorded the birth as an event in the Gokarn family. And for four decades, his mischief lay hidden in the municipal files, cocking a snook at the Karnads.

This was aggravating but not a cause for any major upset. Bhalchandra applied to get the certificate corrected and we assumed that was the end of the matter. His children were by now spread around the world as Karnads and had themselves had children to whom a change of family name two generations ago would be an insignificant event in a largely forgotten past. But Indian families have an immense capacity for keeping grievances alive.

In 1978, Bappa expired at my house in Dharwad at the age of ninety. Both Bhalchandra and Vasant rushed down from Bombay to be with us. Bappa was an atheist and couldn't stand priestly Brahmins. 'You are not to let those rascals into the house in my name when I die,' he had told me. 'And I am not going to return in the form of a crow to accept any oblations.' Accordingly, his funeral took place without any religious rites. Bhalchandra lit the funeral pyre.

But Aayi felt that while what happened on the cremation grounds was none of her concern, the ritual cleansing of the house polluted by death had to be performed as ordained in the texts. This meant that rites like the homa (fire sacrifice) and pitrudaana (offerings made to the spirits of the ancestors) had to be performed.

This in turn raised the question about who was to make the offerings. Traditionally, that right is vested either in the youngest son of the deceased or in the eldest. I was the youngest, but an unbeliever. Besides, I was not going to participate in Bappa's name in rituals which he had explicitly forbidden. So I refused. It thus devolved on Vasant to perform the rites. But I said to him, 'Look, we have grown up believing that Bhalchandra was Bappa's eldest son. He too has discarded his own father's name and taken Bappa's. We should therefore acknowledge him as the eldest son and request him to perform the rites.' Vasant agreed instantly.

The decision met with opposition from the priest who had come to conduct the fire sacrifice as well as some of our distinguished neighbours like Shankar Rao Shirur, of whom I shall speak later. 'The pitrudaana is offered only to one's progenitor,' they insisted. And since Bhalchandra was not Bappa's natural son, they argued, he did not have the right to make offerings to Bappa's soul. I had little patience for all this mumbo jumbo and refused to yield. Aayi, too, took me aside and asked in a worried voice, 'But isn't this wrong? We hadn't even adopted him as a son.' I argued, 'That's your fault. You should have adopted him ritually instead of merely changing his name.' She remained silent.

Bhalchandra agreed to my suggestion. The ritual was completed as per the texts and was followed by a feast celebrating the final release of the departed soul from human bondage.

The next day, I was supervising the clearing up of the hall in which the sacrificial altar had been built. At a little distance from the altar, in the direction in which Bhalchandra had offered oblations, I saw an unfamiliar object concealed by the cupboard. I went and picked it up. It was a group photo. Four gentlemen dressed in suits and ties in the fashion of the 1940s were posing stiffly in chairs arranged in a row. I recognized two of them as the younger brothers of Bhalchandra's father. I was flabbergasted. There was no possibility of Bhalchandra's father being in the photograph since he was by then long dead. It was however quite evident that the photograph was meant to represent the Gokarn family. Someone had obviously borrowed it from the Gokarn house and brought it into our house. But who? And who had arranged to have it placed in the direction in which Bhalchandra was to make his offerings? I found it inconceivable that Bhalchandra could be so perfidious. At that moment, Aayi entered the hall, saw me staring at the photograph and, without batting an eyelid, took it from my hand. She said, 'Oh, this has to be kept inside,' and, mumbling to herself, disappeared into the interior of the house.

I have never seen the photograph again in our house.

2

SIRSI

Though, when I think back, the house of the resident medical officer in Sirsi seems spacious, I suspect it was in fact a fairly small bungalow. Its location, high on the hill above the main road running in front of it, invested it with a special gravitas worthy of a government officer's residence. Built very near the edge of the compound, it was separated from the property of the Roman Catholic church next door by a simple wire-and-flowering-plants fence. On the other side, the undulating grounds of the hospital seemed to stretch endlessly. In front of the house, spreading their shadow even on the main road from their high perch, were incense, banyan and peepul trees, seemingly competing with each other for aerial space. In the backyard were trees of pulpless mangoes, jackfruit and cashew. I am sure we spent as much time scrambling up and down the gargantuan branches of these trees as we did in the sports ground.

Sirsi was in the heart of the dense, wild jungles of the Western Ghats, with the wilderness even invading the town wherever it could force its way in. When our dogs – all, needless to explain, pies – gave birth to puppies in the outhouse, they were certain to be visited either by a wild cat or a panther in the night. It was generally believed that there were spots in the heart of the jungle between Sirsi and Siddapura where the foliage was so thick that no ray of the sun had touched the floor in centuries. I distinctly remember the four or five striped tigers stretched out on the winding main road of Devimane Ghat which, one night, brought the bus by which we were travelling to a delighted halt. (Aayi has often corrected me, saying that there was only one tiger there, but my memory refuses to adjust to her facts.)

The Pandit Cottage Hospital was spread shapelessly on the hill that, starting from our house, rolled on the side away from the church to meet the same main road further downhill. A series of worm-eaten wooden stumps from which the wires had disappeared demarcated the grounds of the hospital from those of the house, thus effectively combining the two into one vast open space. There were three or four wards surrounding the main hospital building, and a row of houses for the hospital staff – headed by a Marathi-speaking Brahmin compounder – in the furthest corner of the compound. All the rest of the open, undulating space seemed designed for us to romp around.

The fuel scarcity created by the Second World War ensured that there was almost no traffic except for half a dozen buses fuelled by coal gas that ran through the town on their way from Hubli to Kumta or Siddapura. And there couldn't have been more than four privately owned cars in the town.

Thus, the great gift of the war to our childhood was that even the boundary that separated the hospital grounds from the settlements beyond was quite simply irrelevant. We were as much at home in the slums of the Bhovi community facing the hospital as in the only marginally more middle class hutments of the Catholics a little further down. I do not remember either me or my younger sister – who was forever attached to me – or our constant companions, the children of the compounder, ever being asked who we were or what we were doing at that time of the day or night by anyone in any corner of the town. Our parents were too deeply immersed in their own chores to worry about whether we had got into some scrap with the other kids. When I returned home after on-foot expeditions to different corners of the town, the only person likely to throw up her hands in horror and shriek 'How do you manage to get so filthy?' was my elder sister Prema rather than my mother.

If Bappa needed to visit a patient in the countryside, he had to travel by a bullock cart sent from the village. This meant there was always enough space for us children to accompany him on the jaunt. So, though we lived in Sirsi, the surrounding villages – the term was usually a euphemism for a large house in the heart of an areca nut plantation backed by servants' quarters – with their narrow footpaths bordering ditches and running through cleft wooden gates meant to control the small and agile cattle, the perennial streams running down from some mysterious source deep in the jungle, the dank interiors of the long, parallel rooms that made up the house, all became part of our landscape.

I learnt about adult life within the compound of the hospital itself, where highly charged occurrences manifested without warning and followed each other relentlessly. Leena, the compounder's children and I would rush out of our houses the moment we smelt drama. Of course, there was no one around to shoo us children away. A child was treated simply as a small adult.

We kept away from the post-mortem room which was located in the furthest corner of the compound, almost at the point where the jungle broke into the town of Sirsi. The bodies brought for autopsy were accompanied by whispered accounts of accidents, murders or suicides. These remained circulating in the hospital precincts even after the doors shut upon the unfortunate victims, and they kept us away from this tiny building. It is likely that the image of Bappa tearing open bodies inside was alone sufficient to keep us at bay.

One day, a woman brought to the hospital in a serious condition died. She had five children with her: an adult son, three girls in a row, and then a young boy. We gathered from the hospital staff that the woman's husband was living with a mistress and had simply abandoned his family. Aayi brought the three girls to our house, wrote off letters to friends and acquaintances in Hubli and Dharwad, and placed two of them as permanent residents with families of relatives. The third, Vimla, lived with us and looked after Leena. She attended Hindi classes and got a degree from the Dakshina Bharat Hindi Prachar Sabha, but refused to become a Hindi teacher in the local convent school despite Aayi's encouragement. She remained a part of the family until we left Sirsi.

Nagappa Earappa, who belonged to a tribe living in the vicinity of Siddapura, came to the hospital to have a wound on his leg treated and never went back. He became the man for all seasons in our house. Leena and I grew up sitting on his muscular shoulders or swinging on his jet-black arms. He was friend, guardian, servant, and a key to the unknown beyond our social world. It was with him that I watched all-night shows of Yakshagana in the open fields, which my parents never attended.

One day, our entire family travelled by car to Sonda – a medieval town in the heart of the forest, some twenty kilometres away from Sirsi – at the invitation of the head of the Swarnavalli mutth. The swamiji received us graciously. We were shown a small sandalwood figure of the goddess Saraswati riding a lion and carrying a long sugarcane stick. The swamiji explained the statuette's iconography according to some ancient text. Then we were taken round the mutth, shown the medieval ruins surrounding it, invited to attend the deity's pooja, and fed a sumptuous meal. The swamiji then escorted Bappa into his inner chambers and I followed them in.

'Doctor, we wanted to discuss a delicate matter with you,' he said, referring to himself in the plural as per tradition. 'Day before yesterday, when we went to bathe in the temple tank, we overheard two women gossiping. Apparently, a woman belonging to our mutth came to consult you about her illness. Now we Havyakas in this area normally go to Dr Kollali in Sirsi when we need medical advice. Why had this woman then decided to go to the government hospital and see Dr Karnad? Was there something to hide, the women were asking, something suspicious?'

Bappa reassured him that there was nothing to worry about. The woman had come to him for some minor ailment. With that, the conversation moved to other topics.

Back home, when I repeated the conversation to Aayi, she laughed and said, 'I was sure it would be something like that. But doctors never discuss their patients' ailments with anyone else. They take an oath to the effect when they become doctors. Clearly, the swamiji doesn't know about it.'

On another memorable night, we were all in bed when there was a frantic call for Bappa from the hospital staff. Since Bappa hated being disturbed unless there was an emergency, this promised something dramatic, and I (along with, I think, Leena) followed him to the hospital. From afar, it looked as if an open-air play was being performed: we could see outside the maternity ward a few members of the hospital staff, their family members and some patients gathered in a large circle lit by hurricane lamps. A withered, grey-haired man, thoroughly inebriated, was demanding in a loud voice that his wife, who had delivered only two days before, should accompany him home immediately. 'If she doesn't come with me, I'll kill her,' I remember him railing in Marathi. 'I want her home. Now.' The woman had come out of the ward and was sitting crouched on the steps, clutching her infant child, pleading with the staff to let her go. 'If I don't go now, he will really kill me tomorrow,' she kept repeating. When the hospital staff tried to reason with the husband, he became abusive and almost physically violent.

On Bappa's arrival, the man turned aggressively on him. Bappa walked up to him, watched him calmly for a moment, and then, without warning, slapped him so hard that he fell reeling to the ground. 'Take the woman in and keep her in the hospital until I let her go,' Bappa ordered in a matter-of-fact way, turned around and walked home, followed by us.

My brother and I had on occasion received slaps from Bappa while he was disciplining us, but there never was any anger behind them. He was not a man to anger easily. Sitting in his chair and seething in wrathful silence was more his style. That night, I saw his official anger for the first and last time.

These incidents in the hospital often brought forth an echo in our lives many years later. It was impossible to say when those indebted to Bappa's professional services would make an appearance and acknowledge their gratitude. Twenty years after we left Sirsi, Aayi came to visit me in the remote town of Sringeri where I was acting in the film *Samskara*. As I was leading her to the unit's residential quarters (a house rented temporarily for the purpose), a boy appeared out of nowhere and asked if she was Dr Karnad's wife. When I said yes, he led her directly to his house where his mother was waiting. Aayi never reached the official residence of the film unit. The woman insisted that Aayi stay with them for the entire week she was there. Her husband explained that in Sirsi, when the birth of their first child seemed fraught with peril, Bappa had worked away for hours and saved both the mother and the child. 'Buckets of blood flowed,' he said, holding out his arms wide, as though to indicate the size of the buckets.

I remembered the nights on which we siblings, sleeping next to each other on the floor of the middle room of our house, had woken up to the sound of

Bappa entering the house, only to see Aayi let in a figure drenched in blood from top to toe.

Childhood in Sirsi meant eczema on the arms and legs every year, with the scabs drowned in a thick purple syrup called gentian violet. Then, there was the regular downing of castor oil to clean out one's insides, and endless doses of quinine, which kept malaria at bay but left the tongue bitter for days. Homes like ours, with pretensions to being middle class, had cod liver oil as well.

But the gifts that Leena, I and the compounder's two children looked forward to were the heaps of yellow 'case papers', on which symptoms of illnesses and medicines were recorded. Once the patient finished his or her treatment, these were left piled on the compounder's table for recycling, being handy as pieces of paper in which to package 'powders' or as stoppers for medical bottles containing the compounder's 'mixtures'. We were allowed to snatch as many of these case papers as we wanted, which kept us from using the hospital walls for our impromptu drawings. My first novel began its short life on these papers.

As the shadow of death was spread out thick and perennial on the hospital grounds – and the Catholic cemetery was next door – we grew up unafraid of death. When news reached us that someone had died in the hospital, we peeped in mainly to see the kind of mourning surrounding the deceased and moved on. While we were not bothered by death, who could say when it came to the spirits that were said to roam the precincts on certain nights?

One day, while Leena was watching, along with Vimla, a Catholic funeral procession pass in front of our house, a huge pig, chased by a stray dog, rammed into her from the back and tossed her such that she was prostrated right in front of the cortège. That is the only time I have really seen Aayi frightened. On this occasion, all the rituals common in Sirsi households but rare in our agnostic house were performed elaborately – the circling of a tray of kumkum water in front of her face, the breaking of a coconut, a lemon waved round her head to avert the effects of evil.

Whenever Aayi went to Dharwad, which was about a hundred and twenty-five kilometres away, it would be dark by the time her bus arrived in Sirsi. As the skies darkened, all kinds of anxieties and fears sprung up inside me. The bus would meet with an accident on the winding mountain road between Hubli and Sirsi, but Aayi would arrive home, talk to us casually as if everything was fine, eat with us and go to bed. In the morning, we would discover that there was no sign of her trunk. The mattress she was meant to have slept on would be unused. And it would dawn on us that it wasn't Aayi that had returned in the darkness, but her ghost come to take a last look at us and her home. When she actually appeared, all these anxieties vanished and the house filled up with the pleasure of having her back.

My fears about Bappa were of a totally different kind, though. The moment I saw the big-bosomed woman with heavy hips, who was known to be the mistress of a local plantation owner, come panting up the hospital hill, I trembled lest she tempt him away.

There were only half a dozen Saraswat families living in Sirsi at the time, and of them all, the Nilekani family headed by Venkat Rao was the most prominent. The family had left Karki at the end of the nineteenth century and migrated to the village of Nilekani outside Sirsi. There they had settled down to farming an areca nut plantation, a profession foreign to the Saraswat lifestyle. The house consisted of long, rectangular rooms built snugly next to each other and was typical of the Havyaka houses of the region. It was built with its back to a cliff, so that the house and the plantation on the low grounds in front of it were protected from the heavy monsoon winds which could shake unripe areca nuts off the trees. If you walked further down, you came to a temple with a tank in front. The temple was of Lord Subramanyeswara, represented by a lingam with the serpent Shesha coiled protectively around it. As plantation owners, they had little of the white-collar ease of a normal Saraswat home, and a distinct air of authority which would have embarrassed the middle-class Saraswat, who is usually averse to the flaunting of power. Venkat Rao sported a heavy moustache, wore a turban and a long coat, carried a walking stick with a silver handle, and possessed an ostentation which was dated even at the time.

Every Champa Shashthi day, a temple fair was organized on the main Kumta–Sirsi road. It was probably the only fair in Karnataka privately sponsored by a family.

Within a couple of years of our arrival in Sirsi, Bhalchandra got married to a granddaughter of the Nilekani family. This immediately created a close bond between their family and ours. Which created its own problems.

During his annual holiday, Bhalchandra would come down with his family from his North Indian station. After spending a few days with his in-laws in Dharwad, he was obliged to come to Sirsi to spend a few days with us. But they would have barely unpacked before a cart from Nilekani would be standing in front of our house to take his wife and children away. My siblings and I would walk the three or four kilometres to Nilekani in the morning – there was no other means of transport – spend the day with them, and walk back in the evening. We were charmed by the prospect of spending a day in the Nilekani house. Its front yard was covered with a pandal of bamboo poles and thatched roof. We could walk through grounds at multiple levels, cross fences meant to discourage cattle, jump across perennial streams. The areca nut and spice industry involved scores of workers, and had a dramatic visual quality missing from our normal white-collar existence. But it upset Aayi who would continually fulminate: 'Does Suman come here to visit us or is she here for a holiday at her grandfather's?' But there was no way she could say it out loud, for that would be a challenge to Venkat Rao's familial authority. In any case, Bappa was impervious to the whole thing.

Every year, the swamiji of the Chitrapur mutth at Shirali, who is traditionally accepted as the spiritual head of the Saraswat Brahmin community, would come to Sirsi and stay in the Nilekani house. On this occasion, the entire community in Sirsi flocked to Nilekani to seek his blessings. I remember Swami Anandashram as an unusually attractive person: he had a pleasant smile which seemed to make his entire face glow, a soft voice, a gentle sense of humour, and very liberal political attitudes which endeared him to Bappa. Once we came to live in Sirsi, Bappa started inviting the swamiji to our house for the ritual of having his feet washed, and thus renewed the estranged relations between our family and the mutth.

There was a story behind this estrangement. During the tenure of Swami Pandurangashram, who headed the mutth before the then swami, the Saraswat community had woken up to employment opportunities offered by the British government and started going to England for higher education. So the most ambitious and adventurous of the Saraswats had all gone abroad. But the swamiji had orthodox views on this new craze: traditional wisdom held that a Hindu lost his caste the moment he crossed the seas. And in his zest to maintain the purity of the community, the swamiji had excommunicated not only those who had defied the prohibition by going abroad, but even their relatives and associates who had continued to maintain normal relations with them. Thus, you lost caste if you went abroad. Those who were married into your family also lost caste. And even those who may have had an occasional meal in your house lost caste, regardless of whether they were aware of your status. Since most enterprising Saraswats fit into one of these three categories, almost half the community was ostracized during the swamiji's regime and the mutth was reduced to penury, which did not seem to bother him too much.

It was during this period that my grandfather – Bappa's father – who lived in Mangalore, decided to visit the district of North Kanara. Since it involved an arduous journey not to be undertaken easily or too often, he visited all his relatives living in the region in towns like Gokarna, Honnavar and Bankikodla. On his way home, he had to pass Shirali, where he naturally decided to visit the mutth for a darshan of the swamiji. He was met at the main door by a priest who took down the names of all the people with whom he had taken food during the trip. The priest asked him to wait and disappeared into the interior of the mutth.

He re-emerged after a while and told my grandfather in a voice heavy with concern: 'You have eaten with many excommunicated families. I am afraid that by so doing you have ostracized yourself from the community. You will have to go through penitential rituals before you can enter the mutth.' My grandfather had no choice but to mortify himself by submitting to a ritual cleansing which involved consuming panchagavya, a concoction made from five exudations of the cow, including cow dung and urine. Thus readmitted to the fold, he was eligible to have the swamiji's darshan. But after that, he never visited the mutth again, nor did he allow his children to do so. Though Sirsi was no more than three hours away from Shirali by bus, Bappa continued to uphold the grudge against the mutth and never encouraged us to go there.

The later swamiji's visits to Nilekani appeased Bappa. He invited the swamiji home and offered him all the customary honours. Still, Bappa never visited the mutth. And I did so only once, at the invitation of the next swamiji, who had organized a literary conference. But I never felt the inclination to go there again.

On one side of our house was the Pandit Cottage Hospital while on the other side, as though on the other shoulder of the hill, was a Catholic church. They have replaced it with a new and hideous building now, but the flat-visaged structure with curlicued tops that then stood next to our house could have provided a model for the primitive churches seen in the spaghetti westerns of the sixties. It formed the core which the Catholic community of Sirsi hugged, so that if you descended from our house to the low-lying main road in front, the simple homes of the community could be seen spread out along the road on either side. Our Sundays, too, began with the Konkani hymns that poured out of the church. We Karnad children felt entirely at home in the church and often joined in the prayers without any self-consciousness, either on our part or on the part of the Catholic faithful. Leena, when she saw Jesus bleeding on the cross, was reputed to have said when she was around four: 'Why don't we take him to the hospital to be bandaged by Bappa?'

Since the road winding up to the church lay in front of our house, it was normal for us to join wedding processions, or attend funerals and accompany the bodies to the cemetery at the back to add our fistful of dust. The band playing at these events was made of Hindus, and it was only some ten years later that I discovered that one of the marches they played during weddings was the Marseillaise, the national anthem of France.

It was in these Catholic homes that I first saw poverty at close quarters (though there was a settlement of people from the Bhovi community in front of the hospital which was even poorer). Though proximity to the church lent their lives a measure of dignity, one still casually passed by scenes of utter poverty and degradation.

Every morning on our way to school, at a road junction known as Five Roads, we inevitably ran into Mariam – tall, well-built, her rough uncombed hair flying wild in the wind, drunk to the gills and shouting out curses against the world that had brought her to this plight. Her husband, shrivelled and bent, scuttled around her, perennially dressed in the same khaki shorts.

Antony, the hunter, was never seen without his gun and often brought his game to the hospital, essentially to impress Mary, a lovely young woman who, along with her mother, worked as an ayah at the hospital and lived in the hospital quarters. The adults all felt she was too good for him and pitied her, but they couldn't see a way out for her, particularly since Antony was known for his violent temper. One day, tired of being rebuffed, Antony aimed the gun at her forehead and threatened to kill her and himself if she didn't accept his proposal within twenty-four hours. Next morning, Mary had disappeared and was never again seen in Sirsi. Antony hunted high and low for weeks without finding any trace of her. It was only many years later that my elder sister, Prema, met her in a train and recognized her at once. She was still as lovely, but had converted to Hinduism, was now called Meera, and had two grown-up children with her.

On Good Fridays, I saw the boys of our neighbourhood catch a chameleon and nail it to a tree trunk with its legs spread out in a mock crucifixion. Then they decked it with flowers while it bobbed its head and flicked its tongue in silent agony. One of the boys told me that this was the punishment ordained for the whole species, because a chameleon had mocked Jesus while he was on the cross.

Mrs Fernandes lived in a single-storeyed bungalow which was unlike any of the traditional houses in the town and which, to our young eyes, looked always freshly painted. It was next to the bus stop, far away from the squalor of the rest of the Catholics. In the shop attached to her house were ranged bottles of cold drinks of various shades, sold by an attendant. Mrs Fernandes was never seen in the shop. But she would proudly invite us to another section of the house where a man gave music lessons to young Catholics from families that were economically better-off and took care to live in areas sufficiently distant from the poor families.

Unlike the other Catholic women of Sirsi who all wore saris, Mrs Fernandes wore a dress that always looked freshly ironed. She wore her hair short, used shoes rather than slippers, and carried a handbag and a ladies' umbrella, all of which set her apart from everyone else in town. She had an air of authority about her and a confidence in her gait which would immediately have been considered unladylike in a Hindu woman, but which marked her as a woman of good upbringing in a Western upper-class context. Aayi got on with her extremely well. Her circle of friends included the richer Gauda Saraswat women, but she admitted that she found it tedious to be with women of Lingayat and other castes, as they were innocent of both English and Konkani.

When we all saw a Kannada play based on the life of Kittur Chennamma, the nineteenth-century queen who fought the British imperialists, Mrs Fernandes was vociferous in her admiration for the anglicized Kannada of Colonel Thackeray, played by an actor who had probably never heard an Englishman speak. Bappa thought he had hammed his way through the role, and Aayi felt that Mrs Fernandes's stance was required of her.

One day, Aayi mentioned to Mrs Fernandes that my brother Vasant was hooked on music. She immediately said, 'Oh! But I have a violin we never use. He can have it.' And when Vasant, after a great struggle, taught himself how to play the instrument, she praised his musical gifts but would accept no credit for her contribution.

It used to upset the Reverend Father Figueredo, who looked after the spiritual welfare of the Catholics, that Mrs Fernandes hobnobbed only with Hindu upper-class women and refused to mix with the Catholic poor. He gave vent to his frustration at what he considered her social snobbery to Bappa. But when Aayi once tried to broach the subject with Mrs Fernandes, she smiled and changed the topic.

Bappa and the padre were the best of friends. Since the padre's residence formed a wing of the church, he was our closest neighbour. When they met and chatted, the conversation was in such low tones – almost in whispers – that we children had no idea what they spoke about. When the swamiji of the Chitrapur mutth visited our home, we did not have a seat high enough for him. Father Figueredo would generously lend us the seat meant especially for the bishop when he made occasional trips to Sirsi. It did not seem to bother him that a Hindu religious head would occupy it for his own special rituals.

He was fond of children. And I still remember that, one evening, he and I walked endlessly around the pillar in the compound of the church, planning a bilingual journal in which he would edit the Konkani section (in the Roman alphabet) and I would look after the Kannada.

He was tall, with horse-like features, and always wore dark glasses, even indoors. He had a deep voice and an extraordinarily mobile face which could change expression with startling suddenness. And he utilized all these features to the greatest effect in the discharge of his duties, particularly in the sermons he delivered every Sunday. There is no question that inside him was an actor struggling to get out, and get out he did during these weekly narrations of Biblical tales to the assembled congregation. I know my Job and Abraham and Judas through his vivid performances – there is no other word for them – and the more tempestuous the content, the greater the range of emotions he could unleash. He wept as the father when the prodigal son left him, he hammed details of his self-indulgent life and made the congregation laugh at his stupidity, he raged as the son's siblings when the father welcomed the son back, and he shed tears of joy at the happy ending. The congregation, always hungry for some entertainment and now presented with material which had ecclesiastical blessing too, listened transfixed.

Around the time my family arrived in Sirsi, another Catholic organization entered the town – the Ave Maria Convent, which started a primary school on the road in front of the hospital. The nuns lived in a building on the other side of the church, not too far from our house, and inevitably Bappa became their physician.

Bappa had been transferred from Poona directly to Sirsi, which meant the family had been plucked out of a Marathi-speaking city and plunged into the backwoods of an area where the only language of instruction was Kannada. At that time, my elder siblings, Vasant and Prema, were already halfway through a Marathi curriculum. They faced the prospect of having their education disrupted by this sudden change, and so were both sent to Dharwad and lodged in the homes of different uncles – a common arrangement in those days – while Leena and I entered schools where the teaching was done entirely in Kannada. After a year in Dharwad, Vasant came to Sirsi and joined the only high school there, Sri Marikamba High School, run by the town corporation with a staff of local teachers. He had to read Additional English instead of Kannada as his second language paper. Prema, after two years in Dharwad – staying with a different uncle each year – came to Sirsi and enrolled in the Ave Maria High School. This further strengthened our bonds with the Catholic community. She was an instant success with the nuns – as she was always everywhere. She liked the school, and my parents had deep respect for the dedication of the nuns.

In 2009, I received a letter from the principal of the Ave Maria High School. She gratefully recalled the services rendered by my father to the school and invited a member of our family to Sirsi to receive felicitations in his memory. Vasant and his wife, Sunanda, attended the function in which tributes were paid to Bappa's generosity. But when one considers that we had left Sirsi for Dharwad in 1952 and that the secondary school had started in 1959, the tributes virtually reached back into the school's prehistory. We were moved, for we felt that the letter was not just a tribute to the close bond between my parents and the convent, it was also a tribute to the innate civility of Christian organizations.

If I have ever had an experience I could describe as 'genuinely religious', it was thanks to the sisters of the convent. I was probably about eight years old then, and was in the convent, to which we had free access. The walls had pictures of Jesus Christ and I must have asked the young sister there about one of them. She immediately took down from the shelf an illustrated book on the life of Jesus, sat me down next to her and took me, picture by picture, through the entire life of Jesus. I remember that the moment she finished, I got up and ran home, where Aayi was washing clothes in the bathroom. I clung to the frame of the door and burst out: 'Aayi, Aayi, I have just heard the story of Jesus Christ!' I poured out the entire narrative to her. Aayi listened intently as though she was hearing the story for the first time, nodding her head and wiping her eyes. When I came to the crucifixion, she almost sobbed: 'Isn't that terrible? This world is so wicked! It is not meant for good people!' It is possible that her empathy further inflamed my passion, but I spent the rest of the day in a sort of inner glow. It cannot have taken too long from the moment the sister started telling me the story to Aayi's exclamation, but I have always felt that this short period immersed me in the core experience of Christianity – or should I say Catholicism? – giving my various interactions with Catholic society a definite shape and meaning.

What is funny is that, looking back on the event after nearly seventy years, I remember vividly only one among the pictures the sister showed me: Jesus clearing the temple of fake scholars by laying into them with a lash. Even while I was stimulated by the life of that messenger of peace, it was the sole moment of violence in his life that seems to have left a lasting impression.

Fifty years after we left Sirsi, Aurora Figueredo (later Couto), whom I later met in Dharwad, wrote about her family and, in particular, about her father in a beautiful book called *Goa: A Daughter's Story*. While writing about what the Church meant to her, inevitably Aurora had to write about the savageries of the Inquisition in Goa during the fifteenth and sixteenth centuries. While she was writing the section, right-wing Hindutva had suddenly emerged as a frightening force on India's political horizon. Those close to her – including her husband, Alban – advised her against dealing with the Inquisition honestly and writing about its atrocities in detail, since for a devout Catholic to admit to those horrors would be to place more ammunition in the hands of the fascists. After spending several sleepless nights over it, Aurora wrote to me asking for my response.

I replied: 'I think you should be guided by the following considerations. Most important of all, you should go by what you know or feel in your bones to be right. Indians are past masters at whitewashing history, and if you are to be influenced by considerations of what is the politically correct thing to say in the present context, morally you are no better than the RSS or the communists, who construct history which is ideologically correct. Your exposition, for the first time in India, brings out an existential (almost Greene-like) paradox: that even if conversions were forced or violent, the faith that people gained from them could prove to be culturally and spiritually enriching. No one so far has had the courage to state that so convincingly … I fear the venomous ideologues of today can have no comprehension of such existential complexities.'

I could not have written about the spiritual richness of Catholicism, whatever its early history in Goa, with such clarity and conviction if I had not spent six years amidst the Catholics of Sirsi.

A great advantage I derived from Bappa's position as the government doctor was that the moment a touring company of actors set up camp in Sirsi, free passes for the entire family would land at our doorstep. Sirsi was the central market for areca nut, pepper and betel leaves and was, therefore, one of the more prosperous towns of the district. But in those days, apart from two cinemas that showed films which had finished their run elsewhere and often arrived in tatters, the only entertainment available was the Yakshagana performances. And these were considered fit only for illiterate villagers. It was the 'modern' plays staged in semi-permanent halls on an improvised proscenium stage that were seen as entertainment worthy of the cultured. So it was in the company of Nagya, our servant, that I saw Yakshagana – a traditional, semi-classical but largely folk form with elaborate costumes that presented stories from the Mahabharata and the Ramayana in the open air. My parents considered it crude and unsophisticated, and instead were happy to be seen gracing the chairs in the front row of the natak companies' tents.

The monsoons usually faded away in September, and the season for the travelling companies would begin. Most companies of North Karnataka set up 'camp' in Sirsi every other year. Though free passes were seen as the automatic prerogative of all government officials such as the mamlatdar or the local police officer, Sirsi was a malarial dump and it was essential to keep the government doctor benevolently disposed. So, between 1945, when I was considered old enough to accompany my parents to all plays, and 1948, when Bappa retired, I had the good fortune to see the best offerings of some of these companies.

My parents were both crazy about theatre. They had seen the Marathi stage at its height, and frequently reminisced about its glorious music, its stars, the spectacle. Bappa's memory went back to the last decades of the nineteenth century, to the trick scenes, the sudden scene transformations and technological feats of Parsi theatre productions such as *Khoon-e-Nahak* and *Asuri Lalsa*. When Aayi came of age, it was Bal Gandharva who was presiding over Marathi theatre. She blushingly remembered wearing saris in his style, exiting with a jump as he did, and repeating some of his phrases that drew continuous applause. Even after she was widowed, she travelled alone to Hubli to see one of Bal Gandharva's plays.

In the summer of 1947, the Jayakarnataka Nataka Mandali, owned and managed by Hulimane Seetharama Shastry of Siddapura, set up camp in Sirsi. My parents patronized the company for its good taste, literary ambition and high standards of production. Shastry himself played the 'heavy' roles in his plays, but the company was particularly known for the comic abilities of a Shanth Kumar, some of whose funnier moments I can still clearly remember.

It is likely that the company was so successful that they stayed on longer than intended. Or perhaps the monsoons, which were expected to begin exactly on 6 June every year, arrived a few days earlier. Whatever the reason, the company was trapped in the rains of the Western Ghats which, in those days, tipped down uninterrupted once they started. They were unable to pack their heavy curtains, property and costumes and move out of Sirsi for three months, which meant commercial disaster. The rains discouraged viewers because they had to walk through the jungles surrounding the town, and attendance was further reduced by repetition of the same fare. To draw an audience, Shastry hurriedly mounted a new play called *Dharma Samrajya.* It dealt with the Mahabharata war, but made heavy contemporary references to the partition of India and the accompanying bloodbath. It didn't do too well, since the painful experiences it referred to were still raw in people's minds. But by then, I had become friendly with the entire cast, and this gave me a chance to see a new play being discussed, written, rehearsed and brought to stage. I was mesmerized by the process.

Shastry's company was already struggling when it moved on from Sirsi, and it soon came to a disastrous end in Raichur, in the state of Hyderabad, where its visit coincided with the rise of Qasim Razvi and his goons, who were fighting for the independence of Hyderabad. The Razakars burnt the theatre tent to the ground. We heard that Shastry somehow managed to escape and turn up at the Hubli railway station with only the shirt on his back.

In 1997, I was commissioned by BBC Radio in London to write a play for the fiftieth year of Indian independence. I wrote *The Dreams of Tipu Sultan.* Writing it was an exhilarating process – I was delighted by the ease with which I could recreate the person of Tipu, his court and its ambience. Nearly ten years later, I received an invitation to the launch of a biography of Seetharama Shastry by R.P. Hegde. The invitation card showed Shastry in his role as Tipu Sultan. As I looked at it, I realized with a shiver that my imagining of the court of Tipu had been shaped by long-forgotten images of Shastry's production of *Tipu Sultan* which I had seen as a boy of nine.

Bappa at last retired from government service in 1948. We all yearned to move to Dharwad where there was Saraswatpur, a hill on which Saraswat Brahmins had built an urban extension exclusively for their caste. But there were no houses vacant there, so we had to continue living in Sirsi. Sirsi was then a small town with a population of barely 10,000 and it was impossible to find a decent house on rent.

Somehow Bappa found a house in Rayar Peth. Moving there from the government bungalow on the hospital hill was not like moving from one section of town to another. It was more like moving from one country to another.

The house we found in Rayar Peth was a grim, godown-like structure in which an entire side, from the front of the house to the rear, was blocked off by a windowless wall – probably an effort to partition the house in some distant past. The section of the house we had was a central passage of dark rooms flanked by bedrooms with tiny windows that hardly let in any sunlight. One of these bedrooms had Bappa's bed, with a mattress on the floor for one of the children. The other bedroom was for many months occupied by my aunt Shantakka. I have already talked about how Shantakka's husband, Mangesh Rao, was responsible for bringing my parents together against all social norms. In acknowledgement of that extraordinary gift, Shantakka, who was now widowed, ill and abandoned by her children, had come to stay with us and been allotted a bedroom. Her house in Saraswatpur was occupied by a family that was refusing to vacate, and our only hope of moving to Dharwad depended on their relenting at some point.

Soon after moving into the house, we discovered that smoke from our neighbour's kitchen tended to pour into Bappa's bedroom. He complained to the municipal corporation and earned the enmity of our neighbours for the rest of our stay in Sirsi. The lavatory was a rickety structure with walls of bamboo and a curtain of jute for the door. One had to climb a narrow path up a steep slope in our backyard to reach it. It consisted of a simple hole in the ground from which white worms often used to crawl out and scare my sisters. Even this house became available to us for reasons which we, the children of the house, came to know only six months after we had moved in. A boy from the neighbourhood told us that some years ago a man had hanged himself from a rafter.

Another stressful aspect entered our social life after Bappa's retirement. Until now, he had been a government servant in Sirsi, which in those days was tantamount to belonging to a haughty and powerful aristocracy. Everyone bowed and scraped in front of him in case his special connections with the powers that be were needed in some emergency. Now, the same people went out of their way to show that they did not need to be so respectful towards him any more, and also by extension towards Aayi. Bappa often mournfully commented that one should never retire in the same town in which one had 'done service'.

But along with this bitter experience, we also discovered financial prosperity. Bappa was known for his bedside manner, and patients who had got used to being treated by him in the government hospital continued to flock to him in our house. The narrow front room of our Rayar Peth house soon became a proper outpatient department. Bappa realized how popular a doctor he was. Later, he would often repeat: 'The only time I had any savings in the bank was when I was practising in Rayar Peth.' Which meant that he realized too late the wisdom of Aayi's insistence that he start his own practice in Poona instead of going to Sirsi.

Culturally, too, Rayar Peth could have been on another planet. If the neighbourhood of the hospital was intensely Catholic and poor, Rayar Peth was entirely occupied by the Gauda Saraswat Brahmin community. Gauda Saraswat houses started at the agase baagilu (entrance gate) on the western side, and solidly lined the road as it ran through the town, turned right towards the ancient town of Banavasi and reached the enormous temple to Goddess Maremma. Here, the town, and therefore the Gauda Saraswat residences, came to an abrupt end. And since the nomenclature 'Gauda Saraswat' covers innumerable sub-castes speaking various dialects of Konkani, it was easy for us to get absorbed in its social ambience.

An ironic result of our attempt to blend into Gauda Saraswat culture was that, although we did not hide the fact that we were, like them, fish eaters, we pretended that we were averse to consuming meat. This meant that the meat delicacies that Bappa's Muslim patients frequently sent to us were delivered with the loud proclamation: 'A parcel has arrived from Hubli.'

There was now a sudden upsurge in Aayi's social activities. She now lived next door to the rich Gauda Saraswat ladies whom she had known, until then, only from a distance. Her enthusiasm was largely responsible for the birth of a new Mahila Samaj, devoted to women's welfare. The opening ceremony of the Mahila Samaj was a major event celebrated with a variety entertainment show of dances and skits. But it was only when the chief guest, in his speech at the end of the two-hour-long event, grumbled, 'I am the first person this evening to speak in Kannada,' did it occur to the organizers that they should have included at least one Kannada item in the evening's programme.

As a result of our association with the convent school, I knew several Goan Konkani folk songs. These were essentially comic songs, about the negotiations before the wedding of a cock and a hen, for instance, or about a boy, spoilt by his father, railing against his disciplinarian teacher. The songs sung by the women of Rayar Peth during the many domestic events opened out to me the rich oral tradition of Konkani songs, which celebrated weddings and childbirths with laughter but could draw tears with their description of a bride leaving her parents or pining for her childhood home. The humour, sadness, anxieties, yearnings, pain and humiliations were all expressed in simple spoken Konkani in tunes which were not boring despite their limited repertoire. But all my writing has been in Kannada, so I have always felt a deep sense of regret that I couldn't use those nuances of feeling, that rhythm and the richness of phrasing.

During our last year in Sirsi, the Mahila Samaj invited a dancer from Shimoga called Omkar to conduct dance classes for young girls. Most of these girls were between eight and ten years old, and since I had to accompany Leena to her dance class, I accepted Omkar's suggestion that I try my hand (and feet) at the art. I found myself enjoying the training. In about three months, I was considered good enough to participate in the grand programme arranged for the disciples, and I performed a couple of items with my guru. By this time, Vasant had taught himself to play the violin. I knew even then that I was not as gifted, but the dance training gave me some confidence in my artistic abilities.

Thirty-two years later, in 1984, I played a dance guru in a film being made in Kannada and Telugu. The director, Jandhyala, had assured me that I would not need to dance in the film. But the shooting was in the east-coast town of Rajahmundry, I couldn't understand a word of Telugu, there was no one in the film unit with whom I could spend time, and the television was unwatchable. Tired of sitting alone in the hotel room, reading or drinking whisky, I one day asked Seshu, the choreographer, if he would teach me a few gestures or stances I could use in my performance. He gave me a few elementary exercises and asked in a surprised tone, 'How come you have such excellent coordination in your limbs?' When I described my three months of dance training in Sirsi, Seshu asked, 'Would you mind attempting a couple of simple dance items in the film?' From that day on, I started my Kuchipudi class at six every morning. In a month, I was proficient enough not only to do half a dozen dances, but even a vigorous Tandava whose rehearsals would knock me out. I would ache all over at night, but I escaped the ennui of Rajahmundry. The Telugu version of the film was a huge commercial success. I enjoyed those few weeks so enormously that I almost regretted not having taken up dance professionally.

One of the few people whose feet I have touched in reverence in my adult life was Seshu, who taught me dancing for *Ananda Bhairavi*. His eyes filled with tears when I bent before him. Another person was Guru Omkar, whom I ran into many years later in Shimoga.

Sirsi had only one primary school and one high school. As a result, children from all social strata ended up studying together. Children of rich lawyers, government servants, owners of cloth or grocery stores, gardeners, carpenters, milkmen and goldsmiths, all sat together on long planks which never balanced properly on the uneven floor, and used stems of a watery plant to wipe their slates with. When there was shortage of space, it was not unusual for four or five classes to be conducted simultaneously in a huge hall, students of each class learning their tables by rote, their voices in competition with those of the neighbouring class. As a rich coffee planter described to me later: 'The only difference between the poorer boys and us was that their shorts were torn and ours were not.' Close contact with children of different social classes brought with it an understanding of the complexities of our society.

For example, my friend Shivanand Achari, whose father was a carpenter and lived next to the prostitutes' street, once described to the entire class, with complete dialogue and action, how on the previous night a prostitute had tossed a trouserless police constable out on to the street for having turned up without any money. I was in the fourth standard then. No boy in the class could have been older than ten.

By the time I entered high school, the boys from the poorer families must have left school and joined their families at work. My classmates in high school were more uniformly middle-class. Now girls, freshly arrived from the girls' primary school, formed about a fifth of the class. They sat distinctly apart and we would not talk to them, although teasing and even harassing them was an accepted pastime.

There were about four hundred students in the school. The teachers were local residents. So not only did they know the students, they were also familiar with their educational and financial backgrounds. There was a particularly close bond between the brightest and the naughtiest students and their class teachers.

The high school encouraged students to take part in extracurricular activities, and some teachers individually guided students who were enthusiastic. Every Saturday morning, the entire school would assemble in the central hall and alternately witness 'variety entertainment' and 'debate'. It was this audience that sat in long-suffering silence as Vasant tested out his self-taught technique on the violin over three years. I received an enthusiastic response to my love for public self-display. I certainly owe my success as president of the Oxford Union to my endless hamming in secondary school.

When Gandhiji was assassinated in January 1948, I immediately wrote out a poem on the tragic event and read it out in the assembly. On Monday, Pai-master, our science teacher, confronted me in the corridor and commanded, 'Come and see me this evening after classes.'

Pai-master had a cockroach moustache on his upper lip, and hair cut so short that what little one saw seemed to cling to the skull. He wore thick 'soda-glass' spectacles, a dhoti that was never actually dirty but did not show signs of having been washed either, and a thick, short-sleeved shirt that was always either jet black or dark green because – the rumour went – he did not want to waste time washing it. His science room was an Ali Baba's cave of the most curious objects placed in unlikely proximity. A stuffed owl perched on a pendulum clock had, above it, a caption inspired by the poet Bendre's famous line: 'Have you seen how Time is flying!' Live snakes. Crabs. Spiders.

Once, even a living pangolin that some admiring parent had presented him. It was impossible to predict what lay in wait inside. I trembled with anxiety as I stepped into the room.

'If you want to be a poet,' said Pai-master, as usual staring unsmiling at me from under his glasses, 'you have to learn prosody.' I couldn't believe my ears. I had tried to get some clue to prosody from several people who seemed to know, but had been told it was a difficult art 'not to be mastered so easily'. Now, someone was offering to teach it to me step by step. 'We shall start tomorrow evening after school hours,' he said, and for the next thirty-six hours I could barely bring myself to breathe. By the time Pai-master started his first lesson, I already had several subjects buzzing in my head, waiting to be turned into epics.

Pai-master patiently took me through the entire discipline of versification. 'Now don't make such basic mistakes,' he warned me before concluding. The net result of Pai-master's careful tutoring was that my poetry began to fly out of control. My sentimental descriptions of sunsets struggled breathlessly to fit themselves into complex rhythmic patterns, traditional metres and rhymes. Fortunately, there were students and teachers around me with enough taste and sympathy to dismiss these grandiloquent attempts. I never became a poet in my life, but I have always been grateful for the rigorous training Pai-master put me through. If not my poetry, it certainly gave me control over my prose.

The person who read my poems seriously and cautioned me that a poem was a vehicle for conveying emotion and not for displaying punditry was my Kannada teacher, G.K. Hegde-master. He brought into the class every kind of reading material other than the textbook – poems, stories, news items, essays – and involved the whole class in discussing them. It was a method quite unknown in the pedagogy of those days. He was such an entrancing teacher that my sister Prema, who was studying Additional English instead of Kannada, insisted on attending his classes. The day before my family left Sirsi for good, he ran into me in the market, lowered a leg from his bicycle displaying a muscular calf wrapped in a crisp white dhoti, said, 'Don't desert Kannada,' and rode off.

In high school, my fellow students were largely from two communities: the Gauda Saraswats, who spoke various dialects of Konkani at home that corresponded to their sub-castes, and the Havyakas, who spoke a dialect of

Kannada almost incomprehensible to other Kannada speakers. (There were a few Muslims and Christians, and very few from the 'lower' castes.) When I look back after three-quarters of a century, the two communities seem to me distinct in their attitudes to life.

The Gauda Saraswats had their homes in Sirsi, or came from the many small towns in the surrounding area which lacked adequate educational facilities. They had grown up in streets and areas occupied almost entirely by their own caste members, and had a simple, practical approach to education, jobs, and indeed to life itself.

The Havyakas, on the other hand, had families living in remote villages isolated by areca nut plantations, maintaining which was almost their caste occupation. Even those students who lived in Sirsi were dependent on relatives in the town for a place to live. Sri Marikamba High School in Sirsi was the only secondary school in that section of the Western Ghats. There were very few vehicles available in those years, and it was quite common for young boys and girls to walk several kilometres through dense jungles to come to school. They would return the same way in the evening, without the aid of lights. There were no books to read in the villages except textbooks. Newspapers were avidly read and were the only connection with the world beyond Sirsi. I distinctly remember the enormous enthusiasm with which a new book was greeted. There was a deep-rooted belief that education was a rare gift to be sought at all costs, something prized and almost sacrosanct. Havyaka students dominated virtually every field of activity – theatre, politics, literature, journalism.

A friend of mine announced, at the age of fifteen, that he would write a novel. I don't know if he even started it, but I remember distinctly that it was called *When the Actress Joins the Actor*. The title unambiguously paid tribute to not only the popular fiction of A.N. Krishna Rao and T.R. Subba Rao (ANaKru and TaRaSu to their readers) but also the classical epic *Jaimini Bharata* that we heard recited at community events and the *Sachitra Stree Charitra* that was circulated clandestinely in class.

The most popular play to be staged by a professional group of touring actors during my life in Sirsi was *Devdasi* by Hirannaiah, dealing with the life of a courtesan and her pimp Najukayya. My group of friends, mostly Havyakas, immediately decided to stage the play. Since I was the most popular female impersonator around, the role of the courtesan Manimanjari came to me easily. But the discussion about who should play Najukayya almost ended in a fight. Eventually, the headmaster K. Raghavendra Rao vetoed the entire project, and I missed my chance to go down in the history of Kannada drama as the youngest Manimanjari.

Although the temple of Maremma did not figure prominently in my daily life, it would be unfair not to talk about it before closing this chapter. She was originally a Dalit deity, but the Brahmin priests, who had taken control of the temple, had Sanskritized her name from Maremma to Marikamba.

The temple in those days was just outside town limits. This seemed almost by choice, since it did not have the slightest connection in size, style or atmosphere to the narrow, shapeless streets and congested houses bordered by open gutters that made up the rest of the town. The entrance hall of the Marikamba temple was vast enough to accommodate various groups of children simultaneously playing kabaddi, hopscotch and hide-and-seek. If you went up the wide stone steps, you came to a square, child-sized opening in the wall rumoured to be the entrance to an underground passage leading to Banavasi almost twenty kilometres away. Its unfathomability seemed to expand the dimensions of the temple. Passing by this entrance you came to large halls which were available to the public for dance, yoga, physical exercise, adult literacy classes, and as rehearsal space for local theatrical projects.

The centre of attention in the vast interior of the temple was an enormous, jet-black buffalo tied to the pillar at the right of the sanctum sanctorum with thick, heavy chains. The non-violence movement led by the Congress had saved him from ritual slaughter at the fair of 1942. Since then, he had stood there, fed and tended as an offering to the gods, but otherwise with no role except to grow larger by the year. It was hard to imagine the size and strength of the knife that would be required to cut his throat.

One night, Vimla took me to a house on the Maremma temple street to see the 'hunters' dance'. She woke me up at an hour well past midnight, splashed cold water on my face, and dragged me to a wide first-floor window.

I was collapsed on the bars of the window in sleepy protest, when the beauty and power of the hunters' dance shook me wide awake. The hunters wore tall and shining headgear, shaped almost like temple towers, with long, black plaits decorated with peacock-feather fans hanging off them. Their chests were covered with violently coloured garlands. Their faces, where visible under ferocious moustaches, were striped in black, white and red. They went down the road, charging at the crowd with the shields they held in their left hand, swinging their naked swords with their right. Most terrifying of all were the ropes tied around their waists to control them and pull them back as they charged into the crowd to the rhythm of drums, sending people scurrying into narrow front verandas and bylanes, their shadows fleeing helter-skelter on the walls. I watched transfixed as the hunters declared their dominance over the four directions.

Those ten minutes opened up a mythical world in my imagination that has remained as vivid and fascinating as it was in the moment.

I have no interest in caressing memories. But I must mention two aspects of my childhood in Sirsi which we have lost forever.

The first is the experience of total undiluted darkness. There was no electricity in Sirsi while we were living in the hospital quarters. And the owner of the house we rented in Rayar Peth – or perhaps Bappa – did not get a connection. The result was that, for a total of ten years, my family grew up without electricity in the house and, for most of the period, without lights in the streets. And we learnt to taste the many shades of darkness. I am not trying to romanticize an existence without electricity, for that would be naïve. But I know that, with the ability to instantly turn on a flood of bright, shadeless light, we have lost a certain delicate and ambiguous relationship we had with light and dark. When there is no evidence of light within the darkness surrounding us, the irises pick out floating slivers of light and weave them into changeable amorphous forms. That quality of total darkness, that takes us to the brink of blindness, also has a close relationship with complete silence. The lack of sound itself seems to shape the light one senses. The small kerosene lamp, the lantern, the earthen lamp, the torch, the brash glare of the Petromax, the flickering of the lamp as its wick sank into extinction, the glow of dying embers. Light from these sources played on mud walls, wooden pillars, cow dung-swept floors, on blankets. The innumerable textures that these shades and intensities of light could create have been lost forever to our ability to create an instant flood of incandescent or fluorescent light that is devoid of all nuance.

The other element we have lost along with the world of complete darkness is an abundance of stories. You could run into them everywhere – in side streets, deserted corners, in the thick of the bazaar. In a society where there were only two cinemas to provide ready-made entertainment, people were famished for tales and simple stories. All the novels, radio programmes, harikathas, keertans, folk plays and periodicals put together were insufficient to fill the void in daily life, so tales were born and circulated at the slightest provocation. As soon it got dark, the old woman who served as a cook, children's companion and maid in our house told tales about princes and princesses which remained unchanged over the years (indeed, we did not brook the slightest deviation). Schoolchildren were saved from ennui by the stories they improvised. If the teacher was late in coming to class, a boy took it upon himself to narrate a story and often concocted an entirely incoherent concatenation of incidents that the other children listened to with rapt attention. Boys capable of such invention had a special place in the affections of the class. During the afternoon lunch break, we rushed back to the school from home either to play tag on and around the desks in the class, or to huddle around the boy who had discovered a new storybook in their storeroom.

The monsoons took barely half a day to flood the town. The gutters were then indistinguishable from the safer mid-street section, and this imprisoned us in our houses. For those three months, stories were our saviours. One year, I remember sitting with a group of friends from the neighbourhood, evening after evening, reading out the Marathi translation of the interminable Hindi romance, *Chandrakanta,* having to raise my voice every now and then to be heard over the rain pelting the roof.

Female spirits hung from every branch; every bridge was haunted by the souls of pregnant women sacrificed to ensure its stability; the five fingers protruding threateningly in the outline of a tree near Sirsi's entrance gate announced the treasure hidden under its roots...

The Marathi playwright Vijay Tendulkar, after seeing my first play *Yayati,* asked me, 'There is a definite stylized mould in which characters in mythological Marathi plays are cast. How come your characters feel so different, so true to life?'

I could only reply, 'Oh, I met them all in my childhood in the streets of Sirsi.'

3

DHARWAD

Fifty-One Houses

In Dharwad, where we moved to from Sirsi, Saraswatpur was the exclusive domain of the Saraswat community. Known as guddo – the hill – to its residents, the colony in the southwestern corner of Dharwad sits perched on a high mound that is the last of a huddle of hills. So, if you stand in front of the last house on the western side, the road plunges down a steep incline in front of you, levels off into the plains, and runs across a landscape so flat that you can see the land stretch far into the west, punctuated here and there by smaller hills and valleys. When we first came to Dharwad, that vantage point had an uninterrupted view of the furthest hill behind which was hidden the tiny medieval temple of Someshwara. Visitors often commented on how rare it was to see a city come to an end so abruptly.

On the other side, the hill sloped off more gently in the direction of the city, but no human habitation enlivened the kilometre or two that separated the colony on the hill from the nearest residence. Since the road to the city ran through this desolate space, crossing a Parsi cemetery, a Christian burial ground and a medieval stepwell believed to be haunted, women and children avoided taking it after dark. There was no local bus service, and if you needed a vehicle to take you and your luggage to the railway station, some young man had to be dispatched on a bicycle to the city centre to fetch a horse-drawn tonga. Schoolgoing children walked about a kilometre and a half every morning to school, and women intent on shopping even further to reach the market. College students had to walk up and down a series of winding slopes and past the railway station to reach college. In the mornings, men on the wrong side of sixty negotiated the winding roads in groups of two or three for their constitutionals. Everyone walked.

Occasionally, some enterprising soul would start a shop in a corner of Saraswatpur for the convenience of the residents. But it wouldn't take him long to realize that people preferred to walk all the way to the market rather than pay a little bit extra for the convenience of having groceries available next door. You had to walk to the market even for a matchbox.

During my two years in school, there were still about a dozen schoolgoing children around. We gathered every evening in the plain at the bottom of the hill to play lagori with stone chips piled on top of each other. Jackals slithered around the edge of the rainwater pond nearby, and howled while we chased the ball. Once, I came across a tortoise the size of my palm on the main road, right in the heart of the colony. By the time I entered college two years later, this group of playmates had melted away. On returning home from college, I often went on long walks across the undulating landscape with our one-eyed terrier Hero, named by my father after Hirohito, the emperor of Japan.

Soon, however, I found a companion who was equally keen on these meandering perambulations along the railway tracks from Hubli or up the hills covered with berry bushes. Krishna Basrur, who was two years my senior, had come to Dharwad to continue his education in Karnatak College. Instead of opting for the hostel, he had chosen to live in his aunt's house at one end of the hill. On most evenings, the two of us with Hero wandered aimlessly across the wavelike terrain. By the time we had exhausted dissecting Freud, Marx, Eliot, Yeats, our professors and the girls in our college, had laid plans to escape the claustrophobic atmosphere in India and go abroad, and analysed the prospects of success for Krishna's passion for a Catholic classmate, it would get dark and we would be home. We loved the solitude, rich with half-digested theories, half-understood poems and suppressed ambitions.

The colony had fifty-one houses, each with an outhouse of its own. And so, there were about a hundred families of the Chitrapur Brahmin caste – Bhanaps, as they preferred to refer to themselves for some long-forgotten reason – living there. In fact, the Saraswat Cooperative Society – to give the colony its full name – was one of the first housing societies in India based entirely on caste. Those of us growing up in it were inordinately proud of the fact that it seemed to have a civilization of its own, with its majestic bungalow-like houses, so unlike the poky, clumsy houses of the town.

But why should a group of people intent on making homes for themselves and their children have opted for such an isolated and inconvenient corner to build a settlement? No one talked about it, and it took me some time to realize that though the idea of the colony was perfectly rational to begin with, it had gone awry in the course of being transplanted to the environs of Dharwad.

In 1913, a Provincial Cooperative Conference was held at Poona, and the question of applying the methods of cooperative financing to private housing was extensively discussed. The idea excited a young Bhanap, S.S. Talmakki, who collected together a few relatives and acquaintances and formed the Saraswat Cooperative Society in Bombay. The Society was registered in 1915. Not only did six blocks containing four flats each materialize in Gamdevi at the very reasonable cost of 3,000 rupees per flat, but every flat was occupied and in use before the end of the year. This was the very first cooperative housing society to be built in India. Its spectacular success spurred the Bhanaps to embark on similar experiments elsewhere in Bombay, as well as in Poona, Bangalore and Dharwad, where they lived in sufficiently large numbers.

The founders of the society in Dharwad must have been delighted when an officer called Dhebar, keen on expanding the limits of the city, allotted them the entire hill of Akkitimmanahalli at a throwaway price. It was outside the city, some five kilometres from the centre, and the Bhanaps had historical connections with the spot. In the plague-ridden nineteenth century, it was quite common for entire sections of the city to be relocated to a remote area until the pestilence disappeared. Although these were temporary settlements, abandoned once signs of the plague disappeared, members of individual castes grew habituated over the centuries to moving to the same area every time an epidemic threatened. The Bhanaps normally used to move to the hill of Saptapur, but the Akkitimmanahalli hill, which was further away and more isolated, must have seemed an attractive proposition for permanent residence. With the plague always round the corner, isolation was probably seen as a safety measure.

The Saraswat Society in Dharwad was registered in 1918. With the arrival of a separate post office for the area many decades later, it became Saraswatpur. The hill allotted to the society was situated to the west of the Karwar–Dharwad road just before it merged with the Bangalore–Poona highway, at a point known for obvious reasons as the Toll Naka. The colony was to be built on the eastern face of the hill, and the planners decided to wrap a new road around the hill. It started from near the Toll Naka at the base, went sharply up the hill, and then bumped merrily along the side of the hill, running parallel to the Karwar road. This road – which I shall call the Diagonal Road even though it had no such name – connected the bottom of the hill to the top, and almost every house in Saraswatpur was built beside or within easy reach of it. The road divided Saraswatpur into two zones. The lower half, that is the area between this road and the Karwar road at the base of the hill, was divided into sixteen plots, measuring roughly about ten gunthas each (a guntha is one-fortieth of an acre). The houses built on these plots were classified as C-class. In the upper half, the plots were larger, some twenty to twenty-five gunthas, and had more spacious houses built on them. These were called B-class. Halfway across the hill, having fixed the two zones neatly, the Diagonal Road took a sudden turn and snaked right up to the peak before plunging into the valley beyond, where the railway station sat hidden from view. On the crown of the hill were two enormous houses referred to, in hushed tones, as A-class.

Thus, if you viewed the colony from the hill opposite, you could see the entire economic stratification of the society spread out before you like a chart along the side of the hill – the C-class houses in the lower part of the hill, below the Diagonal Road, and the B-class ones above it. The smaller houses and the lower position of the C-class area did not necessarily mean that its residents were poorer; several of the C-class houses were occupied by middle-class families who were quite well off. Yet, it was taken for granted that those who lived in B-class houses were somehow a little superior socially, their position higher up on the side of the hill a proof of their status.

The houses, despite being classified into three types, all had the same simple layout modelled on the colonial travellers' bungalows. Since most

Bhanaps were employed in the forest or revenue departments or the railways, which provided their employees with official accommodation built on a basic model worked out by the Central Public Works Department, this design was probably seen as a status symbol or a sign of modernity. Each house consisted of three wings, each wing consisting of three rooms of a standard size, strung out in a straight line like compartments of a train. The ceilings were high, which made for excellent ventilation, and it was many years before the need for overhead fans was felt. The coast of Goa was around a hundred and fifty kilometres to the west as the crow flies, so there was a continual if distant supply of sea breeze.

Since plots for building the houses had to be scooped out of the rocky side of the hill, they were not always correctly aligned with the Diagonal Road along which the daily life of the colony flowed. Foundations of houses, too, refused to be level with the ground on which they were built. So, steps were an essential part of the settlement's design. Some compounds, particularly in the C-zone, could be accessed only by the use of steps. For many residents, visiting a person living in the neighbourhood meant you had to first negotiate the steep incline of the road outside your own gate and then go on to climb the flights of steps at the front of the house you were visiting. Seen from the hill opposite, the colony looked like a snakes-and-ladders board, with the snakes replaced by winding roads. Even accepting the belief that old people of that era were used to walking and had strong legs, it is hard to believe that these houses were designed for people on the verge of retirement.

The whole enterprise seemed to be driven more by enthusiasm for the project than any practical planning. Cutting into the rocky hill and building roads across it proved much more expensive than had been anticipated. If the houses in the Bombay prototype had cost a mere 3,000 rupees and had been built within a year, six years went by before the colony was occupied in Dharwad, and by then, the cost of even a C-class house had touched 9,000 rupees. If it was envisioned as a place for retirement, many who had poured their savings into it never lived to see their house completed, or died as they prepared to settle in. A belief spread that those who built or bought houses on the hill were destined to die prematurely – a fear which prevented my father, for instance, from investing in a house there when he could have easily afforded it. Houses built in 1925 for 9,000 rupees wouldn't fetch 18,000 rupees in the 1960s. Financially, the project was a disaster.

Despite – or perhaps because of – all this, Saraswatpur glowed with a certain romantic refulgence in the eyes of the community. It was an impossible vision and, therefore, admirable by virtue of its very existence. If the Saraswat Societies in Bombay and Poona had managed to survive in the hearts of their cities by striking compromises, Saraswatpur sat in lonely splendour, steadfastly watching its own dissolution.

There was another curious paradox behind the very vision of the colony. The founding fathers of the colony obviously believed that their children, too, would continue to live in it, though it is difficult to fathom what this belief was based on given the known history of the community. Unlike the Gauda Saraswat community of which they are a sub-caste, the Bhanaps had, at least since the day they fled their ancestral homes in Goa to escape the Inquisition, a history of relentless peregrination. From Goa, they had spread southwards along the coast right down to Mangalore, and then branched out in North Karnataka and across the former Bombay as well as Madras Presidencies looking for employment. It was a firm belief among the Bhanaps that while they had no head for business or agriculture which the Gauda Saraswats were known for, they were excellent at salaried jobs. So they moved to wherever job opportunities opened up. Most Saraswat family names refer to a village or town, which might suggest that they have a long-standing loyalty to that place, but nothing could be more misleading. When, in the nineteenth century, the British administration demanded that everyone in government service should have a surname, the Bhanaps merely took on the names of the towns and villages in which they were living. Surnames like Mankekar, Karnad, Padukone and Benegal are not proofs of loyalty or even nostalgia, but merely records of the habitations they passed through, with nothing left in those places now to mark even their passage. Like most caste groups in the eighteenth and nineteenth centuries, they moved together and rushed en masse to wherever a new opportunity arose. When some Saraswat secured a position of power, younger Saraswats flocked to fill the jobs under his patronage. When that place offered no further prospects, they moved on. Since the colonial system resorted to frequent transfers of its employees from one administrative centre to another according to the need of the hour, this willing submission to itinerant existence suited the rulers perfectly.

Given this history, it's baffling why the Bhanaps should have believed that their children would settle down in Dharwad, and sunk their fortunes in carving a permanent habitation out of a rocky hill.

The isolation of Saraswatpur was not merely geographical. It was also linguistic and, therefore, cultural. Although Kannada was the spoken language of the area, it was rarely heard on the hill, except when it was necessary to converse with village women who came in the mornings with their buffaloes to sell milk or to vend vegetables. And, of course, no one spoke to the scavengers who passed you in the mornings after cleaning the lavatories in the backyards, carrying baskets of human excreta on their heads. If educated Kannada was ever heard spoken in the vicinity, the residents turned and stared at the source of the intrusion in a sort of feigned surprise bordering on indignation. The mother tongue of the Bhanaps is their own brand of Konkani, but reading and writing in Marathi was seen as a mark of high culture.

Nevertheless, it must be admitted that during the half century that the colony was alive and every house buzzing with life, it became the home of a vibrant, idealistic people who were socially active and artistically gifted. Many of the young men actively participated in adult education campaigns or camps to eradicate untouchability. The Prarthana Samaj and Brahmo Samaj had enthusiastic adherents here, practising and propagating strategies for the reform of Hinduism. Many had a leading role in the Indian National Congress and the independence movement, during which a few had even been to prison.

Saraswat girls were brought up more or less on par with boys, and encouraged to participate in sports and other extracurricular activities at school and college, which was rare in the more traditional communities of Karnataka. The freedom with which young Saraswat women mixed with men made them seem flighty and frivolous, but also objects of desire in the eyes of the young men of other communities. I remember Leena being exasperated that so many Kannada novels depicted Saraswat girls as somewhat 'loose'.

Cinema houses were far away in the city and there was no television. So the younger set was self-reliant when it came to entertainment, often enacting short Marathi plays and organizing fancy-dress balls or musical soirées to which flocked not just the Bhanaps who lived in the city but even those from Hubli. The elders watched and smiled in encouragement but rarely interfered with what the young were doing. The Bhanap society on the hill was known even in Bombay and Poona for its immense sophistication, its conscious avoidance of traditional prejudices, its social involvement, and its passion for education. It was driven into the young that enthusiasm for social activities was welcome but it was unacceptable to make a public display of oneself. But even as the hill was buzzing with youth and activity, it began to be gripped by a pervasive anxiety. As the young inevitably started moving to larger cities like Bombay and Bangalore, and as the population of the hill became thinner, an uneasiness began to grow among those who continued to live there that other castes, such as Deshastha Brahmins and Lingayats, would move in and ruin the poised culture of the hill. A Lingayat lady who had recently moved there had said, 'You just watch – this place won't remain Saraswatpur for long. It is soon going to turn into Lingayatpur.' The comment had travelled with lightning speed, filling every resident's heart with dread. Whatever future the founders had envisaged, they had not allowed for a wholesale takeover of their houses by other castes. Ironically, even this prophesy was not fulfilled.

For the sake of completeness, I should mention that there were a few Bhanap families living in the heart of the city. Prominent among them was Dr Annaji Rao Sirur who, through his daily visits, kept a strict eye on the health situation on the hill, and in the manner of general practitioners of the day, acted practically as a personal psychiatrist to the members of every household. Then there was Dinkar Rao Arur, who was a coffee planter in Chikmagalur but lived in a grand mansion in the city. He also owned another mansion in the heart of Saraswatpur that his family had never occupied. Then there were the financially more straitened families living in a shabby cluster of shapeless houses called Saudagar Chawl, my retired uncles among them. But despite the unspoken economic hierarchies, every Bhanap was treated as an equal on the hill.

My family moved out of Sirsi in 1952. My elder brother Vasant was already in college. My sister Prema had only a year to go before finishing school, while I had two. So it made sense for the entire family to move to Dharwad, which was known for its educational institutions. Besides, it had Saraswatpur.

Fortunately, the house of Mangesh Rao Sashittal had just been vacated by their troublesome tenants. I have already described the critical role played by this Mangesh Rao in our family history. When my mother was a widow without a future, he had casually dropped her into the lap of my father and removed himself from the scene. He was now dead, but his wife, Aayi's eldest sister Shantakka, was still alive, ailing and bedridden. Aayi had taken charge of her and brought her to live with us in Sirsi. She was given a smallish dark room entirely to herself, which was no small gesture since the house had only three bedrooms with seven of us living in it. I remember the devotion with which Aayi and Bappa looked after her. All Shantakka pined for on her sickbed was to get back her house in Dharwad.

That happened in 1952. An ecstatic Aayi and Shantakka led our move to Dharwad. Shantakka died within a week of our arrival, happy to be home at last.

It didn't take long for Saraswatpur to start shaping our lives. In Sirsi, our family had a house to itself. We had almost no contact with the other members of our extended family spread across India, except when they came to Sirsi for a visit or when we siblings enthusiastically came to Saraswatpur during our holidays. Now, Aayi's elder sister Indirakka and her husband Vittal Rao shared the house with us along with their two grandchildren. His daughter had lodged her two children with him as there was no provision for proper schooling in Ranebennur, and she looked after the entire expense of that establishment. They lived in one wing of the C-class house, while we occupied the remaining two-thirds. Shantakka's son, too, now sent his daughter Shailaja to live with us since there were no good schools in the small town where he ran a rice mill. There were, thus, eleven of us crowded into that house. But this was not seen as anything unusual, since the house had actually sheltered fifteen children when Bhalchandra was staying there with his cousins during his schooldays.

Vittal Rao had no income or savings of any description. He was a brilliant man, but was regarded by the residents of the hill as someone to be kept at a distance. From his early youth, he was known for his ambition to be an industrial magnate, but in point of fact this had meant leading the life of an inveterate litigant. In pursuit of his ambition to make it to the top of the industry – I never discovered which industry – he had moved from patron to patron, one employer to another, taking them all to court for not giving him the treatment he considered his due. He kept them running to the courtroom until they agreed to his terms. Indian courts are ideally suited to such manoeuvres, since suits go on for years without resolution. If his opponent in a case employed a Saraswat lawyer to represent him, Vittal Rao immediately registered the lawyer as his witness and knocked him off the case.

It was not long after we moved into the house that Vittal Rao came to know of Bappa's Remington typewriter. He instantly borrowed it. 'I have a little court work,' he told Bappa with a smile that established his position as a close in-law. 'I'll return it in a couple of days.' The typewriter simply disappeared from view. But Bappa could hear it from Vittal Rao's section of the house as he typed his court affidavits through the night. Bappa was a man who would record the date on which he took a new razor blade out of its paper cover so he could keep track of how long it had lasted. The relentless pecking at the typewriter keys started giving him insomnia, but given the intricate strands of customary courtesy in a Saraswat family there was nothing he could do. By the time daily life in the house picked up its pace in the mornings, Vittal Rao was out of the house along with the typewriter in his satchel. We all saw Bappa writhe in anguish at his insouciance, but as junior members of the family we were not allowed to comment or offer help.

Bappa was an early sleeper and, therefore, unaware of Vittal Rao's late-night habits. But the insomnia occasioned by Vittal Rao's relentless industry ensured that he soon became familiar with his nocturnal movements. One night, he pretended to be fast asleep – he had to cover his eyes with a hand towel to be able to sleep at all – when he heard Vittal Rao fill the metal pot at the rear door with water and step out into the backyard on his way to the lavatory. Bappa sprang out of bed. By the time Vittal Rao had washed his hands and feet and returned to his table, the Remington had vanished. The paper from its roller had been removed and placed neatly on the table. Bappa was fast asleep, snoring with the towel across his eyes.

Vittal Rao confided in me the next day that the typewriter had proved to be of enormous service, and half-grumbled that it was such a pity it was being kept unused. But we never discovered what plans for an industrial empire had been sabotaged that night by my father's uncouth behaviour.

Saraswatpur created more complex situations than this. The house facing ours across a narrow road was occupied by my mother's uncle who was in his seventies. He lived with his son, a daughter-in-law who looked after her husband with a devotion we had only seen in Hindi films, and a middle-aged woman who looked after the old man's needs. These four people occupied the main section of the house. The rest of the house was occupied by a maternal uncle, his wife, their three daughters, and the daughter of the uncle's younger brother who had committed suicide when he realized his wife was pregnant. These four girls were more or less of my age, one a year older than me, and the rest separated from each other by almost exactly a year. These four cousins, Leena and my niece Shailaja would keep our two houses busy through the day, running between them, giggling, gossiping and carrying out errands for the older members of the family.

A 'maternal uncle's daughter' has strange connotations among the Saraswats. She is your first cousin and, therefore, to be treated exactly as your sister. You are expected to be protective towards her, and concerned about her needs and well-being. But she is also your rightful spouse; it is a young man's primary duty to marry one of them and relieve the uncle of 'the burden of a daughter'. To complicate matters, we were all in our teens, so we grew up together and stepped into our youth with this unspoken ambiguity about the 'cousin/wife' relationship hanging between us.

Of course, there was no question of our holding hands or hugging or kissing, let alone being seen together by ourselves without an implicit commitment being assumed between us. In fact, the first woman I kissed was at Oxford when I was twenty-three. But the half-spoken sentences, glances, nasty remarks, sulks and hurts that swirled through our houses were enough to illuminate for me the erotic world of a girl growing up.

My uncle, not known for his subtlety, had more than hinted several times that he expected me to fulfil my duty to the family by marrying one of his daughters. But I had my eyes fixed on the possibilities of the unknown future, and was determined not to allow any family obligation or emotional entanglement to ruin those prospects. Nevertheless, the sensuous resonance of this constant proximity to these 'cousin sisters' could be very disturbing, particularly when I found myself alone with one of them.

Our two houses stood facing each other, virtually like mirror images, looking into the depths of each other's interiors. The doors were in the middle of the walls and aligned, so that one could stand in the backyard of one house and have an uninterrupted view of what was happening in the backyard opposite. Every secret, every nightmare seemed to echo back and forth between the houses, creating a persistent air of prying and eavesdropping.

By the time my family had moved into Saraswatpur, the generation born or brought up on the hill had already started deserting it. Most of its houses were occupied by retired officials and their ageing wives, or by the school- or college-going young. The generations in between were conspicuous by their absence. The sense of abandonment was palpable. Even half a century after its founding, Saraswatpur continued to remain isolated, far outside the borders of the city. The city had grown at its other end and simply ignored Saraswatpur. The stretch that separated the colony from the city was still empty. It was common to find scorpions in the houses, snakes of various descriptions in the gardens. At night, jackals still bayed by the rainwater pond at the foot of the hill.

One of Aayi's many unfulfilled desires was to have a house of her own. After marrying Bappa, she had followed him devoutly from one government residence to another, as he was transferred every year if not sooner. Now that he was retired and it was time to settle down, this desire became the primary obsession of her life. To grasp the scale of her ambition, and how its progress was woven into the very layout of Saraswatpur, one needs to understand the geographical placement of the houses her restlessness led us through.

The first house we occupied in Dharwad, as already mentioned, was owned by Shantakka and was a C-class house numbered 38. It was, like all C-class houses, situated on the lower side of the Diagonal Road and not acceptable to Aayi's ambitions. On the other side of the road from 38 was 25, a B-class bungalow now occupied by Shankar Rao Sashittal, the unfortunate contractor responsible for building Saraswatpur, but now penniless and bedridden after a stroke. The house was near enough to 38 for us to hear Mrs Sashittal occasionally give vent to her frustrations and curse her husband for turning out to be a physical wreck and a financial failure despite the empire he had at his command. Beyond 25, in line with 38 and 25, but high up on a bluff, surveying the land stretching out to the east, was the majestic house numbered 18. This house was one of the most beautiful houses in Saraswatpur if not in Dharwad, with its long semicircular garden and a pillared portico, the rooms larger than normal, and an area of some twenty gunthas around it.

No member of the family that built the house had ever lived in it. From the day it was considered fit for occupation, it had been used by the family of Narayan Rao Koppikar, the father-in-law of my elder brother, Bhalchandra. Narayan Rao was a well-respected lawyer. He had been active in the independence movement and associated with the leaders of the Indian National Congress. Naturally, when Mahatma Gandhi came to Dharwad on his tour to campaign against untouchability, he had spent the whole afternoon of 4 March 1934 in this house, meeting local political leaders. Yet, when offered a place in the government, Narayan Rao had turned it down, preferring to continue to earn a living as a lawyer. He was gentle, soft-spoken, and almost twitchy in his desire to be helpful. Bappa always spoke of him with respect.

His wife Lalita came from the Nilekani family of Sirsi, about which I have already spoken. It rankled Aayi that the Koppikars had offered their daughter to Bhalchandra without first consulting her and Bappa on the alliance, as tradition demanded. Narayan Rao's letter to Bappa that Bhalchandra had consented to the alliance was the first they heard of it, and this snub was never forgiven. But more than anything else, Lalita's manner continually reminded Aayi that Bappa was only a retired government servant, living on a small salary and known to be tight-fisted, and that it was Bhalchandra's good looks and brilliant academic career that had induced them to stoop socially.

Unfortunately, the geographical placement of our two houses seemed calculated to underline this social disparity. Our house was below the Diagonal Road, built on an excavated plot, almost cowering behind a compound wall. You only had to turn your head ever so slightly to see No. 18 looming above it, in splendid isolation on the promontory. The disparity concretely expressed a difference that could not be narrowed until Aayi moved into, and hopefully owned, a B-class house on the 'proper' side of the Diagonal Road.

After six years in Dharwad, I spent two years in Bombay for my MA, and then another three in Oxford before going on to Madras to work with the Oxford University Press (OUP). During this period, my father developed a cataract in his eye which, after a careless operation, turned into a glaucoma and permanently blinded that eye. Devastated by this, Bappa refused to have his other eye, which had also developed a cataract, even looked at by an ophthalmologist. It was only when I resigned from OUP and decided to return home that I could persuade him to have his eye operated in Madras. This time, the operation was a success and my father's life brightened up. But by then, he had spent nearly two decades in terror of the enveloping blindness and in a deep depression. He was of no help to Aayi in her efforts to buy a suitable house. She struggled alone, bitter about her lack of success. But she refused to give up.

One day, while I was still working with OUP in Madras, Aayi heard that a B-class house had come up for sale. With no one in the house to help her, she ran to seek the assistance of Shankar Rao Shirur.

Shankar Rao lived in a B-class house opposite ours, which I have already referred to earlier as belonging to the sole coffee planter among Saraswats, Dinkar Rao Arur. The house was huge and looked down from a height, with wings spread out, upon the flight of steps that led to the front door. It thus had an air of grand authority, which was further enhanced by Shankar Rao's lifestyle. He had no children, and he and his wife had willingly taken in, free of charge, any number of students looking for lodgings. As there were no large halls for hire in the city, all Saraswat weddings and thread ceremonies were performed in the vast living room of his house. Most of all, whenever the swamiji, the religious head of the community, came to Dharwad, his entire entourage was housed by Shankar Rao. So all members of the community, including those resident in the city of Hubli fifteen kilometres away, gathered in his house. For a week, the house would come alive with bhajans, religious discourses and musical soirées. Most Saraswat families, thus, needed to visit his house at least three or four times a year. He was a good man, liberal and helpful, but with a fierce temper, inclined to fly into a rage at the slightest suspicion of disrespect or disobedience. These flashes of temper, which were accompanied by flailing arms and his voice hitting a distorted high pitch, were feared as much as his person was respected. Under the circumstances, he was the right man for Aayi to go to.

Aayi told Shankar Rao about the house, which he must have already known about since he was the secretary of the Housing Society. 'It would be a great help,' she pleaded, 'if you could intercede and get the price of the house reduced to a more acceptable amount.'

Shankar Rao burst into a loud and dismissive guffaw. 'Kuttakka,' he said, 'we are getting old. None of us is immortal, don't you realize? Why in heaven's name do you want a house of your own at your age? What are you going to do in it that you can't do in your present house? Look at me. I have lived in this house for over three decades now. But I don't own it. It's Dinkar Rao Arur's, and he is happy to have me as a tenant. Be sensible. You are quite all right where you are.'

Aayi felt rebuffed, and climbed down the steps biting her lower lip.

When I returned to Dharwad in 1973, Bhalchandra, who was in Dharwad on his holiday, said to me, 'Listen, the owners of the house occupied by my father-in-law [No. 18] want to sell it. Why don't you approach him if you are interested?'

This was the regal house I had always yearned for. I rushed to Narayan Rao, who was living in it because the owners, like most homeowners in Saraswatpur, lived in Bombay. I had some money saved from my OUP provident fund and the Homi Bhabha Fellowship, which I hoped would be adequate for the purchase. But it was not easy to bring up the subject with Narayan Rao. He and Lalita had lived in the house from the day it was certified habitable. All their children and grandchildren were born and raised there, and everyone had assumed they would live in it forever. I remember trying to control my tremors as I asked him if the house was for sale.

'No,' he replied, with more than a touch of surprise and asperity. 'It's not for sale. I can guarantee that. But the house above yours [No. 25] is. Why don't you think about that?'

I was downcast. I knew B-25 was for sale since the bedridden contractor who had lingered at death's door for years in that house was now dead and his wife had moved to Bombay. But the house occupied by Narayan Rao was the one I was after, and here he was, explicitly telling me that he was not vacating it. There was no point in nursing that hope any further. And there was no way to ask Bhalchandra why his account differed from his father-in-law's. Saraswat etiquette simply did not permit such uncouth behaviour.

But I was determined to make Aayi the mistress of a B-class house. Besides, since the day my first play *Yayati* was published to an enthusiastic response, I had decided to make Dharwad my home so I could immerse myself in the local idiom of Kannada. I bought 25 Saraswatpur.

Aayi was ecstatic. As she and I walked up to inspect the interior of the house that was now ours, Aayi said, 'Good. Now we can sell this house and buy a better one.' We never did get a chance to live in the house. Just then, I was offered the directorship of FTII in Poona. I let out 25 Saraswatpur, and moved to Poona with Aayi and Bappa.

We had barely settled down in Poona when news arrived that Narayan Rao's residence was indeed up for sale. It was clear he had deliberately misled me, but who could blame him? To die in a house of one's own is every Indian's dream, and Narayan Rao would be justified in assuming that his daughter Suman and son-in-law Bhalchandra would buy the house and make it available to him for his retirement. That was a normal Indian expectation, but in pragmatic terms it made no sense for Bhalchandra to do so. His own future as well as his children's seemed to be in North India if not abroad. The house I had always eyed was now up for sale, but all my money had been invested in No. 25. I cursed Narayan Rao under my breath. Then, a fresh development gave events a happy turn.

My sister Prema and her husband Dr Vasant Nadkarni had, until then, lived in Malaysia. Now, Vasant felt the political situation was becoming unsafe for émigré Indians and decided he wanted a refuge of his own in India should the Malaysian situation get out of hand. He, therefore, bought 18 Saraswatpur with the intention of retiring in Dharwad. But there were no immediate plans to move. Prema was anyway reluctant to leave Kuala Lumpur, where her children were now settled and where she had a vast circle of friends. So, when I finished my two years with FTII and we returned to Dharwad, Aayi and Bappa, in effect, became the caretakers of No. 18. I moved in with them in the fashion of unmarried men in Indian families. Aayi had completed her dream journey with the entire Saraswat community witnessing her literal elevation. She had started in a C-class house on the lower side of the Diagonal Road, skipped over the B-class house which was hers by rights, and landed in the most prominent of the B-class houses – that too, one on the heights from which she had once sensed her in-law Lalita looking down upon her.

Another strand in this web of relations made this plot-twist particularly painful. Narayan Rao and Lalita were keen that my sister Prema should marry their son. Since Bhalchandra, Prema's brother, was a son-in-law they were attached to, this connection was seen as completing a traditionally ordained symmetry in marital relationships. But just as this relationship was about to materialize, Prema met her present husband and rejected Narayan Rao's son. This rejection had naturally turned the already-strained relations between our two families to bitterness. Now Prema had topped it all by purchasing their house.

After vacating No. 18, Narayan Rao moved with his family into a B-class house nearby. It is not hard to imagine the anguish the move must have caused. The whole family was viscerally entangled with the old house in which they had spent half a century. One day, after my return to Dharwad with my parents, I was supervising some changes in the structure of the house when Narayan Rao walked in on some errand. He was aghast at the changes I was proposing. He blurted out in horror, 'No, no, you can't do that. That door has to remain where it is!' Even as he said the words, he realized he was overstepping his bounds, flushed violently, turned and almost ran out. I hate to think of the pain it must have caused Lalita to see us running around in her house, and worse still, to receive regular reports of all that was being done to the interiors she had once ruled as being hers in perpetuity. After a few months, Narayan Rao and Lalita moved to their son's place in Poona. They never came back.

The Arur house, in which Shankar Rao Shirur continued to live, was directly opposite our new residence. Aayi said to me one day, not without a certain smug satisfaction, 'There! Shankar Rao continues to be a tenant in that house, and I have two houses owned by my children right in his front yard.' This proximity also caused a certain amount of wear and tear in the social decorum that was the pervading characteristic of Saraswatpur.

One day, Aayi was reading in the pillared porch of our house when she noticed activity in the neighbouring compound. The maid employed in Shankar Rao's house had begun to have a small house of her own built. Since she could not afford to pay for tiles, Shankar Rao had generously allowed her to take away the tiles of his outhouse. But he had no authority to give away these tiles. As he had loudly proclaimed to Aayi years ago, he was only a tenant in the house. The tiles rightfully belonged to Dinkar Rao Arur who lived in Line Bazar.

So Aayi phoned Mrs Arur, who visited Saraswatpur that evening on the pretext of attending a bhajan organized in the house next to Shankar Rao's. On her way home, she casually sauntered through Shankar Rao's compound. It wouldn't be the done thing to comment on the missing tiles, of course, but she paused long enough while staring at the bare beams of the outhouse to register her comment. Shankar Rao realized someone had tattled and was instantly convinced it was the lady of the house in which the bhajans had taken place. The moment Mrs Arur left, he rushed to the gate of his house and started, as usual, at the top of his voice, heaping imprecations on the 'mischief-makers' of Saraswatpur and its 'venomous snitchers'. 'Jealousy, that's what it is, rank jealousy!' he raved. The lady at whom these curses were aimed heard him from her house, and walked up to her gate nodding her head in commiseration with no idea what he was shouting about. Aayi stood calmly listening to him from our compound, playing the sympathetic neighbour.

Much later, my brother-in-law in Malaysia became increasingly involved in spiritual pursuits. He began to seriously consider returning to Dharwad to continue his studies. This scared my sister, who was simply not willing to move away from her two sons, their wives, the grandchildren, and of course the large network of friends with whom she shared the Bhagavad Gita as well as rummy evenings. There was also the additional argument put forward by their sons, that it was far too inconvenient to come rushing from Kuala Lumpur to Dharwad if there was a sudden crisis. Prema told me she had no other recourse but to sell the house and asked if I would buy it. I did so with absolute delight. I would have done so years ago if it were not for my brother-in-law's frequently mentioned intention of returning to India. The house I had wanted to possess for forty years finally became mine.

Saraswatpur was already going downhill at the time and did not last long after I moved in. But it did not 'lose caste' as my contemporaries had feared. Perhaps its essence was in its forlorn solitude – its end came when the prosperity that had left it untouched for so many decades finally came its way. In the 1970s, the Heggade of Dharmasthala built a college on the Karwar road further down from the colony. The city also flowed in the direction of Hubli, replacing the hundreds of guava plantations along that route with buildings. This drew the attention of real estate developers to the hill. It was not the spacious houses that attracted them, but the open grounds they were built on. The craze for high-rise blocks of flats – regardless of whether they were right for the terrain, regardless of whether there was enough water to meet the needs of occupants – led to real estate gobbling up Saraswatpur. Only a couple of Saraswat families are now left on the hill. A colony that was considered a folly in the twentieth century has fallen victim to the follies of the twenty-first.

4

DHARWAD

Karnatak College

My family left Sirsi and moved to Dharwad in 1952. I lived there for six years, until I moved to Bombay in 1958. My first two years in Dharwad were spent at the Basel Mission School, but from the moment I stepped into the city, my eyes were firmly set on what was certainly the most magnificent as well as the best-known building in the area: Karnatak College.

In 1952, India had not been reorganized linguistically, and the districts of Dharwad, Belgaum, Bijapur and Karwar were part of the Bombay Presidency. These four districts stood apart in a huge administrative unit that sprawled from the northern borders of Mangalore district to Gujarat, because these were areas where Kannada was spoken. The rest of the Presidency was dominated by Marathi and Gujarati. Bombay was the capital of this Presidency, but Kannada was not heard in the city except in the homes of those who had moved there for education or employment. Even sophisticated Marathi literature of the period is replete with mocking references to Kannada, calling it crude and uncouth. North Karnataka, as these four districts were known, was remote from the capital and an economically neglected area. Culturally, it was dominated by the Marathi language. Aayi often lamented that, by accepting the transfer to Sirsi, Bappa had deprived us of the rich and vibrant culture of Maharashtra and Marathi.

As a student at Karnatak College

It was not just that North Karnataka was remote from the political centres of Bombay and Poona, it also lived a life sundered from the princely state of Mysore, which considered itself the acme of pure Kannada culture. Even the spoken idiom of North Karnataka was considered rough and uncivilized compared to the polished court language that emanated from Mysore. The district of South Kanara – Mangalore – which formed a part of the Madras Presidency had benefited from the attention paid to it by Christian missionaries, who built excellent educational institutions there as well as the rudiments of industrialization. While banks originating in North Karnataka had sunk without a trace, the four from South Kanara – Canara, Corporation, Vijaya and Syndicate – had gathered strength and would go on to become banks of national importance.

Isolated from Mysore and South Kanara, North Karnataka had found a local cultural centre in Dharwad. The city was on the western edge of the Deccan plateau, around a hundred and fifty kilometres from the Goan coastal strip, situated on an outcrop before the Western Ghats plunged down to the sea. It had, therefore, a temperate climate. The British had built many educational institutions there, and Dharwad was admired as a place suitable for retired government servants, college students and poets.

In the Marikamba School in Sirsi, we had been brought up to believe that literary figures were endowed with divine grace. And Dharwad was bursting with such celebrities. One day, while I was still at the Basel Mission School, my Kannada teacher invited a few of us students home for tea. While we were animatedly discussing the state of Kannada literature, a gracious old man in flowing clothes and with a resplendent beard walked in, sat down, chatted with us and left. It turned out to be Aluru Venkata Rao, one of the founding figures of modern Kannada literature. I was so thrilled by the encounter that I went home and wrote a poem about him. Later, I met several such revered figures (though none of them again inspired a poem). In fact, the high density of poets in Dharwad was not particularly conducive to a young man aspiring to be a poet. The cliché was that the city's population was divided into two species: poets and critics. Another saying went: 'If you stand in a corner and randomly fling a stone in Dharwad, it will land on the roof of a poet.' To which a local poet Chennaveera Kanavi added, 'The stone thrower is invariably a poet too.'

One day, the writer V.K. Gokak came to our school to judge a poetry contest. He was also the principal of Karnatak College, where I hoped to study, and so I observed him intently. Since coming to Dharwad, I had visited Karnatak College several times, gazed longingly at the building, and thrilled at imagining myself in its corridors. The college building had originally been constructed by the Madras and Southern Mahratta Railway for its offices, but a governor of Bombay had been generous enough to acquire it for the education department. It was a magnificent structure in redbrick and steel. The arches of its elegant façade, the wide corridors and spacious classrooms, the grand steps at the front of the college, the spiral staircases at the ends of corridors, all gave it a grandeur in keeping with the stature of the college.

Gokak's personality matched the college he was principal of: he was a tall man who walked with a long stride and a slight stoop; he had a smiling countenance and a deep, somewhat nasal voice. And in my eyes, he possessed all the glamour of a leading literary figure. As if this weren't enough, his academic prowess shone about him like a halo: he had studied English literature at Oxford and been awarded the rare 'congratulatory first'. So, it could be said that he had surpassed our British rulers at their own literature.

Gokak was also known for being an excellent administrator. Karnatak College was a government institution, and it was believed that the then director of public instruction in Poona, D.C. Pavate, had appointed the best teachers he could find, expecting the college to one day be part of Karnatak University. The professors who taught there were authorities in their fields, and Gokak received much praise for being able to manage them all without giving occasion for any friction.

But what made the deepest impression on students was Gokak's boundless enthusiasm for teaching. Since he taught at all stages of the four-year degree course, every class had the opportunity to interact closely with him. As a result, he too had some idea about what was going on with the students in different classes.

Soon after I joined college, I spoke to him in the corridor after a class. 'I write poetry,' I told him. 'I want to understand modern English poetry. What should I read?' He took me to his office and said, 'Sit. Write this down.' I sat in front of him, practically trembling with eagerness. He said, 'Had you asked this question to anyone else, they might have asked you to read T.S. Eliot.

He's a good poet, of course. But he's a difficult poet. Don't start with him.' He gave me the names of W.H. Auden, Stephen Spender, Cecil Day-Lewis and Louis MacNeice. I ran at once to the college library.

The evolution of my artistic sensibilities seemed to begin the instant I set foot in college. I could experience this myself from day to day. The novel I had read and adored a week ago would start to feel ordinary. 'At last, I have written a good poem,' I would congratulate myself, but the same poem felt childish after a few days. It was the kind of feverish stimulation that the poet Adiga described as 'Everywhere the hand extends – a switch, a switch.' Going to the library became a cause for anxiety. It was like stepping into a minefield: there was no telling where a new bud might sprout, when a lightning bolt might strike.

One day, a classmate held out a book and said, grumbling, 'I borrowed the book thinking it would have a good story, but this...' It was B.C. Ramachandra Sharma's *Elu Suttina Kote*. I sat down at once to read the poems. On another day, I was looking at books through the glass pane of a bookcase when I saw on a spine the name Frost. I drew the book out from curiosity, and was immediately transported by the poems. Robert Frost remains one of my favourite poets to this day.

Similarly, I began to read a book called *A Key to Modern British Poetry* after it caught my eye in the library. It was by a then-unknown writer named Lawrence Durrell. He wrote that the scientific advances of the nineteenth and twentieth centuries had changed what lay at the heart of poetry, and that it was impossible to write poetry any more without responding to the world that science was opening up. He described with examples how poetry had been transformed by the work of scientists like Einstein, Freud, Darwin and others. Durrell would go on to make a name for himself as a novelist. When I was at Oxford, copies of *The Alexandria Quartet* were invariably found on every student's bookshelf. But I have not to date met anyone who has read or even heard of *A Key to Modern British Poetry*. In addition to its bold ideas, I also benefitted from the writers it quoted. It brought to my attention Eliot, Dylan Thomas, Freud and others, and made them part of my consciousness.

My four years in college can be bookended by two great poems. In the first year, I had read the poems in my English textbook even before classes began and marked the ones I had found difficult. So, when Gokak asked in class, 'What poem should I teach today?' I immediately said 'Kubla Khan' (for which my classmates cursed me later). Gokak nodded gravely. He started with Plato, expounded upon Beauty, Truth and Goodness as philosophical concepts, and went on to explain how the early nineteenth-century Romantic poets incorporated these ideas into their work. 'Kubla Khan' had come to Coleridge in an opium-induced reverie, and Gokak unlocked for us the magical world hidden in it. I grew obsessed with the poem after he taught it. In the next three years, I translated it thrice into Kannada.

When I was in the fourth year, my friend Kitti – Krishna Basrur – who was in the MA course, brought news that V.M. Inamdar was about to teach 'The Waste Land' in his class. I had begun looking up to Inamdar when he taught us *The Mayor of Casterbridge.* He brought Hardy's Wessex to life as if it were all happening on a stage in front of us. The story, in which tragic characters grapple with fates that toss them about, made my hair stand on end. In his classes, one had a chance to feel the throbbing heart of a novel. Gokak, on the other hand, had a greater affinity towards poetry. I don't recall ever having heard him speak of modern novels with any enthusiasm. His sensibilities, too, were of the Romantic period, and he regarded Shelley as the greatest of poets. Inamdar's teaching of 'The Waste Land' took me by the hand and led me to the modern. I recalled Gokak's warning that Eliot was a difficult poet. But now, he was mine. Later, Kitti, Aurora and I sat in a corner reading 'The Four Quartets', savouring it line by line.

Even though the most memorable events of my college life have to do with poetry and literature, it was mathematics I was studying for my BA. Mathematics filled me with terror, but there was a reason why I still chose it as my main subject.

By the time I stepped into college, I had begun to feel suffocated by the cultural atmosphere in India. It felt stale and lethargic, and I was convinced my talents would go unrecognized here. I vowed to somehow go abroad and make an impression in the lands that had produced giants such as Eliot, Pound and Hemingway. But how was I to go abroad? My father was not wealthy enough to send me, so it would have to be through a scholarship of some sort. And to get a scholarship, it was necessary to have a first-class BA or BSc. But how was I to be sure of getting such a result? The subjects I was truly interested in were English literature and philosophy. Economics was

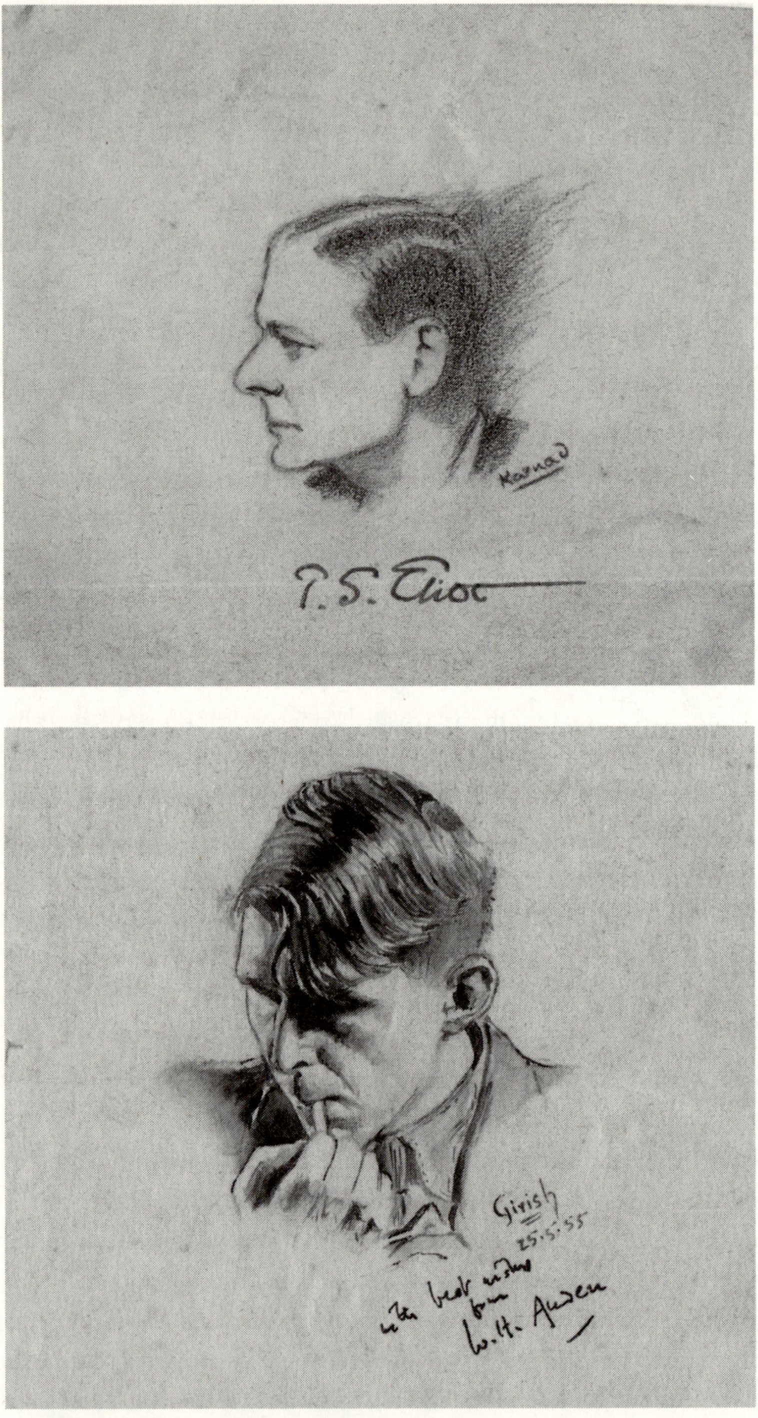

Sketches of Eliot and Auden, autographed by them. I also had Agatha Christie, P.G. Wodehouse, Pearl S. Buck and Tenzing Norgay, among others, sign my sketches of them.

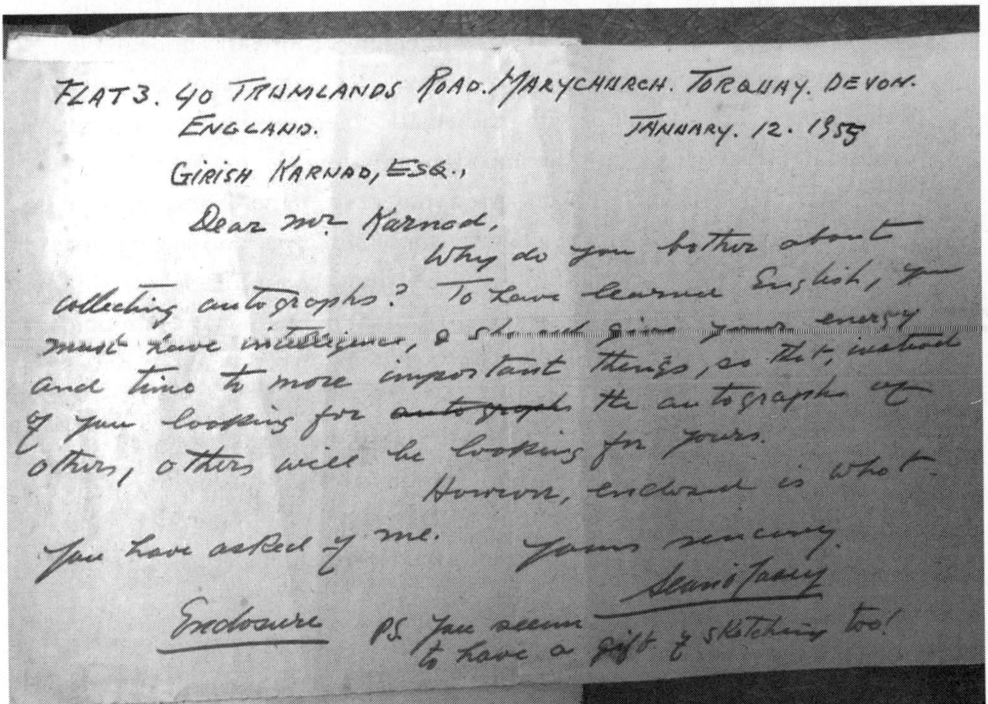

FLAT 3. 40 TRUMLANDS ROAD. MARYCHURCH. TORQUAY. DEVON.
ENGLAND. JANUARY. 12. 1955

GIRISH KARNAD, ESQ.,

Dear Mr Karnad,

Why do you bother about collecting autographs? To have learned English, you must have intelligence, & should give your energy and time to more important things, so that, instead of you looking for ~~autographs~~ the autographs of others, others will be looking for yours.

However, enclosed is what you have asked of me.

Yours sincerely.

Sean O'Casey

Enclosure

P.S. You seem to have a gift of sketching too!

A letter from the Irish dramatist, Sean O'Casey, suggesting that I stop pursuing other people's autographs and get them to pursue mine.

an attractive option from the perspective of employment because the system of five-year plans had just been introduced and was certain to absorb a large number of economics graduates. But the trouble with all these subjects was that the evaluation of answer scripts was subjective, at the discretion of the examiner.

This was not the case with science subjects, where questions have precise, well-defined answers. But if I were to study science, I would have to spend hours every day in a laboratory, the very thought of which was unbearable. One thing was certain – whatever subject I studied, it would take a great deal of effort to get a first class. But with mathematics there was neither the grim prospect of the laboratory nor the uncertainty of the examiner's opinion.

So, after all this calculation, I became a student of mathematics at the age of sixteen. I worked hard and my plan was successful. I went on to get a first class in my BA and I stood first in the university; I received a scholarship and went abroad. I was not a very sincere student of mathematics though, given that my sole purpose in studying it was to obtain more marks. But as the examinations approached and I immersed myself day and night in the subject, I began to see in it patterns, arrangements, rhythm, elegance. In one of Aldous Huxley's stories, a character is moved to tears by the beauty of the Pythagorean theorem. Such a reaction was not surprising to me once I had begun to relish how mathematics – ripple upon ripple, branch growing from branch – led one to the uncanny and wonderful.

It was only later, when I was in Oxford and writing *Tughlaq*, that I realized how studying mathematics had shaped my working process. While proving a theorem, it is important at the outset to identify its constituent parts, the relationships between those parts, and how they are held in balance. It is mathematics that taught me that, while working out an individual part, I always had to be vigilant about the effect it had on the other parts, and how it changed the overall structure as well as the interrelationships between various parts. This is essential technical training for a playwright.

It was at Karnatak College that I met Krishna Basrur, who remained a friend until his death. Kitti and I recognized our obsessions in each other the instant we met. Our family backgrounds could not have been more different, but this only created more room for each other's experiences and drew us closer.

My parents had made sure their children were bound by the glue of familial love. Even when there was some friction amongst us, we never lost the feeling that we were all born together. We never grew emotionally distant. Our families are now scattered in far-flung corners of the world, and with the birth of children and grandchildren we have new loyalties to contend with. Still, we have all kept in close contact.

Kitti's parents divorced when he was a child. His father started another family and gave him little attention. His mother was one of the first women to have studied law in India, but since her work was in the provinces of North India, Kitti was entrusted to a public school from a young age. He grew up alone. His relationship with his mother was volatile, marked by anger, insult and betrayal.

He told me one day that, when he was an adolescent, he had found and read a letter from his mother to her younger sister. His mother had written: 'It's a moment's madness that leads to the birth of a child. Then we regret it all our life.' Kitti asked me, laughing, 'Don't you think it's strange she left the letter lying around on the table? Maybe she wanted me to find it?'

As a consequence of his solitary childhood, Kitti was able to relate sensitively to the pain, despair and longings of others. He could meet a stranger and form a close bond almost instantly. Equally, there were occasions when he abruptly broke off close friendships without good reason.

Cigarette smoke emanated from Kitti's lips all day long. He was copiously talented, but paid no regard to success and spoke with contempt about matters like long-term security. In spite of being a reflective person with a deep interest in literature, he struggled with his BA and passed with a third class. He later had well-paying jobs, but he seemed allergic to the word 'wealth' and never bothered to save money. Kitti had an enormous fondness for language, literature and poetry. If someone did an injustice to language, in speech or in writing, he would be outraged as if that person had attacked a child.

Kitti once wrote a poem and showed it to Gokak, who pointed out that the entire poem was nothing more than a garland of adjectives. Kitti was disgusted with himself for a week after that. And then, Gokak read out his new English poem in a large gathering. When he read the lines –

And you my friend
Standing by the pool
So nice and cool

– Kitti burst out laughing loud enough for everyone to hear. The next day, Gokak threw him out of his class and said, 'Don't come back.' But Gokak forgave him after he apologized.

I have already mentioned that Kitti lived in his aunt's house in Saraswatpur, right next to our house. We would return from college together and set out to roam the hills of Attikolla, Someshwara and Nuggikeri while we talked. Kitti's aunt was his anchor, the one who provided him with the affection and understanding he did not receive from his mother.

An equally close friend was Aurora Figueredo, whose family was from Goa. Her father came from an affluent family and was a good pianist, but he happened to be an alcoholic. Since the Bombay Presidency was under prohibition, Aurora's mother led a move to Dharwad with her husband and their seven or eight children. Because the family was struggling financially, Aurora had learnt stenotyping even as she went to school, and was preparing to work as a secretary. But when she passed her SSC with a first class, Father Suarez of St Joseph's Church extended financial support so she could go to college. Aurora seized the opportunity. She studied English and French, and graduated without missing a first class in any year. Thanks to my association with Aurora, I gained an appreciation for French literature and for the traditions of thought associated with philosophers like Blaise Pascal and René Descartes.

Our world was rapidly expanding around us. And it was beckoning: I believed that the opportunities this wide world offered had to be grabbed, that I had to move beyond the confines of India into the international realm and take on the cultural, intellectual and artistic challenges this entailed. Kitti and Aurora shared my naïve enthusiasm. I have to admit that the intellectual stimulus I found in their company led me to gradually move

Krishna Basrur

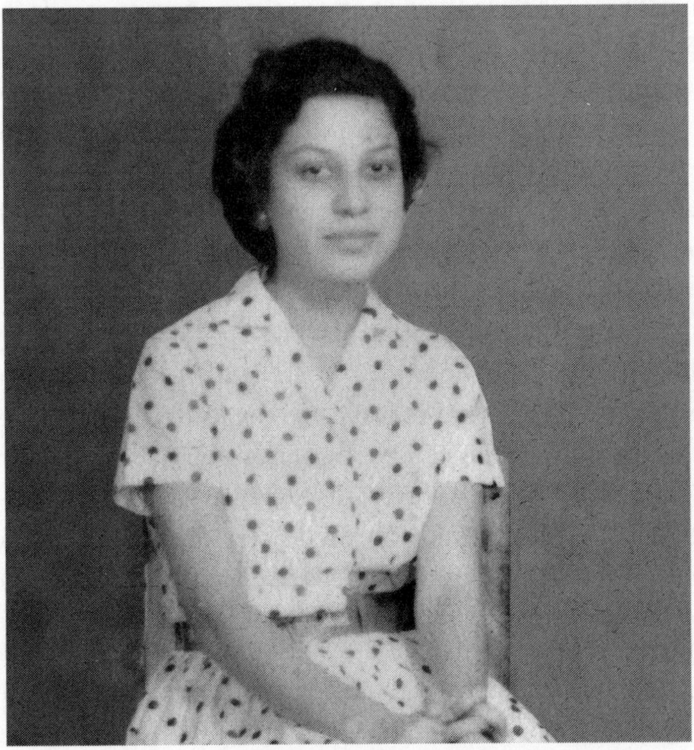

Aurora Figueredo

away from Kannada. I immersed myself in English cultural activities during my last two years at college.

This transformation also had something to do with my changing views on Gokak. I had initially been enamoured of him, but increasingly I found myself disenchanted. When I was in the second year, one of our professors, S.R. Malagi, directed Gokak's play *Yugantara*. Since the play lacked humour, Malagi asked Gokak to add a few comedic scenes. These pasted-in scenes turned out to be the most popular with the students and only served to highlight the weaknesses of the original play. I was part of the cast, and I agonized over the thought that I was wasting my time. I decided to stay away from such mediocre plays in the future. I also began to doubt Gokak's abilities and question if his sensibilities were modern enough.

At that age, what stood out starkly to me were Gokak's antiquated views on how men and women were to behave around each other. The young men and women of Karnatak College had always interacted freely, but Gokak took it upon himself to impose restrictions. I remember that there was even a screen put up, so that girls could not stand in the gallery outside the ladies' room and communicate with boys standing in the opposite gallery.

I had grown up sceptical when it came to things like holy men and sacred ash, and found it hard to come to terms with Gokak's eagerness to bow before anyone wearing ochre. He had an affinity for students who were interested in literature, and would invite them to his house. At some point, I started distancing myself from that group. One evening, he ran into me in front of the college and said emotionally, 'Girish, you don't come to me. You boycott me.' I didn't know what to say and could only mumble something in response.

It didn't take me long to realize that he was not a particularly important poet. Instead of directly confronting his own anxieties and desires, he tended to seek consolation in spirituality. This meant that his poems, unable to explore human experience, were forced to rely on techniques like rhyme and alliteration. More than anything, he was deeply troubled by modern culture and science, and he sought to express this in language that was poetic and spiritual. The muddled train of thought that ensued was insufferable.

Once, while giving a speech, he launched into a fierce criticism of Freud's work. He said with revulsion, 'It is ugly. Horrible.' After the speech, I stood up to ask a question: 'Freud was a psychoanalyst, and the purpose of his work was to treat mental illnesses. It's important to know whether his ideas are successful in treating patients. Why should we raise questions of beauty and ugliness when it comes to medicine?' Gokak only said, 'But there is no beauty in it! No poetic justice!' I sat down quietly. Kitti, sitting next to me, slid a piece of paper in front of me. He had written: 'Clichés.'

Kitti, Aurora and I, along with Vinayak Shirke and a few other students of philosophy, started a discussion forum called the Socratic Club. The idea was to list issues we had read about or were grappling with ourselves. We would then write papers proposing our solutions and discuss them. Our first rule was to stay away from the self-satisfied pretentiousness of Sarvepalli Radhakrishnan that was in vogue as 'Indian Philosophy'. (He was vice president at the time too.) The idea for the club had come from a professor of philosophy at the college, K.J. Shah. Besides Shah, there was also P. Nagaraja Rao who taught philosophy. But since he never tired of repeating 'I am the leading Indian philosopher after Dr Radhakrishnan', we gave him a wide berth.

Shah must have been around thirty-five at the time. Not only had he gone to Cambridge, he had been a close student of Wittgenstein while he was there. Shah was languidness personified with his loose, often-unbuttoned shirt, his long, uncombed hair, slight stoop, and a constant air of abstraction. If you asked him a simple question, he would listen intently, think for a while, and then answer carefully, pausing in the middle of every sentence. We had heard that this was a characteristic shared by Wittgenstein's entire academic lineage. Shah's room was truly a bachelor's den: stacks of paper everywhere, thick books and journals of philosophy, essays submitted by students for their exams. It was here that I first heard the names of philosophers such as A.J. Ayer, Iris Murdoch, Gilbert Ryle and others.

Yet, there was a kind of order within that mess. The announcement soliciting applications for the Rhodes Scholarship had gone to all the professors, but it was only Shah who kept it aside and remembered to give it to me with the advice to apply. Shah was close friends with the professor of French, Kashinath Mahale, and it was a delight to spend time in their company. They were straightforward and unaffected, and there was always a good-natured discussion going on about philosophy or literature.

Shah's teaching method – he followed the Cambridge tradition – often proved too difficult for students, and there had been occasions when they went on strike against him. Those students usually wanted notes and fixed answers to questions that might appear in the exams. But I took every opportunity to sit in Shah's classes. Even if I didn't follow everything he was teaching, I would try to understand the broad direction in which his questions were taking us. Later, when I was a student of philosophy at Oxford, this unofficial guidance received from Shah came to my aid.

The most valuable thing I learnt from Shah was to choose with great care the words used for analysing ideas. The connection between language and philosophy was deep and delicate. Before using a word, it was important to examine how it was used in everyday speech, and to take utmost care that incongruous meanings were not foisted upon it. Only then, Shah convinced us, could any meaningful intellectual enquiry take place. Such precision was exhilarating at a time when the elaborate web of words spun by Radhakrishnan and Nagaraja Rao was being held up as the essence of Indian philosophy.

Shah knew Sanskrit well and had been a Dakshina Fellow in Sanskrit at Bombay University. So, he had an understanding of the concerns of Indian philosophy. He initiated work on the similarities between Bhartrihari and Wittgenstein, a path down which many others followed him. He argued that the Indian intellectual tradition evolved from the tight intertwining of the ways of thinking contained in texts such as the *Natyashastra, Manusmriti* and *Arthashastra*. As a result, these texts could not be understood in isolation; they had to be grasped as a whole, along with the interrelationships between them. (Here, it must be said that Shah had absolutely no interest in oral traditions. The oral literature in Kannada and Tamil that A.K. Ramanujan studied, translated and brought to the world's attention both complements and challenges the area of Shah's interest.)

But Shah and Ramanujan were in agreement when it came to language: that one should not fall prey to easily or traditionally available clichés, that a word must be tested against its daily use and then employed with a precisely defined meaning. Having this idea drilled into me at a young age proved very useful: going forward, it helped me steer clear of many meaningless ideologies.

Shah once shared a story about Wittgenstein. They were walking together when, in the course of their conversation, Wittgenstein asked, 'What do the Jains believe about the dead?' Shah said mischievously, 'Oh, all kinds of things. Souls float up like balloons and stick to the sky, and so on.' Wittgenstein stopped and stared at Shah. He said, 'You think you're very clever, don't you?' Shah still squirmed at the memory.

Though I liked philosophy, I had chosen mathematics as my subject in college after calculating that it would improve my chances of a first class. It was Shah who gave direction to my studies by making me aware that the two subjects were closely related and shared common underpinnings. At Oxford, I studied in a tradition that equated linguistic analysis with philosophy. On my return to India, it was Shah who cautioned me: 'If we don't accept that there are human experiences beyond the construct of language, then all philosophy is reduced to wordplay.'

Marathi had a strong presence in Dharwad until the linguistic reorganization of 1956 made North Karnataka part of the new Mysore state. In addition to the Marathi-speaking families that lived in Dharwad, students from other parts of Bombay province came there in large numbers. Students also came from Goa, and to them Marathi was as familiar as Konkani. These Marathi speakers all had a great enthusiasm for theatre, as a result of which Dharwad had more plays performed in Marathi than in Kannada, and though there was the occasional visit by a professional theatre company, most of this vibrant theatre scene was the work of local amateur groups. I myself played a small part in Pu La Deshpande's *Amaldar*. But Marathi theatre became less active after 1956.

In 1956, the government organized a National Youth Festival in Delhi in which my elder brother Vasant participated as a violinist. The next year, Kitti, Aurora and I put up a performance of A.A. Milne's *The Ugly Duckling*, won a regional contest, and went to Delhi. As a play, *The Ugly Duckling* was not any more memorable than Gokak's *Yugantara*, and the professor who directed us, W.W.S. Bhaskar, had no clue about direction. But by virtue of directing this play, he got to attend a theatre workshop for teachers organized in Bombay by Ebrahim Alkazi. Though he didn't learn direction there, he brought technical concepts like composition, choreography and ensemble acting to Dharwad and sowed them in our group. He began rehearsals for Jean Anouilh's *Antigone*, which he had read in Bombay. Kitti was to play Creon. I was given the not very important role of Haemon. The project was abandoned for some reason, but not before we had read the play thoroughly five or six times.

That was all I needed. For the first time in my life, I had been part of an important, serious play. Those five or six rehearsals gave me the sense of possessing a living connection with the tradition of Greek drama, with French plays, and because Laurence Olivier and Vivien Leigh had performed it in London, with the world of English theatre. The play, constructed beautifully and written in France under the influence of existentialism, inspired me in many ways. For one, the Chitralekha–Yayati confrontation in my play *Yayati* is directly inspired by the conflict between Antigone and Creon.

As luck would have it, the same year Karnatak College was hosting the All India English Teachers' Conference. English teachers from various universities across India participated in vigorous discussions about teaching the English language and its literature. It hardly needs to be mentioned that we were involved as volunteers, only too thrilled to be around the leading lights of English education in India.

Kitti, Aurora, I and some others put up a play: Bernard Shaw's *The Man of Destiny*. Shaw was not yet a mature playwright when he wrote this play. It is set around an imaginary event from Napoleon's early life, before he had consolidated France into an empire. Kitti took the lead role of Napoleon and I played an innkeeper. In its rasa, the play was the very opposite of *Antigone*. Shaw evokes laughter line after line, and it was a delight to feel the audience respond to his humour. But what I found exemplary about the play was its taut dialogue, its lean form with nothing superfluous.

When the conference was over, I wrote an English play. There, too, the situation was that of an older man in an exchange of words with a sharp-witted young woman. Kitti dismissed it as 'pure imitation'. Still, I had passed through the crucibles of Shaw and Anouilh, both excellent playwrights but each entirely unlike the other. My understanding of theatre had begun to grow.

As far back as I can remember, I had wanted to be a poet. In college, I read, wrote and imitated poems. I gazed longingly at poets and envied them. But looking back now, I realize that all my personal growth came from plays. *Yugantara, The Ugly Duckling, Antigone* and *The Man of Destiny* all mark different stages of my evolution.

The conference was attended by three well-known professors: Dr Stock from Jaipur, Dr S.C. De from Allahabad, and Prof. Dastur. Stock was a woman and Aurora would later remember her fondly for her perceptiveness about colours, flowers, the texture of cloth. De wore an achkan with dhoti and looked every bit the Allahabadi. Dastur wore a suit and spoke English with a polished accent.

In her speech, Stock argued, 'It is true that Indians write poetry in English. But these poems lack the emphasis and rhythm that are natural to the English language, and so they tend not to flow off the tongues of those who speak English as their mother tongue.' A.K. Ramanujan, who was there representing Belgaum's Lingaraj College, addressed Stock and read out some of his poems. She was impressed by his facility with English and spoke highly of him to other delegates. It was no small thing to be praised by Stock. Ramanujan's standing soared at once. That evening, Dastur met Ramanujan in the college staffroom and had him read his poetry. The long discussion that followed was meant to be private, but I had hidden myself outside the staffroom window to listen to them. All I remember now is that one of them – I can't remember who – said, 'In poetry, one should absolutely avoid evocative language.'

At the time, Ramanujan's poems were being published in *The Illustrated Weekly of India*. We had always thought of him as a considerable talent, and this was established beyond a doubt during the conference. He would visit Dharwad with students when there was a debate or drama competition organized between Karnatak College and Lingaraj College. And when we visited Belgaum, we got to spend time with him, thanks to our mutual friend Ashok Kulkarni. Ramanujan revelled in conversation, and had a special enthusiasm when it came to analysing his own poetry. It was while reading Lawrence Durrell that I first encountered the idea that 'a poem must be scientific'. In describing how he had applied the dictum to his own poetry, Ramanujan dragged in figures such as Coleridge, Eliot, Leavis and Allen Tate, and set them to work on behalf of his poems.

Ramanujan was of short build, had somewhat protruding teeth and a slightly upturned nose, and spoke in a high-pitched voice. I had thought that these had led to Ramanujan suffering from an inferiority complex. But soon after meeting him, Aurora declared: 'He has no lack of self-esteem. You can see his boldness in just the way he looks at a woman.' With time, I realized that he had a fine sense of humour, and a perceptiveness that allowed him to spot the incongruous in something entirely ordinary that someone had said. He could delicately brush aside pomp and pretension, but was also capable of cutting sarcasm. He had an endless enthusiasm for poetry, literature and people he held close to him. The better I got to know him, the higher he rose in my esteem. Even so, I was particularly attracted to two qualities of his.

The first was that, unlike other English teachers at the time, he could talk about contemporary Western writers without valorizing them. To use his own term: without any 'lowly-me-ness'. At the time, it was rare to find an objectivity that could praise Western writers as well as examine their flaws.

The other was his exceptionally wide range of interests. He had a deep interest in cultural processes. He collected proverbs, riddles, songs that accompanied games, grandmothers' tales sourced from old women he visited in villages, folk tales. To the rest of us, these did not seem related to literature and felt meaningless in the context of Eliot and Pound. It took me another two decades to realize the importance of the work he was doing.

It must be admitted that we did not anticipate the extent to which he would blossom after going to the United States, or foresee the heights he would eventually rise to.

It was in Karnatak College that I fleetingly met a person who would later change the course of my life – Kirtinath Kurtakoti. I first heard of Kirti from

A.K. Ramanujan

Kitti, who was his classmate. Kitti had said with wonder, 'This man spends day and night discussing literature. He is not interested in anything other than writers.' Kirti had done his BA from Gadag, and not having the means to pursue his studies any further, had worked for five years as a schoolmaster. Now, he had come to Karnatak College for his MA. I was curious about him for one reason only: he was close to Manohara Grantha Mala's G.B. Joshi and was always found at his house.

Back then, college students flocked to Subhash Road every evening. It was an important part of the day's routine for boys to stroll from Vidyavardhaka Sangha to Gandhi Chowk, chatting amongst each other while discreetly eyeing girls who were there for the same purpose. But every time I passed by Manohara Grantha Mala, its nameboard drew my attention more than any girl could. I yearned to somehow gain entry to the atta – Kannada for 'attic', and the term by which the Mala's premises were fondly known.

In those pre-television days, gathering at the atta for conversation was a well-known Dharwad institution. Writers past, present, and future thronged the place. I entered one evening to see GB sitting on a chair, his dhoti-clad legs tucked under him, laughing and nodding at something. His trademark black cap was on the table in front of him. Kirti was right next to him. The 'chief guest' was the writer V.G. Bhat, brimming over with eloquence. The topic of Bhat's unfinished novel came up and GB threw out an open invitation: 'Just finish it and give it to me. I'll bring it out at once.' I burned with envy. Maybe, I fumed, a day will come when he would say something similar to me.

I paid no attention to Kirti after this evening. And since I had not written anything, there was no place for me in his consciousness. Later, I would become a playwright as a result of Kirti seeing merit in my *Yayati.* But he also made another contribution that I must record.

My mother had a deep love of Sanskrit and was in the habit of sprinkling subhashitas into her conversations. As a result, I too developed a fondness for the language. When I studied it in college, one of the prescribed texts in my first year was Kalidasa's epic poem *Raghuvamsha.* I was captivated by its elegance and lyricism, and could even recite the first two cantos from memory. But I remained entirely indifferent when it came to Sanskrit drama. This was because of the inferior plays we were studying: Harsha's *Ratnavali*

With G.B. Joshi, D.R. Bendre and Kirtinath Kurtakoti (partially visible)

and *Nagananda*. They convinced me that Sanskrit drama was extremely contrived, used conventions from some distant age in the past, and lacked any human dimension. I turned away from the form altogether. A decade later, when I was in Madras, my interest revived after reading Kirti's essays on Sanskrit drama in the journal *Manvantara*. It was then that I deeply read all the Sanskrit plays I could find. I studied and savoured plays such as *Shakuntala, Uttararamacharita* and *Mrichchakatika*. Later, when I went to Chicago on a Fulbright Fellowship (1987–88), I even delivered a lecture series on Sanskrit plays. Though I came to it late, I eventually discovered the treasure that is Sanskrit drama. For this, I have Kirti to thank.

Because I neglected Sanskrit in college, I missed the presence of another excellent scholar. K.T. Pandurangi wore, along with shirt and trousers, the traditional Madhva markings on his forehead. He was slight of build, and he walked the corridors shrunk into himself as if he would be defiled by so much as a whiff of air from someone passing by. And so, I barely noticed him while I was at college. I might have ended up forgetting about him, but later in Bangalore, I sought his guidance on several matters. By then, he was renowned around the world for his scholarship.

Right opposite the college was the All India Radio broadcasting station. Several capable directors came and went in the four years I was there. People like N. Iqbal Singh (who wrote Amrita Sher-Gil's biography), Rangacharya (and his wife), M. Shankar and H.K. Ranganath kept us continually interested in Akashvani programmes. Not only did we hear these people on the radio, we saw them in person too, usually at Dharwad Restaurant which had turned into a haunt for Dharwad's intellectuals and where they joined in on conversations between the likes of Shah and Mahale. Once, when I compared Shaw's *Saint Joan* (based on the life of Joan of Arc) to Anouilh's *The Lark*, Shankar said, 'Anouilh is a child in front of Shaw.' I revered both playwrights, and I thrilled at Shankar's remark. It is through such steps and half-steps that my intellectual development progressed.

In 1958, Akashvani organized an all-India debate competition. I had been enthusiastic about debates and speaking events right from the time I was at school in Sirsi. That training proved useful when I took part in college competitions and began to win – initially in Athani and Belgaum, and later as far as Nalanda and Waltair (now Visakhapatnam). The Akashvani contest came to be particularly significant because Kitti, Aurora, I and Mala Gokak (V.K. Gokak's daughter) were invited. We won the Bombay stage of the contest and went to Delhi. The debate itself had to do with art and literature, the very things we discussed among ourselves daily. We easily won second place at the national level. Mala only played a minor role, so in effect it was the three of us who had participated and won, that too without any supervision from teachers. With this journey, it felt like we had successfully taken on a responsibility and grown up. The affection between us, restricted until then to student life, took on a more emotionally mature aspect that would hold us together for the rest of our lives.

My elder sister in Bombay along with her husband had listened to the event broadcast from Delhi. My brother-in-law later asked, 'All the books, writers, works of art and anecdotes you brought up were from the Western context. Do you have absolutely no familiarity with Indian culture?' I could not think of anything to say. His question had laid bare our intellectual limitations.

The poet D.R. Bendre loomed large during my six years in Dharwad.

In naming his son Vaman, perhaps Bendre had sought to make a sly joke about the extent of his own body. Or perhaps he was referring to his stature: a towering genius who could barely be contained in the firmament of modern Kannada literature. Bendre was a short man. Maybe it was for this reason that he had taken to speaking loudly and at such a high pitch that it was impossible for anyone to ignore him. Moustache, topi, umbrella, dhoti, a stubble – he looked so much the archetypal schoolteacher that it was no wonder GB addressed him as 'master'. Whatever his attire, his face glowed with an extraordinary liveliness (as if his line 'What sparkle in the eye, what radiance in the face' was describing himself). It is impossible to find even a photograph in which he looks dull or impassive.

When Bendre read his poetry, he read it with his entire body. If he held the book in his left hand, he'd wave his right around as if his index finger was prodding at the secret heart of the poem; he would smile, frown and nod as he read, his voice brimming with light and life. The effect on the audience was electrifying. It wasn't hard to imagine the sensation he had created at the Belgaum Sahitya Sammelana in 1929 when he had read his poem 'Hakki Harutide Nodidira'.

I was still at school when I took Varadaraj Huilgol's advice and went to Bendre's house with my poems. He emerged through the open door and I read him my poems. I had read about existentialism somewhere, and had inserted some of its ideas here and there. Bendre was friendly and willing to discuss my poems with me. He said, 'It's inaccurate to translate the word "existentialism" as "astitvavada". Astitva means "being", which is a deeper concept than "existence".' At one point, he told me, 'It is not important what Sartre is saying. What is important is how you have internalized it.' He finished his comments, and as I began to take leave, he put a spoon of sugar on my palm, as was his custom, and said: 'The lines in your poems that have important ideas – print them in bold letters.' I was alarmed at the suggestion and suspected he was pulling my leg. I later learnt that such mischievousness was not beyond Bendre.

Bendre was endlessly fascinating when he spoke – and so it was easy for the listener to be deluded into thinking he had understood all that had been said. Once he started talking, he could wander freely between modern physics, the Vedas, Colin Wilson, Aurobindo, Freud, algebra, and so on. Though it was stimulating at the time, it was impossible to later put a finger on what exactly had been said. Akashvani's M. Shankar went to the extent of saying, sorrowfully, 'Bendre's brain was once brilliant, but now it has lost all direction and rambles incoherently.' In contrast, the renowned physicist George Sudarshan is supposed to have met him and said, 'He is an extraordinary intelligence.' Whatever it was, I went to meet Bendre a couple of times, and then stayed away to protect myself. I witnessed many young poets who were my peers flock to him, follow his suggestions to the letter – 'Write a poem on this sutra in the Upanishads' – and squander whatever talent they possessed.

He developed a regard for me after reading *Tughlaq*. I had heard that there was a history of mental illness in his family, and that he was tormented by the fear that he, too, might lose his mind. Perhaps he responded to *Tughlaq* because the main character grapples similarly with madness. Bendre praised me lavishly at the ceremony marking the publication of the play. 'If this play is performed in Delhi, they will not allow him to return to Dharwad,' he is supposed to have said. I was pleased to hear of it, but I also felt fortunate not to have been present when he said it. Kirti would tease me: 'Only two people have ever been blessed with praise from Bendre. One is Shankar Mokashi Punekar who wrote *Gangavva Gangamayi*, and the other is you!' His theory was, 'Tughlaq should have been a mystic but he ended up a mistake. That, and the way he dreaded the madness closing in around him, must have touched a hidden anxiety in Bendre.'

Later, when I was making a documentary on Bendre for the Karnataka government, I asked him if we could take a shot with him standing in front of Karnatak College. He said, 'No. It has no significance in my life,' and dismissed the idea. Now I am including him in a chapter titled 'Dharwad: Karnatak College'. I am certain he would not have approved.

The script for the documentary was written by Kirti and the cinematographer was Govind Nihalani. I spent about a week with Bendre while shooting the film, and saw for myself the extraordinary consciousness he crackled with. He knew all the monkeys that lived around his house – to the extent that he had named each one of them, and only had to call out a name for that monkey to emerge and run up to him without fear. The film has a scene showing this. Had I asked him to climb on to the roof and recite a poem, perhaps he would have been ready. He was an artist with such great self-confidence.

But he was reluctant when I asked him, near the end of the film, to speak about his vision of life. He had Kirti write out something for him to read. It was surprising that someone so articulate about his philosophy had Kirti write it out when those views were to be recorded. It is also a sign of the extent to which he trusted Kirti.

When I was in preschool, I used to delight in singing Bendre's poem 'Pataragitti Pakka' with my classmates. It had childish rhymes and was playful with its language, but it was only when I was in Karnatak College that I understood the poem properly. This autobiography owes its Kannada title – *Aadaadta Aayushya* – to one of Bendre's poems.

There is the custom among us of naming daughters after rivers: Ganga, Yamuna, Narmada and so on. When my daughter was born, my wife and I thought: 'Why go so far? The river Shalmala that arises in Someshwar, right next to our Saraswatpur, makes for a good name.' In Bendre's poem 'Sanna Somavara', he affectionately calls the river Shalmala 'little girl Shalmali'. And so, my daughter, too, became Shalmali.

5

BOMBAY

After my BA examinations, I decided I had to look for new horizons beyond Dharwad. In the days before the linguistic reorganization of states, all paths to employment led north, to Poona or Bombay. Though Karnatak University was now an independent institution, it had still not completely cut its umbilical cord to Bombay University. So, my first-class BA was recognized there too, and I was assured of receiving a Dakshina Fellowship.

It was the era of five-year plans, and the prevailing belief was that these plans would absorb statisticians and economists and give them a respectable living. Bombay University's department of statistics was well regarded across the country. So, with my future prospects in mind, I applied to the department and was accepted.

Had I been even somewhat sensible, I would have done an MA in pure mathematics, which had begun to give me great joy as my BA exams neared. But if I was to do an MA in pure mathematics, there was no need for me to go to Bombay – Bappa would argue for me to stay on at Karnatak University.

I was eager to go to Bombay, but Bappa was not in favour of the idea. My education until this point had not cost anything since it had been supported by scholarships. Now, if I went to Bombay, there would be hostel charges and the overheads of living in an expensive city.

Fortunately, Bappa had bought, with an eye to the future, a flat in Bombay's Mahim. It was in a housing cooperative called Karnatak Buildings, and my elder brother Vasant was living there at the time. I told Bappa, 'I won't stay in a hostel, I'll live with Vasant Dada,' and convinced him to let me go. Besides, he too must have felt that this experience of the world outside would do me good.

Karnatak Buildings was a beehive of Chitrapur Saraswat Brahmins. It was a spacious compound of six buildings with four floors each. Of those, our block alone had been somewhat hospitably designed. The flats here had three rooms – a kitchen, a bedroom in the middle, and a hall with a large gallery – and so were more spacious than the other buildings, which were built like chicken coops. Despite the large house, my arrangement with Vasant Dada was that we would share the middle room.

Dada was a talented violinist. There was no doubt that, had he pursued it seriously, he could have become an excellent musician, but Dada did not have the patience to persist with his art. He got a job and left it. Then, he burnt his fingers with various businesses. His sensibility allowed him a deep understanding of musical notes but not of business partners, and he was repeatedly done out of the money he had invested. Finally, his wife Sunanda grew exasperated with his attempts to become a big businessman and insisted that he pursue music alone. He met his guru Dhondutai Kulkarni when he was fifty, and his life at last found purpose and direction.

But when I came to Bombay he was still unmarried, and his sole aim in life was to somehow become immensely wealthy. And so, with the hall rented out to four young Malayali men, the kitchen to three others, and the two of us sharing the middle room, he had turned our flat into a Kishkindha of nine people. According to his calculations, installing a ceiling fan in each room would increase his expenditure, and so it was each to his own as far as ventilation and cooling were concerned. As a result, our room had a single table fan.

From its map, the city of Bombay looks like a man extending his arm into the Arabian Sea. This peninsula used to be seven or eight islands which were joined into a single landmass in the nineteenth century by depositing earth into the sea. All major movement in Bombay takes place along a north–south axis: such as the city's three local train routes that run parallel to each other.

The city is slender in extent along the east–west axis. Bombay University was near Churchgate station, the southern end of the railway line that ran along the western coast. (And because of the Rajabai clock tower, it looked spectacular even from a distance.) The suburb of Mahim was twenty-five minutes by train from Churchgate. Karnatak Buildings was between Mahim station and the sea. Bombay had a constant sea breeze, and in theory, this should have kept the city cool, but tall buildings had come up close to each other along the seashore. Together they were like a fort wall, and the interior of the city didn't get as much as a whiff of the sea breeze. This is the historical backdrop to our fan in the middle room.

Sweating has been a problem for me since I was born: rivers of sweat can flow from me without any cause. (Later, this caused trouble when I began to act in Hindi films. Studios were not air-conditioned then, and we often filmed under a roof made of metal sheet. There have been times while shooting romantic scenes when a drop of sweat formed at my brow and began to slide down slowly, and just as it was about to fall on the actress in my arms, I have prayed, 'Oh god, why won't this shot end?') I would finish my classes at three in the afternoon and leave from Churchgate in good spirits. By the time I entered the flat in Mahim, I would be completely drained. I would spread a mat on the floor and go to sleep sweating.

I won't blame Dada alone for this state of affairs. After all, I had participated willingly in the arrangement. We had both grown up with lower-middle-class parents who had been cautious about every paisa they spent. We had come to believe that being frugal was of paramount importance, even if it meant being uncomfortable. It was also essential to me personally to prove that my coming to Bombay did not mean any increased expenditure for Bappa. So, all the scrounging and scrimping in our daily lives was with my full assent.

Among our societal preconceptions is the carefully nurtured notion that 'brothers are one'. Or rather, 'brothers *must* be one'. But the fact of the matter was that, while we both had affection for each other, there were aspects of our day-to-day lives in which our expectations were entirely different. Words were exchanged at every step, disagreements happened all the time. But according to the boundaries set by tradition – 'Don't talk back to your elder brother' – I could not protest outright. I had to be cautious when it came to expressing any difference of opinion. And then, he had been staying in that flat longer than I had. There was no choice but to silently accept his way of living.

After a year, I decided I could not live like this any more. I went and asked the head of my department, Prof. M.C. Chakrabarti if it was possible to join the hostel for my second year. He said it wasn't.

That year, I had a strange experience. I returned home to Dharwad by train for the December vacations, and the very next morning my throat was swollen to the extent that I could neither swallow nor cough. Bappa examined my throat and grew alarmed when he saw it had a thick white coating. I had never before seen Aayi and Bappa so scared. Dr Kamalapur came home, examined me and said: 'Nothing to be scared of, it's just diphtheria. Give him these tablets.' As evening approached, Aayi and Bappa were, if anything, more worried than before. Bappa even sat next to me quietly for half an hour, something he had never done before. Finally, when Aayi was alone, I asked her why they were so anxious. She was stronger than Bappa in these situations. She told me why: 'You haven't urinated since morning. It's possible that your kidneys have stopped functioning. If the waste in your body isn't being washed away, it could be poisoning your entire system. If you don't pass urine soon, you might even die.'

For a while, I contemplated death. So this is what death was like! I was lucky not to be in any pain. To lose consciousness and float off into death is a fate reserved for the truly fortunate. No complaints there. But there was an incompleteness to my life. Sex. What kind of a fate was it to die without ever having caressed, embraced or kissed a woman? Without having made love? I had read and heard about the intensity of these acts. I had imagined them. It was unbearable to think I had been cheated of these experiences.

As it grew dark, I started to get better. I urinated. Bappa and Aayi broke into smiles. While I was convalescing, our cat gave birth to three kittens. Since there was no space anywhere else, their shelter was made up in my room. The kittens grew more lively and playful by the day. I recovered while watching their antics. After staring at death from up close for half a day, it was a delight to watch the kittens take to life.

Nearly twenty years later, Bappa was diagnosed with cancer of the oesophagus. If I had to leave town for work at this time, he would grasp my hands firmly and beg: 'Don't go. I am afraid of being alone.' It was not enough that Aayi was with him. It was as if he believed that the more people there were around him, the slower death would approach.

While sitting next to Bappa holding his hand, I was reminded of my own brush with death all those years back. I was twenty-one then. While I might have told myself I was dying, I doubt I was convinced about it in the depths of my being. It may well be impossible to comprehend death at that age. Maybe the prospect of one's own complete extinction becomes more tangible when one is old and frail.

When I returned to Bombay, I was healthy in body but troubled in mind. I had begun to feel strongly that the way I was spending my days was a waste of time. If I was in the flat, I could sit and sweat. Or, I could go to the kitchen on the pretext of making small talk with its occupants and look out of the window. It was the only window in our house from which one could observe the next building's ground-floor flat, in which lived the extremely attractive Nadkarni sisters. I could stand there and kill time watching their comings and goings.

When I wanted to escape that boredom, I would abandon plans of trying to study after returning home and loiter near the department building. Prof. Chakrabarti noticed my listlessness and warned me once: 'Be careful! This department has been a graveyard of reputations.'

All around the Bombay University campus were bookstalls, showrooms, cinema theatres and restaurants. There was no dearth of entertainment and intellectual stimulation. And then, to one side of our department building was the department of economics. It didn't take me long to realize that the students there were sharper and more lively than my classmates.

One of them was Ashok Kulkarni, whom I had met in Dharwad. He had been a student of Lingaraj College in Belgaum, and our paths often intersected since he participated in drama and debate competitions. What also helped cement our friendship was that he was close to Ramanujan. He had now come to Bombay to study economics. We ended up spending much of our two years there together.

Meghnad Desai was then a brilliant student in the economics department, always participating in debates, continually taking part in Gujarati plays. He went on to be a professor at the London School of Economics, became one of the leading lights of Britain's Labour party and ended up as Lord Desai. In 2000, I was at a party in London when a deep voice called out, 'Girish!' It was him – large of body, a shock of white hair surrounding his face like Satya Sai Baba's halo, and just as open-hearted forty years later.

When I was not keeping the company of economics students, I could spend the entire day at the libraries of the United States Information Service (USIS) and the British Council. The cold war between the US and the USSR was at a critical juncture. Even as the two countries threatened to reduce each other to rubble, and with them the entire world, they were involved in an equally fierce cultural battle to win over to their side 'third-world' countries like India that were just emerging from colonial rule. I must accept that the Cold War came as a blessing to someone like me with a keen interest in culture. Bombay was buzzing with jazz musicians, classical instrumentalists, photo exhibitions, poets, critics, dancers, scientists, and thinkers that America was continuously sending our way. It was thanks to the extraordinary exhibitions organized by the USIS that I came to realize that photography was an art form.

Ashok and I watched plays at every opportunity we got. In our enthusiasm to watch all kinds of productions, we once ended up viewing a junior boxing championship. But we could not stand it for very long. The scenes involving Irani, Parsi and Anglo-Indian boys pummelling each other mercilessly proved too much for our South Indian Brahmin stomachs.

There was no shortage of new Marathi plays. Among them, Pu La Deshpande's *Tujhe Aahe Tujpashi* was regarded a triumph for both its intellectual and dramatic content. I still remember the stage design of *Pathan*, performed by Prithviraj Kapoor and Zohra Sehgal at Prithvi Theatre. And I remember rolling with laughter at the comic melodrama of their *Paisa*. Around this time, the Oxford Playhouse company brought to Bombay two plays directed by Frank Hauser. As luck would have it, I knew both plays line for line, and was constantly filled with wonder at their presentation. I had studied *Twelfth Night* as a college text, and after watching it, Kitti said, echoing my own amazement: 'I didn't know Shakespeare could be performed like this.' The Shakespeare we knew from college was a writer. It was a revelation for us to see those words transformed into action on stage. The other play was *The Man of Destiny*, which Kitti and I had performed in Dharwad. We saw it and patted our own backs, saying to each other that our production was better. But I had noticed the professionalism of these productions, and I had begun to realize that there was still a lot for me to learn about theatre.

The first time I became intensely aware of accomplished playwriting technique was not while watching a play, but while watching a film. I had absolutely no interest in films and had decided they were a form of entertainment that I had nothing to do with. Then I saw David Lean's *The Bridge on the River Kwai* and was stunned. As I watched it, I felt as if someone was teaching a class on screenwriting – or, in a sense, playwriting. The film is set during the Second World War, and a Japanese unit is trying to use Allied prisoners of war to build a bridge near the Burma border. The fate of every character is entangled with the construction of the bridge, and they all respond to the situation in different ways. The technical mastery involved in bringing these strands together to build up to a tragic climax was so staggering that while watching the film I found it difficult to breathe at times. For many days after, I was in a sort of daze, as if I had toiled in a playwriting workshop and emerged after learning many new things.

At around this time, a textbook of literary criticism given by Ramanujan became for me a manual for effective writing. Written by Cleanth Brooks and Robert Penn Warren, *Understanding Poetry* was an influential book in the New Criticism movement that was taking over American universities. It held that the best way to understand a literary work was not by placing it in its historical context, or by tying it to the life and personality of the author. Instead, every creative work was to be seen as having an independent existence, as being held together by a set of internal relationships. It was only by teasing apart these relationships and subjecting them to analysis that a meaningful appreciation of the work was possible. Today, this method is out of fashion. To me, however, it was valuable not so much as a method of criticism, but as a principle of composition, as a means to bring rigour to creative activity.

Later, I was astonished to learn how similar the principles and assumptions of New Criticism are to Sanskrit criticism. Ramanujan pointed out to me that Indian scholars such as S.C. De and others, who had been disparaging of methods of Sanskrit criticism and had adopted wholesale the ideas from nineteenth-century English criticism, were now bewildered by how 'modern' Abhinavagupta and Anandavardhana were turning out to be.

Ramanujan had been a mentor and guiding light every step of the way. So, an episode around this time involving him and Karnatak University caused me much anguish.

When Ramanujan was in Baroda, he was called to interview at Karnatak University for the position of reader. On his way to Dharwad, he happened to meet an English graduate on the train who was going there for the same job. But not as a candidate. He said, 'I've already been selected for the job. The interview is just eyewash.' Ramanujan recounted this to the interview committee and said, 'Three or four days of leave is a financial burden for me. In addition, I've had to bear my own travel expenses. Karnatak University should not have toyed with me like this.' The chairman of the committee, Vice Chancellor D.C. Pavate, did not show any reaction. One of the members, the English professor Armando Menezes, later justified his role in the sham by telling someone, 'I took Ramanujan to one side and told him he should consider himself fortunate to have escaped this place.' But it turned out he had not said a word to Ramanujan.

Hearing about this episode only strengthened my resolve to escape India. Perhaps this was a sign of my naïveté. I have come to accept that this sort of favouritism is an integral part of public life in India, but I am to this day agitated by the incident. In any case, the missed opportunity proved fortunate for Ramanujan. He received a Fulbright Fellowship to go to Indiana University, where his brilliance blossomed and expanded into new horizons.

When I was still at Karnatak College, Prof. K.J. Shah had urged me to apply for the Rhodes Scholarship. A Rhodes candidate needed to have a first class at every stage, and have excelled at various extracurricular activities. I had a first class in every examination from my SSC to my BA. I had also won prizes in several inter-college and inter-university speaking contests, drama competitions and debates.

It was also useful that I had been in the National Cadet Corps (NCC) for two years in college. (My elder sister, younger sister and wife were all Under Officers in the NCC during their college days. After two years, all I could manage was a lance corporal's single V-shaped stripe!) One of the Under Officers above me in the NCC was a student named Shrinivas Vaidya, who later worked at a bank and rose to the top. He gave no sign then that he would go on to write, at the age of sixty-five, as fine a novel as *Halla Bantu Halla*.

There was only one Rhodes Scholarship for all of India. Candidates staked their claim to it by writing what was practically an autobiography describing the glories they had attained in various fields. I wrote mine and was asked to attend an interview in Delhi's St Stephen's College. St Stephen's was one of India's best colleges, regarded as 'India's Oxford–Cambridge'. The scholarship went to a student from St Stephen's at least once every couple of years.

My immediate problem was that I did not have a suit to wear to the interview. I did not want to spend money on buying one either, given that I had little chance of succeeding. What I did have was a dark blue blazer I had been given to wear when I represented Karnatak University at speaking events. I had trousers stitched in a matching blue to try and approximate a suit. Approximate is what I ended up with.

The candidates were to have dinner with the committee on the evening before the interview. It was a formal, Western-style dinner, something I had never been part of or even seen. I bought a book of etiquette that described how to behave appropriately in different situations while moving in refined society. In those days, the train from Bombay to Delhi had a dining car in which Spencer & Co. supplied Western-style meals to those who wanted it. I sat in the dining car with my book of etiquette open in front of my plate, eating according to its instructions. 'The first course is soup. Use the rightmost spoon for it. Soup is only served once. You cannot ask for a second helping…' And so on. Over the course of a few meals between Bombay and Delhi, I did my best to learn how to eat like a gentleman.

The dinner and the interview were both at St Stephen's College. The college's 'English' atmosphere was intimidating, but the meal went off without complications. The interviewers were chatting and laughing with us, and didn't appear to be testing our etiquette.

We were around fifteen candidates from various universities across India. We sat together in a room and were called in one by one for the interview. It hardly needs to be said that as each candidate emerged from the interview the rest of us fell upon him: 'What did they ask? What were the interviewers like?' One of the candidates, a tall young man from St Stephen's who wore an elegant suit and spoke with a flawless English accent, exited the interview room. He told us, looking pleased with himself, that he had responded to one of the questions with: 'The subject is outside my specialization, so I am unable to provide an answer.' I was immediately impressed by his manner and audacity.

During my interview, the chairman of the committee, a well-known ICS official named Sir Penderel Moon, asked me a question to which I could not think of an answer. I blurted out, 'The subject is outside my specialization, so I am unable to provide an answer.' He said, 'A Rhodes candidate is expected to know at least this much.' My heart sank. Another interviewer asked, 'What do you know about Sir Cecil Rhodes, who established this scholarship?' I said, 'He must be some philanthropist I suppose.' The entire interview panel burst out laughing.

I did not get the scholarship that year. Sir Penderel announced the name of the winner and the committee dispersed. The rest of us, silent in defeat, were still standing as a group when the secretary of the scholarship trust, Reverend W.W.S. Jarvis, came to us and said softly, 'We have only one scholarship, so we have no choice. But do apply next year.' I decided those words were addressed specifically to me. I resolved to try again, and to come better prepared.

I met Ramanujan in Bombay. He heard what I had said about Cecil Rhodes and chided me: 'If I had heard that answer, I wouldn't have given you the scholarship either. If you're trying to get a scholarship, it is your duty to find out as much as you can about the organization, to take some interest in its founder. How will you get it if you go without doing your homework?'

I began my preparation for the next year's interview. I had noticed something significant during my interview: the interviewers were not trying to intimidate or confuse the candidate. All their questions were at least somewhat related to the 'autobiography' I had sent them. I wrote out a fresh application for the next year. I came up with a thorough list of questions I might be asked and wrote out answers to them. Every day, I read news articles, essays and editorials published in *The Times of India* and the *Free Press Journal*, and made notes. I prepared jokes that I could deploy here and there. I memorized quotations and statistics.

This time, I did not talk much with the other candidates. I kept to myself.

The interview began. I was going to use my entire year's preparation to show that I was a quick-witted fellow with great presence of mind. I had barely got started when the committee chairman Lovraj Kumar said, 'That's all, Mr Karnad, thank you.' I was stunned. All that preparation had been for nothing, and my dreams of going abroad ended here.

I was despondent when we gathered in a group to hear the result. Lovraj Kumar announced – could I be hearing him correctly? – 'Girish Karnad.' My brain was saying there had to be a mistake somewhere even while the interview committee came one by one to shake my hand.

I am not easily overcome by emotion. But at that moment, I was on the verge of breaking into tears.

My recollection of what followed is hazy, as if it all passed by me through layers of mist. Lovraj Kumar took me to his house and had me fill out all sorts of forms. He saw me filling out a telegram form to inform the people at home and struck out a long-winded message – 'The Rhodes Committee has kindly honoured me ...' He said, 'Why do you need all that for your parents? Just write, "I got the Rhodes."' That was the telegram that went to Dharwad.

I needed to list six colleges I wanted to go to, in my order of preference. I knew the name of only one college – Balliol – because of Gokak, and was in a quandary about how to go about choosing the others. Finally, Lovraj Kumar made a suggestion: 'Magdalen College has a deer park.' That was good enough. Then we went to a house nearby for tea with Prof. Reddaway of Cambridge, who was spending a few months in India. While discussing what course of study I might follow, Prof. Reddaway let slip: 'Didn't he win the scholarship last year as well?' Lovraj Kumar bit his tongue theatrically. Reddaway said, 'Oh! Maybe I shouldn't have mentioned it,' and laughed. That was when I found out that I had been tied for points with another candidate the previous year, and there was only one scholarship to be awarded. He was twenty-five, I was twenty; he could not apply again, I could. The scholarship went to him. But for some reason, the fellow never went to Oxford. He missed the opportunity, and he made me miss it too. Among the jumbled memories of that evening, what stands out clearly is the interest taken in me by Lovraj Kumar and Reverend Jarvis.

Just two days after returning to Bombay, I received an inland letter from Aayi. 'I was listening to the radio in the evening. I heard the sound of a cycle outside the door and thought it might be a telegram. I rushed to open the door and receive your telegram. Your father was fast asleep. You know he doesn't like to be woken up. Still, I woke him up and read out your telegram. We are both very happy.'

I must have read those lines at least twenty times that day.

Though Bombay was the capital of a bilingual region in which both Marathi and Gujarati were spoken, the corresponding cuisines were not very popular in the city's restaurants. Both kinds of cooking could be delicious at home, but they lost a subtle aspect of their flavour when cooked on a large scale. So, the food at a restaurant could begin to seem tasteless after one had eaten there a couple of times. This allowed enterprising members of the Bunt and Billava communities from Dakshina Kannada to storm Bombay, and soon their vegetarian restaurants were everywhere. (If one developed a craving for meat, there was bound to be a Punjabi restaurant not very far away.) Because Dakshina Kannada restaurants took over Bombay so quickly, the Shiv Sena began to regard them as the mark of an invading Kannada culture.

Thankfully, when I was a student there, the Irani restaurants, which were an integral part of Bombay's history, were found all over the city, and especially around the Flora Fountain area (now Hutatma Chowk). Like the Parsis, these Iranis were followers of Zarathustra, but the Parsis migrated to India over a thousand years ago. The Iranis came to Bombay in the nineteenth century and created a café culture of their own. These cafés had an important place in student life – they were inexpensive, and once your tea and snack were on the table, you would not be rushed, no matter how busy the café was.

On your way out, as you reached the cash counter near the entrance, the boy who had served you would call out the entire bill from a distance. The owner – or his representative – at the cash counter was invariably a man with heavyset, sloping shoulders, a round face, thick black eyebrows, a toothbrush moustache, and a double chin. He would revive for a moment, wordlessly push your change towards you, and return to his sleepy-eyed stateliness. Every Irani café looked similar enough that they all seemed to have been designed by the same art director: a large, high-ceilinged hall with rows of tall mirrors on the walls that made the hall look larger. These mirrors also made it inevitable that anyone stepping into the café, and especially a young man, would quickly adjust his hair and straighten his collar. At a prominent place in the café could be found a picture of the creator, Ahura Mazda, with his long, white beard and turban, rising from clouds to bless the world. If there was room between the mirrors, one might find tall, thin pictures of young women adorned with flowers in the style of Pre-Raphaelite paintings. Some cafés had a jukebox. And as if it were demanded by the rules, every Irani café had square marble-topped tables with a dotted tablecloth, and black ebony chairs that had arched backs and woven seats with a pattern full of holes.

After watching a film or play, the evening would be incomplete if we didn't go to an Irani café for a cup of thick chai made from boiled tea leaves, hot milk and condensed milk. (If you plunged a spoon into this chai, its reputation went, the spoon remained vertical.) To go with it: pav, keema or egg bhurji, vegetable puff for the vegetarians, and if not anything else, at least a khari biscuit. It is unfortunate for the younger generation that Irani cafés are vanishing as the city grows more prosperous.

A young man who moves from a medium-sized city such as Dharwad to a metropolis like Bombay has to face all manner of insult, suspicion, temptation, incitement and annoyance. I experienced them too. (Except, unlike some of my classmates, I did not seek the company of prostitutes.) If that had been all, those two years spent in Bombay would have dissolved unremarkably into the past. Though I didn't realize it then, it is clear in hindsight that those years were significant because of one person: Ebrahim Alkazi.

Today, Alkazi is widely regarded as the founding father of modern Indian theatre. Then, he was a young man with a small theatre company, directing plays in a style that was all his own. His father was a wealthy Arab who had settled in Poona, where Alkazi was born. As he was growing up, he joined Theatre Group, started in Bombay by the gifted Sultan Padamsee, and went on to marry Sultan's sister. Alkazi went to London to study at the Royal Academy of Dramatic Art after which, though he had a chance to work with the London theatre establishment, he chose to return to Bombay. He started a group called Theatre Unit – because by then Sultan had died, and Alkazi did not want to share directorial control with Sultan's brother Alyque.

In the years following Independence, the presiding deity of Indian theatre was the English playwright, George Bernard Shaw. Shaw believed that theatre's responsibility was to discuss social issues and the playwright's aim was social upliftment. This corresponded with a philosophical belief underpinning the Indian independence movement: 'To become eligible for independence we must wash away traditionally handed down evils from society and purify ourselves.' Further, it was possible to sit back and enjoy Shaw's plays since they were mainly comedies. From beginning to end, his dialogue threw up lines that elicited laughter. To him, humour and irony were devices to bring about social change.

There was the practical aspect as well: since Shaw's plays were all about middle-class family troubles, they only required a living room set. This was in contrast to company theatre, which demanded elaborate sets and scenery, costumes, accompanying music, and so on. Plays in Shaw's style were affordable to middle-class organizers of performances. The middle-class audience could relate to them since they were seeing on stage the problems of their own living rooms, and it was palatable to them since it was sugar-coated with humour.

In Marathi, beginning with the generation of playwrights that moved away from the company tradition to write exclusively for cultured audiences – Mama Varerkar, P.K. Atre, Mo Ga Rangnekar – and continuing into my own generation – Vasant Kanetkar and Vijay Tendulkar – almost every play was written in this style. In Kannada, it was Kailasam and Sriranga who wrote plays in this tradition.

As a result, our epics and the puranas found no place in contemporary urban theatre. To this 'modern' sensibility of theatre, stories from the puranas or our folk literature were not only ridiculous but also politically regressive. At a 1956 seminar on Indian theatre organized by the Sangeet Natak Akademi, left-leaning critics branded traditional forms and literature a regressive temptation that would take us away from contemporary reality.

Alkazi revealed to Bombay's audiences an entirely new body of drama. He pushed aside Shaw and social issues, and took up tragic plays by European playwrights like Anouilh.

As a consequence of his 1958 workshop for college teachers, I had already read Anouilh's *Antigone* in Dharwad. Now, I saw it on stage, directed by Alkazi. He kept his stage compositions simple, using platforms of different sizes and shapes, benches and canvas flats. The demarcation of scenes was achieved more through lighting than through sets. Though the best actors in Bombay acted in his plays, my attention was captured by his young, quivering heroines.

I watched two versions of Alkazi's *Antigone* while I was in Bombay. In one, the lead role was played by a young woman named Kusum Bahl. She had a beautiful face, was petite with an endearing physical presence, and had a style of acting in which she conveyed emotion in a low, breathy voice. In the other production, Antigone was played by Alaknanda Samarth. She was tall, thin, and had pronounced cheekbones with large, flashing eyes above them. A voice that could give you gooseflesh. When she made her entrance, the stage crackled with electricity and it became hard to notice anyone else on it.

Alkazi also brought Anouilh's *Eurydice* to the stage, but it was not as successful as *Antigone*. The attempt to modernize a mythological story seemed to have ended up distorting the original. Some of the situations in the play were muddled and hard to comprehend. But when it comes to understanding what a playwright is attempting with his craft, the ambitious failure is often more useful than a flawless play. I watched two shows of *Eurydice* and made notes about its weaknesses. Alkazi and Anouilh both entered my consciousness more deeply.

The production that truly astounded me was the Swedish playwright Strindberg's *Miss Julie* directed by Alkazi. It is a tragedy about an aristocratic young woman named Julie, who sleeps with a servant named Jean and, unable to bear the shame, kills herself. Jean was played by Alkazi himself, who was not a particularly talented actor. But Alaknanda's performance as Julie felt as if a valve had been released on a boiler bursting with steam. She did not shed a single garment, but her realization of the character was such that it made Julie stand naked in front of us. It can be said that there was something obscene about the way the playwright had exposed the ghosts writhing in the crevices of Julie's mind, about his merciless portrayal of the sexual games and struggles between the two characters. I had never before seen such a depiction on stage.

The technical precision of the production left me dazzled. At one point, Julie was delivering a long, poignant section of dialogue. As she spoke, the music in the background underlined her emotions in a way barely noticeable to us. She finished speaking, and as if in response, Jean lit a cigarette. With the sound of the match being struck, the music stopped and the lights, which had been slowly fading, turned bright. These changes appeared to be controlled by the match being struck.

It was a new experience for me to see lights gently fade or grow bright. Ashok and Meghnad were with me, and I later asked them about this. Meghnad explained to me what a dimmer was. I was naïve when it came to technical matters: it had never occurred to me that, just as we changed a fan's speed using a regulator, it was possible to control the intensity of light by turning a knob.

The science of quietly taking the viewer deep into the netherworld of the character's mind, and the technology that allowed light to be modulated easily – they both took my awareness of theatre to a new level.

I never met Alkazi when I was in Bombay, and I saw him at close quarters only once. It was in the auditorium of Siddharth College, where I had gone to watch one of Alkazi's productions along with a friend named Kaveh Munshi. We were sitting in the gallery and the play was about to begin when two students next to me started singing loudly, banging the benches in accompaniment. A young man emerged from backstage, jumped into the viewing area and began to rush towards us. 'That's him, that's Alkazi,' Kaveh said to me. Alkazi climbed the steps to the gallery and materialized in front of us. He thundered at the students sitting next to me: 'Who are you?

Where have you come from? Are you students or goondas?' The boys slipped out of the auditorium. Alkazi went back and the play began.

My MA examinations were of no consequence since I had won the Rhodes Scholarship. Still, I remained in Bombay and wrote two papers. I then became convinced that if I finished the exams, I would not do very well, and this would only end up spoiling my academic record. I abandoned the remaining papers and went back to Dharwad. On the train with me was Ashok, who had also given up on his MA exams. We returned in high spirits.

Bappa was not expecting me. Nor did he accept my weak excuse. Even after I returned from Oxford after finishing my studies, he would occasionally say, 'You could have finished your MA in statistics.'

I had never fared poorly in an exam until then. So, even though the MA exams had no bearing on my future, the humiliation of leaving them halfway nagged at me. To escape, I went to visit my elder brother Bhalchandra, who was working as a railway official in Varanasi. I stayed with him for three weeks. (In those days, it was common practice when visiting a relative's house to set up camp for weeks at a time. I only learned to think about the inconvenience this caused to the hosts from my wife Saras, after we were married.)

I felt I should read our epics and puranas once before leaving for England, and so I picked up C. Rajagopalachari's concise Ramayana and Mahabharata. He had managed to pare down the Mahabharata to three hundred pages, and that too without leaving out all the side stories. Some of the important ones are included and narrated beautifully. Among them, I was excited by the story of Yayati, where a son exchanges his youth with his father's old age. The situation was both dramatic and tragic. But the question that bothered me even as I was finishing the story was: If the son had been married, what would the wife do? Would she have accepted this unnatural arrangement?

This was the first scene that formed in front of my eyes: the confrontation between Yayati and Chitralekha. Here, the essence of *Antigone* and the manner in which Alkazi's young heroines had resisted injustice came to life again. As I thought about it, the rest of the play began to take shape around this climax. I did not feel as if I was writing a play. The characters came to life in front of me, and all I had to do was take down what they were saying to each other like I was a stenotypist. It was as if a spirit had entered me. Never again in my life did I experience this kind of loss of control while writing a play.

Though the eminent dramatist Sriranga would later write in his critique of *Yayati* that 'the eight-page-long argument between Yayati and Chitralekha, who makes her entrance in the last act, feels contrived' (*Prajavani*, 9 October 1961), the play was born from that argument.

When I reflect upon the play now, I see Puru as a personification of my own angst at the time. I was leaving the country and going to the West. It was an uncommon experience at the time, and certainly so in my family, where I was the first to do so. It was not a simple journey either. It would take me three weeks to reach, and then I would not be able to return to India for three years. My parents were worried that in those three years I might decide to settle there. Aayi even feared that a white woman might ensnare me and keep me there. I was eager to come into my own in the West and make that world mine, but my parents had told me that they expected me to return to India. I had started to feel resentful that my parents were imposing a limit to my freedom, that they wanted me to circumscribe my future for their sake. It can perhaps be said that Puru embodied the serious misgivings I had about the demands of my elders.

Yayati manifesting itself suddenly in this manner was disorienting in several ways. First, in preparation of my victorious march upon the West, I had decided that I was only going to write in English. The play had come, without warning, in Kannada. When I was returning from Varanasi, Ashok Kulkarni met me on the platform of Belgaum station. He was astonished to hear about the play. 'You wrote it in Kannada?' he asked incredulously. 'How? You didn't write it in English?' Second, I had lost touch with puranic stories since leaving Sirsi. I could never have imagined that this umbilical cord would sprout again, and that too through the medium of Western influences. Third, it had been my ambition since childhood to become a poet. With the arrival of this wretched play, I began to realize that I was not a poet but a playwright. I was greatly disappointed.

On returning to Dharwad, I revised the play. (I still revise my plays endlessly.) I ran to the Manohara Grantha Mala atta and asked GB to read it. He said, 'Come back after two days.' When I went, he returned the manuscript and said, 'The dasi's monologue in the final act has come out well.' That was all.

I don't recall now just how dejected this made me feel. I was rushing about, getting ready to go abroad. But when the publisher returned the play, I decided: 'My connection with India is now broken. I will go abroad and dedicate myself to England.' I left India.

6

OXFORD

ARRIVAL

Sea travel was coming to an end across the world when I left for London from Bombay's Ballard Pier on 7 September 1960. My ship, the *Strathnaver*, pride of the P&O Steam Navigation Company, had been in service for around thirty years. It was a stately ship, celebrated for its pristine white hull and copper-coloured funnels, that had once thrived on ferrying mail and affluent passengers between England and Australia. Now, it had no first class and carried all its passengers in ordinary. We learnt during the voyage that it had only a year's service left. The *Strathnaver* easily held around 1,800 passengers, and since it sailed from Australia via Ceylon and India, and since this sailing was to reach Britain near the end of September, when the new term began in British universities, it was filled mostly with students.

Though my older sister Prema had married and moved with her husband to Malaysia, I was the first from my family to travel to the West. So, my journey held a historical significance, and the entire family came to the dock to see me off. From the tears that were shed as I stepped on the gangway, it seemed as if they were seeing me off for ever. Behind those tears were apprehensions that I might marry a white woman, that I might choose to

In front of the *Strathnaver* as I leave for England

settle abroad. I, too, was unsure if I would ever see them again. Because those were possibilities I had considered seriously.

The journey from Bombay to London was to take three weeks. I had bought the cheapest ticket and been assigned one berth of four in a cramped jail-cell-like cabin somewhere in the innards of the vessel. Luckily, there were the decks to walk about on all day. The cabin's discomfort was limited to the night.

Four days from Bombay to Aden. It was then a British protectorate, and a free port where goods were not taxed. Aden seemed like Ali Baba's cave to someone who had grown up in the heavily-regulated socialist economy of a poor India. It was believed that goods here were cheaper than anywhere else in the world. Passengers on our ship were raring to mount an assault on Aden's markets. They disembarked, spent all day buying goods of Western manufacture using what little foreign currency the Indian government had reluctantly parted with, and staggered back happily with enormous packages.

Even as the ship left Aden and entered open seas, the new transistor radios fell silent one by one. Expensive Terylene-nylon shirts were unfolded to find they lacked backs – they were samples meant only for display. Appliances like grinders and mixers seemed to be missing some of their parts. Along the length of the ship, consumer delight turned to consternation. Asian sellers in Aden had a reputation for cheating, but many of the passengers had been confident they couldn't be taken in, and so had become willing victims. I went to the house of someone who knew someone I knew and delivered presents. Under their local guidance, I went to a trusted shop and bought a beautiful Olivetti portable typewriter. I believed firmly that a typewriter was of utmost importance if I was to write in England. But then, I never learnt typing and the machine stayed packed in my cupboard for three years. I returned to India and gave it to Vasant Dada as a present.

Though my three cabin-mates were working men, the ship was full of students. With no first class, the entire ship became our playground. It didn't take long to meet others from different cultures, to start conversations if not friendships. On the third day of the journey, I learnt that we had a Rhodes scholar from Australia on board. Through him, I met another Rhodes scholar from New Zealand. We made elaborate plans for all the things we would do together once we reached Oxford. Of course, once we got there we never bothered to meet.

All of us Indian male students on board realized quickly, and to our amazement, that it was possible to talk to Indian women on the ship with a familiarity we couldn't have dreamed of in India. I myself did not venture beyond conversation, but I delighted in watching romances blossom and fade around me with astonishing speed.

It's hard to explain the gradual cultural and emotional exploration of those three weeks to someone who today enters a plane, crams himself into a seat, and reaches London in eight or ten hours. Back then, there was no television, and everything we knew about the culture of the West was from books or word of mouth. There were Hollywood films, but they announced themselves as set in a kind of dreamworld that was clearly beyond the reach of ordinary people. Here on the ship, we were meeting new people every day, hearing new languages and accents, coming upon new lands – it was like being in the Nilekani village fair in Sirsi and somehow managing to enter the bioscope machine that flitted from scene to scene with an incessant soundtrack of '*Dilli ka raja dekho, Bambai ki madam dekho*'. Aden, the Red Sea, the Suez Canal, Cairo, the Sphinx and the pyramids, the Mediterranean Sea, Marseilles, Gibraltar. We thrilled in saying those names, in exploring those places with our senses. We had the time to savour new encounters, to assimilate them. We had the opportunity to wonder about encounters to come.

My friend Vishwanath and I had been assigned a table to ourselves in the ship's dining hall. The prospect of having only each other's company at mealtimes for three whole weeks felt insufferable. Not only that, a table nearby with only white people had two unoccupied chairs, and we were incensed at being segregated for being Indian. We got ourselves transferred to that table. I had studied my book of etiquette thoroughly and mastered its contents. I was confident that I would not be the cause for any embarrassment. Still, it did not take long for something to happen that made me feel there might, after all, be some merit to seating Indians separately when they lacked a good grasp of Western table manners.

One day, there was lobster for lunch. I had no idea how one went about eating it. An elderly Australian woman seated opposite me saw that I was gazing at the lobster in bewilderment. She held up the two-pronged fork next to her plate and said, 'Use this.' I ignored the fork next to my own plate, leaned over the table, snatched the fork from her hand, and thrust it into my lobster. Even as I did this, I knew I was making a fool of myself. I was so flustered I didn't even thank her. I continued to eat without looking up. My self-loathing intensified when I noticed that she had discreetly called over a server to ask for another fork. I apologized that evening at dinner, but she brushed it off, saying, 'It happens to all of us.' It must be because of such incidents that the Bangladeshi and Goan servers on P&O ships had a reputation for treating all Indians as uncultured idiots.

Before reaching London's Tilbury Docks, ships pass by the sheer white cliffs of England's southern coast. In the travel accounts I had read, English passengers returning to the motherland would be overwhelmed when they spotted the cliffs. They would congratulate each other and swell with pride, saying things like: 'This land of mine, that has built an empire unmatched anywhere in the history of the world.' Or just express their eagerness to get home: 'At last I can enjoy a proper British roast beef.' I was born as a subject of that empire, and I felt proud too, in my own way: 'We are independent now.' As the *Strathnaver* neared England, I stood against the railing on the deck. Tears of fulfilment welled in my eyes. England at last! I looked to my right and left. All along the deck were Indians stuck to the rails, weeping tears of joy at having reached England.

We spent three or four days at the International YMCA on Tottenham Court Road, thankful to be here and assimilating into the greatness of Britain, while at the same time fiercely asserting our newfound sense of equality now that we were independent from it. Three or four of us Indians went to a well-known shop named Harris and bought tweed jackets. While we were walking around together wearing the jackets, one of us said, 'Who can say that we're not Englishmen?' When we had our shoes polished, another of us said, beaming, 'I could never have dreamed that, one day, a white man would polish my shoes.' Some months later, an Indian who had just slept with a white woman for the first time boasted, 'I felt as if the whole empire was crumbling under me.'

When I boarded the train at Paddington station, I was looking forward to my first view of the legendary 'dreaming spires' of Oxford. But I fell asleep as soon as the train started. When I woke up, the train was at Oxford station, and I got off in a hurry. I had a number for Magdalen College. I stuffed four pennies into a payphone, dialled the number, and asked if I could speak to the tutor, Mr Worswick. 'He just left for the day,' came the answer. I then called Rhodes House, the organization behind my scholarship, and asked to speak to the warden. No luck there either. I didn't know what else to do, so I stayed on the platform. As the evening progressed, it got windier and colder. After a few hours, I called Rhodes House again and this time found the warden, who was appalled that I was still at the railway station. 'Go to the college at once,' he ordered. I left the station.

Outside the station was a board: 'Welcome to Oxford, Home of Pressed Steel'. I might have crossed the seven seas to reach this world-renowned university town, but the board was reminding me at the very outset that, to the public here, the automobile manufacturer Morris Motors was far more important.

I realized when the taxi reached the college that 'college' here meant the student hostels. I should have come here straight from the train. At one time, all the students of a college lived in it. Now, it is only the first-year and some second-year students, and a few unmarried professors. Older students live in their digs – private residences outside the college.

A tall man in a deep-blue suit with shining, neatly combed hair welcomed me at the Porters' Lodge – the college's reception area. His name was Woodley and he was a porter (only a title, he didn't actually carry luggage). He showed me to my room and handed me three letters. One was a map of Magdalen, placed there by the college. The second was from Westminster Bank, welcoming me and asking me to open an account with them, along with a helpful map showing the location of their office on the High Street.

The third was an Indian air letter from G.B. Joshi! I was thrilled to see it. It had been three weeks since I had left home. I was yearning for a familiar voice. In later years, there would be many reasons for me to feel a deep affinity with him, but near the top of that list was the letter that greeted me when I reached Oxford. Twenty years before me, V.K. Gokak had come to Oxford as a student. GB had published extracts from Gokak's letters to him as a book: *Samudradaacheyinda*. Now, if I wrote him letters regularly, he urged, he could bring out another such book.

I had been assigned a room on the floor above the Porters' Lodge. I was delighted by its size. It was impossible to think of such a spacious room in any hostel in India. It was already dark, and I could only see the silhouette of the ancient structure that surrounded me. The dining hall was large as a cathedral, with high, pointed arches in the ceiling, and long tables and benches for the students to eat at. At the front of the hall, perpendicular to the students' tables, was the high table, where the fellows dined. On the walls were portraits of luminaries who had a role in the history of the college, all looking down upon the students with raised eyebrows. I was exhausted. I ate and went to sleep.

When I was in Dharwad, I had read authors like P.G. Wodehouse and Evelyn Waugh describe upper-class life in England. It was a matter of wonderment to me to find in these novels young men who stayed in bed until ten in the morning, or even into the afternoon. As someone who grew up in the heart of Malnad, my eyes opened of their own accord by 6 a.m. regardless of when I had gone to bed. I simply could not comprehend the lifestyle of such late-rising idlers. But after I came to England, it didn't take long for the cold, the feeble sun and the cloudy skies to make leaving bed feel like torture.

I was in deep sleep when I was woken up by someone saying, 'Good morning, sorry to disturb your beauty sleep!' I jumped out of bed, trying to remember where I was. Standing in the middle of the room, with his hands on his waist, was a bald man in a long-sleeved white shirt and waistcoat. He must have been at least sixty, but he had the bearing of someone much younger. He introduced himself – 'I am Edwards, your scout' – and asked how my name was pronounced. He apologized for waking me, but the dining hall would close for breakfast in twenty minutes. 'I am here to look after you,' he said. I was alone in England, and his manner, which had the familiarity of someone who had known me for years, was reassuring.

A scout was someone appointed by the college to look after students. His duties included waking up students in the morning, making their beds, cleaning their rooms, emptying wastebaskets and generally being useful if there were errands to be run. Apparently, at one time, when Oxbridge was open only to the wealthy upper classes, students were accompanied by their personal servants. Now, the college had taken it upon itself to provide scouts – which suggested that, even if the social and economic profile of students had dropped, they were still considered incapable of looking after themselves.

Over breakfast, I unfolded the college map and glanced over it. To the east of the college was an area marked as Addison's Walk. I had read Addison's celebrated essays, so why not start with him, I thought. I walked in that direction, crossed a bridge over the river, and stepped into a magical world. I had never until then seen such a dazzling range of colours in nature.

I had grown up amidst the green of Malnad's thick forests. Around Dharwad too, other than the red and black of soil, it was green that dominated the landscape. The riot of colours that was autumn in England drove me to a frenzy. Addison's Walk looped around an expanse of meadow, with the river Cherwell flowing to one side. On either side of the path were tall trees, their leaves glowing red, yellow, copper, brown and gold. The water flowing below shimmered with the reflection of those colours. On the path was a bed of dried leaves. The squirrels were larger than any I had seen in my life. In front of me, to the left of the path, was a herd of thirty or forty grazing deer.

I decided then and there that, whatever England ended up doing to me, it could be forgiven.

COLLEGE

Magdalen College was established in 1458. Like other old colleges in Oxford, it was started as a seminary for the instruction of priests who would later work in the church. But the founder of the college, William Waynflete, was also a high-ranking member of the royal court – Lord Chancellor – and this ensured that the college had considerable wealth and financial support. During my time there, Magdalen was one of the richest and most beautiful colleges in Oxford. When I was offered the Rhodes scholarship, I had picked Magdalen without knowing anything about it except that it had a deer park. I was delighted at my good fortune when I finally saw the college in all its beauty and splendour.

You enter the college passing the Porters' Lodge into the expansive St John's Quadrangle. The college is constructed around four abutting quads of different sizes. Along the sides are the buildings in which students live. If you stand in the middle of any of the quads and look around, you are greeted by rows of doors leading into those buildings. If you step inside one of those doors, there's a room each to the left and right, and the same arrangement again if you take the steps going up. The staircase connecting the four rooms served as a student's address. It is said that there was a plan to build another quad with a building around it some distance away from the main chain of quads, but only one side was completed, creating the beautiful New Buildings.

It was to the New Buildings that I went to meet my tutor – a combination of teacher and mentor – David Worswick. He was not a world-renowned figure like some other economists at Oxford. Still, he was well respected as an intellectual guru to Britain's Labour Party. He was a tall man, always with a pipe in his mouth. He was deaf in one ear and used a hearing aid that screeched from time to time during a conversation. At the beginning of our hour-long tutorial, he would give me a mug full of coffee – without milk or sugar – and take one for himself. He had a special affection for students from India and Pakistan since these were newly independent countries. He was to go to the United States during my second year, so he taught me economics himself for all three terms of my first year. Though I hadn't finished my MA in India, I had been a postgraduate student, and so had decided to do a BPhil at Oxford. Worswick asked me to sit down, and enquired about my background in great detail. Then he said, 'Look, it's true that if you do a BPhil you will be qualified to teach economics. But why do you insist on becoming a teacher? And if you do a BPhil, you will have to be a bookworm in the library for both of your years here. You've travelled abroad for the first time in your life, so my advice to you is this: do a BA instead of a BPhil. Our PPE course [philosophy, politics and economics] is an excellent and thorough introduction to Western thought and culture. It's a good opportunity to study this country and life here, its art and culture. Finish your BA in two years. If you feel like spending another year here, there's always the Rhodes scholarship. The university has a rich life outside studies – sports, debates, drama, political discussions. Take part in them. Enjoy yourself!'

That remains one of the best pieces of advice I have received in my entire life. I gave up the idea of doing a BPhil, took a step down and did a BA.

Without much academic pressure on me, I revelled in everything Oxford had to offer.

METHOD OF STUDY

Learning at Oxford and Cambridge occurs mainly through the system of tutorials. A student is expected to write two essays every week. Each essay is read out to and discussed with the concerned tutor. The topic for the next week's essay is decided at the end of the hour-long tutorial, and the tutor assigns a relevant reading list. There is barely time to breathe as a tutorial approaches: life is consumed by reading, discussion and making notes. But what joy to emerge from a tutorial! Once again, there is the breeze, the chirping of birds, the sunset. Picnics by the riverside with girlfriends. Drinks and conversation at pubs. And the next day, it's back to the grind.

In addition to these two tutorials every week, professors give lectures on their subjects at the university's main building. It is the student's responsibility to identify topics and professors relevant to their studies and attend those lectures.

To this day, I find it a torment to sit still in an auditorium and listen to a speech or lecture. I cannot sit for five minutes without my attention wandering, and my notes from lectures always tend to be disconnected and lacking in context. When I was at Oxford, there were lectures by thinkers such as A.J.P. Taylor, A.J. Ayer, Iris Murdoch and Gilbert Ryle. At the time, I thought these lectures boring and could not benefit from them, which is something I regret now.

MUSIC

A friend at Oxford suggested: 'If you want an easy introduction to our music, start with Mozart's Fortieth Symphony and Schubert's Unfinished.' I went out at once and bought an LP record with these works on either side. I went to my friend John Keay's room, which was near mine, and listened to them on his LP player. I liked Mozart more than Schubert, but still, no matter how much I listened, I found myself utterly incapable of grasping the composition.

My friends were taken aback when I admitted, somewhat sheepishly, 'I didn't understand Mozart's music.' In the world of Western classical music, Mozart is renowned for the beauty and virtuosity of his compositions, for his ability to effortlessly move people. But all I heard in his Fortieth Symphony was a downpour of dainty scales that only occasionally resolved into something I could enjoy.

One autumn evening, I was at a friend's room toasting crumpets on the electric room heater when my ears perked up at the music he was playing. I asked him what it was. 'Bach. Johann Sebastian Bach,' he said. As I listened, not only did I find Bach pleasing to my ears, I could also see his music unfolding its geometric structure in front of my eyes. It had a clearly defined outline, of the sort present in Carnatic music compositions. Bach was a giant of Western classical music, and I let him lead me into it. I went on to appreciate Mozart and Schubert too, and came to worship Beethoven. Western classical music played a vital role in expanding my horizons.

Magdalen College has had a choir since its inception five hundred years ago. It is made up of college students and children from the Magdalen School, and they sing in the chapel every day. My room was near the chapel for two years, and during that period, I had the good fortune of being able to listen to the choir daily.

Every year, at daybreak on the first of May – the event is called May Morning – university students, townspeople and visitors throng Oxford. They are everywhere – on boats on the Cherwell river with the college spires towering above them, on bridges on the nearby highway, on the island that Addison's Walk circles around. At six precisely, the choir begins to sing a hymn from the bell tower. It is a wonderful moment, when it feels as if not only the people gathered there, but also the surrounding trees, the swans swimming in the river, and the deer standing somewhere out of sight, are all listening quietly. All creation seems entranced.

When I was a student at Oxford, the end of the hymn marked the beginning of raucous revelry: dancing, drinking, shouting, drunk students jumping into the river from boats and struggling to the bank. There would be boats damaged and, often, students injured. Now, I've heard that colleges and boat owners have stopped giving out their boats, and this has put an end to the madness.

While speaking of Western classical music, I must admit to a failing of mine. I am interested in all forms of theatrical activity, but I have never been able to make sense of one of the main forms in the Western tradition: opera. I went to a performance of Mozart's *Magic Flute* and I am ashamed to confess that I fell asleep in the first act itself.

MANOHARA GRANTHA MALA ONCE AGAIN

One day, I received an air letter from India. It was from Kirtinath Kurtakoti. He had written: 'Yesterday, G.B. Joshi told me about the play you have written – *Yayati*. I am intrigued. Send it to me so I can read it.' I hardly need to say how thrilled I was with this unexpected interest in my play. But Kirti's letter also had a comment that alarmed me: 'Playwrights like Eugene O'Neill have tried to stuff mythological stories with the masala of modern Freudian psychology. But those are meaningless attempts.' Kirti's disapproval of O'Neill perplexed me. At Oxford, I had been blown away by reading O'Neill's play *Mourning Becomes Electra*. He takes the story of Aeschylus's trilogy *Oresteia* and recreates it in the context of the American Civil War. In the Greek play, Orestes's mother kills her husband to be with her lover. At his sister Electra's urging, Orestes kills his mother. In O'Neill's retelling, the son's desire for his mother and the daughter's unfulfilled attraction towards her father all take on a Freudian significance and build up to a dance of destruction. The force of those feelings, the playing out of distortions coiled deep within the subconscious, the powerful depiction of lust and hatred, all completely overwhelmed me. At some of the more intense moments in the play, I felt myself unable to breathe, and I stopped reading and rose to my feet. I had sworn to myself that if I wrote a play it would have to be like O'Neill's.

Still, I kept Kirti's cautionary words in mind, edited the play, and sent it to India. Kirti changed what seemed like every letter in the play and sent it back. I made a few more changes, and GB published it through Manohara Grantha Mala. Kirti wrote a foreword that I don't know how many times I must have read. *Yayati* was received with great enthusiasm. The writer and critic C.H. Prahlada Rao praised it in *MysIndia*: '*Yayati* ranks among the best in Kannada.' The journalist and prolific translator from Bengali to Kannada,

Ahobala Shankar, wrote in *Bharat Jyoti*: 'The playwright has dramatized this short tale ... investing it with an epic force reminiscent of the great Greek tragedies.' Sriranga's criticism appeared in *Prajavani*: 'While it can be said that there is a new perspective here, it cannot be said that there is a play here too.'

It had been a year since I had come to Oxford. England's cultural life had inspired me in all sorts of ways, but the enthusiastic reception given to *Yayati* back home raised new questions for me. I had lived a year as an outsider in several ways to English society. I had lost any illusions I might have had that it was easy here for talent to be appreciated or to find success. Now, after the passionate response *Yayati* had earned from Kannada critics, I wondered if I could ever expect anything similar from the English intellectual establishment. I asked myself, 'When there are people in Kannada who will read my play and be excited, angry, critical or appreciative, why aspire to lay down roots in the soil of another language?' After *Yayati* was published, I grew convinced that my original idea of settling abroad was not only unnecessary but even actively harmful to my interests. The confusion in my mind abated somewhat. I decided I would return to India after my time at Oxford. But the question of what I would do there still hung by a thread above my head like the sword of Damocles.

SOCIETY

Since Oxford and Cambridge universities were born together, grew in parallel and have similar methods of instruction, they are referred to jointly as Oxbridge. To understand student life there, it is essential to first understand Britain's class system. Just as the caste system forms the basis for Hindu society, the foundation of the British society I encountered was its unique class system.

At the bottom-most level of society – the weakest economically and socially – was the working class. At the top was the upper class, which, despite its inherited wealth and property, was covered in mildew and had become socially and politically inconsequential. In between lay the middle class, with distinct social divisions of its own.

The upper middle class was composed of those who had been successful in areas such as law, medicine, finance, the military and the civil service. The reins of the country's administration were in the hands of this class. They had created a special system of education for their children through 'public schools'. Though these institutions were called public schools, they were in reality private schools – the entire cost of education had to be borne by the students' parents. These schools imparted to their students a specific idea of what British culture was, how to behave in accordance with it, how to use language, how to conduct oneself in day-to-day matters, and shaped their entire outlook towards life. For over two centuries, these public schools had been tasked with melting down the behaviours and mindsets of their pupils and pouring them into exquisite moulds to produce young men who could take on the responsibility of administering and protecting an empire spread across the world.

The lower middle class was made of shopkeepers, traders, schoolteachers, nurses, accountants, clerks and office workers. Children from lower middle class families had traditionally been educated at government-run 'state schools'. Until the Second World War, an Oxbridge education was beyond the reach of this class because it was too expensive.

This class division was clearly seen in all aspects of Britain's social life and conduct, but it was most easily noticeable in the use of language. The upper middle class pronounced words differently. 'Here' sounded like 'hiyaah', 'really' like 'ray-alleh'. The same object could be described by different words depending on who was speaking. What the lower classes called a 'toilet', the upper classes called a 'lavatory' or a 'loo'. A 'napkin' to the upper class was a 'serviette' in a lower-class home. The lower class wore glasses on its nose; the upper class wore spectacles.

Along with language, there was a subtle difference in how things were done. On being introduced to someone, a person from a lower class might say 'Pleased to meet you'. The upper-class man only said 'How do you do' as a statement, not a question. If you answered 'I am well', then you had let your class show. While preparing tea, the lower classes poured milk first and then the decoction; the upper classes did it the other way round.

The main difference between our caste system and their class system was that there was no way to free oneself from the caste of one's birth, but in

British society, there existed a single important means to rise from the lower classes to the upper middle class: education.

Since it took place through education, the transition to the upper classes took at least two generations. A person from the lower classes might work hard, become wealthy, and manage to afford a public school for his children. There, the children could absorb upper-class ways and gain entry to it.

Until the end of the Second World War – that is, until 1945 – Oxbridge was restricted to students from the upper classes. Some renowned (and expensive) public schools had a close relationship with Oxbridge colleges. This meant that a student who went to one of these schools could, more or less, count on being admitted to one of these colleges. Further, these students came from a background of wealth, and after their Oxbridge stint, were guaranteed a position of power somewhere in the vast British empire. So they were not particularly inclined towards taking studies seriously. The main purpose of an Oxbridge education was the production of a gentleman. A gentleman came from an illustrious background, had been trained in a public school, and was refined in his manner. The hallmark of a gentleman was his confidence, the belief that he could rule any place anywhere in the world.

In 1945, the left-leaning Labour Party won the elections and formed a government. They began to impose heavy death taxes and inheritance taxes. Soon, there was full employment in the country. The income of the lower classes rose while that of the upper classes fell.

The Labour government started a new kind of school known as grammar schools. Here, students from the lower middle class could obtain an education that would prepare them for Oxbridge and other universities. Special scholarships were instituted for students from these schools. The experiment was successful, and students from the lower middle class began to enter Oxbridge institutions via grammar schools.

In 1960, when I set foot in Oxford, it had both privileged students from public schools as well as students from grammar schools who had worked for scholarships and reached there after considerable struggle. What contempt the two groups had for each other!

With the entry of grammar-school students, and with the changed post-World War climate, it was no longer the case that Oxbridge institutions were places where students spent three leisurely years in the process of becoming gentlemen. Students had begun to be competitive. They now cared about examinations and how well they were doing in them. To illustrate, Magdalen in the 1920s was well known for the antics of its rich young men. By the time I went there as a student, it was known for the quality of its tutors and its excellent results in examinations.

Though the old order was fading when I was there, there were still some vestiges. For instance, rich students from the more elite public schools had a club of their own where they could eat and drink in each other's company. Students from grammar schools and the lesser public schools were not allowed to become members.

As Indian students, we had access to all tiers of the British class system. This was partly because we fell outside the existing demarcations and conflicts of that system, and partly due to the great goodwill for India among the British. Their political relationship with the Indian subcontinent went back some two hundred years, and almost every day we met British people whose families had lived in India for generations before returning. We came from a newly independent country, and we also carried with us the halo of having achieved independence through non-violent means. And then, by virtue of having come to Oxford to pursue studies, we had made evident our respect and affection for British culture. For all that, we Indian students strutted about like snobs with an attitude that signalled: 'We are not like workers. We are cultured people.' No doubt our mindsets had been influenced by the British social order.

I celebrated the birthday of an upper-class friend at his house. I lived for two months in the house of a lower-middle-class friend. I celebrated Christmas at the house of an upper-middle-class friend. I spent a weekend at the house of a working-class friend. My wide circle was partly because I was an office-bearer in the Junior Common Room (JCR) and the Oxford Union, but it also helped that I was outside the class structure to which these four belonged. I doubt they were capable of extending to each other the kind of affection and indulgence they all showed towards me.

I had a chance to experience the British class structure from within when I became president of the JCR. The JCR was a vast lounge that students could use in their free time. It had newspapers, a television (just introduced at the time), tea and coffee, cheap alcohol, and other such conveniences. The JCR's president was elected by students of the college. I had contested the election and won.

It was not the power of the position that made me contest the election. It was the spacious living quarters that were set aside for the president: a large lobby, an independent bedroom, a personal telephone (which was quite a luxury in those days). Above everything else: a bathroom to myself! The bathroom was a particularly big lure because the college didn't have showers. Instead, there was a row of bathrooms outside with bathtubs in them. You filled the tub, bathed in standing water, and drained it when you were done. If one of our burly football or rugby players had returned from a game and used the tub just before you, there would be a half-inch ribbon of dirt as a reminder of the previous bath. At these times, it seemed preferable not to bathe.

The JCR president had a scout to himself, a man named Ireland. Ireland came from a vastly different background compared to Edwards, who had been my scout during my first two years in Oxford. They might as well have represented different historical periods. Accent, bearing, conduct – by none of these was it even possible to imagine Edwards as the scout of the JCR president. He had been in a line of work that had nothing to do with the college, and had joined as a scout after retirement. It was simply a job for him. Ireland, on the other hand, had made being a scout his vocation from the age of eighteen. Since he had spent half a century in the role of a scout, beginning at a time when going to Oxbridge was the prerogative of upper-class students, Ireland was a personification of the relationship between young gentlemen and their servants. There was a familiarity to Edwards's behaviour that Ireland could never permit himself. It was embarrassing to Ireland when the new generation of lower-middle-class students tried to treat him as their equal. I was Mr Karnad to him. He was Ireland to me. There was no scope for the intimacy of first names in the rigidly compartmentalized roles we were playing. He had no interest in being friendly or in having a conversation, which might have bridged our separate lives. He was in his place, and I, the gentleman, was in mine.

When I returned to Oxford twenty years later, the tradition of having scouts had ended. A middle-aged woman was in charge of the JCR president's rooms. She laughed in astonishment on hearing that there was a time when only men did the job.

THE BRITISH PUB

Even now, if I have to pick an English village to visit, I look at two aspects. One is the medieval church that the village might have. The other is the local pub, where the residents of the village gather to drink. But drinking is not the main purpose of the pub. It is a place where locals can gather to exchange news and have conversations, where they can argue about politics, sports or TV programmes, or just amuse themselves by playing games like darts.

Though pubs serve all kinds of alcohol, their specialty has traditionally been beer. Draught beer in particular, stored in kegs and served out of taps. In addition, they have bottled Guinness, ales and stouts. The pub is an institution unique to Britain. Though you can find replicas of pubs in India or the United States, the pleasure of being in a British pub is something else.

From a distance on the street, one can see hanging from an iron rod embedded in the wall a signboard with the name of the pub and its insignia. (For example, a pub named George might have an insignia with the legendary St George slaying a dragon.) Pubs tend to have a deep black exterior, and though the windows look on to the street, the people within are hidden from view by frosted glass. Inside, the pub might be a vast open space or (as with old and popular pubs) a dimly lit cave-like room. In either case it is crammed with tables occupied by patrons who, in the pub's shadowy light, can be seen engrossed in conversation. The main feature of the pub's interior is a waist-high wooden bar counter that runs across one side of the room, with barmen serving from behind it and bottles of various drinks above.

My beloved pub was The Turf Tavern, at the centre of Oxford. Tiny building, dark inside, a circular bar in the middle. There wasn't enough room to seat the patrons thronging the bar, so a beer garden had been created in the yard outside, with crude benches and tables made from planks. In all pubs, the tradition dating back centuries has been to go to the bar, buy the beer one wants, and return to the table with it. Snacks, however, would be served – usually by attractive young women from the village – at the table because they take time to prepare.

Though pubs formed around the lives of the working class, they welcome all classes of people living in the village and any strangers who happen to be passing through. Pubs are the focal point of social life in a village, and often the history of the village is contained in its pub. Posters for sporting events and plays, photographs of historical importance, antique objects, fossils found nearby, all make up a local museum. When I stayed in London with my friend Paul Rayment, the nearby pub was called The Case is Altered. The strange name comes from the pub's Spanish origins. Three centuries ago, it was apparently called Casa Altera – which means 'second home' in Spanish.

As pints of beer go down, patrons might argue about matters ranging from what a sportsperson scored in a particular game to the length of the longest river or the depth of the deepest ocean. To answer questions like these, the Guinness company ended up publishing the *Guinness Book of World Records*. Strangely, the book is particularly popular in India, where people think up new kinds of competitive events and create records in them. The publishers have themselves said that there is no other country in the world where people go to such great lengths to see their name in the *Guinness Book*.

One of the most important scientific breakthroughs of the twentieth century was the deduction of the structure of DNA. Francis Crick, who was awarded a Nobel Prize for his work, is supposed to have announced the discovery to the world at a pub in Cambridge, when he burst in at lunchtime and declared: 'We have found the secret of life.'

The atmosphere in pubs is not amenable to the personal; it is a place meant for the social. English literature is packed with dramatic episodes that occur in pubs – brawls, the plotting of conspiracies, the arrival of unexpected news from outside. But what it is not an appropriate place for is romance. In fact, women are not commonly seen there. When I was in love with a married woman named Seskia, we ensured that our attraction would not find a physical expression by avoiding meeting in my room or at her house. We would go to the beautiful pubs in villages around Oxford and sit for hours holding hands under the table.

In those days, restaurants seldom served good British food. Those who wanted tasty British food had to go to faraway pubs. There's a special pleasure to eating simple fare like steak and kidney pie and bangers. Twenty years after I left Oxford, when I went back to Britain in 1984, it gave me no joy to find samosas and 'poppadoms' being sold alongside traditional pub food. I rued the fact that a cultural identity was being lost in the face of commercial pressures.

In 2003, an elderly actress took me to a unique pub whose management, staff, patrons and shareholders were all retired actors and actresses from London theatre. Scenes from old plays were performed on Saturday evenings, and fond memories from their careers were once again brought alive. I found it a moving experience.

In the last decade, I hear that pubs have begun to shut down at an alarming rate. With smoking prohibited in all public spaces, it feels like an important aspect of the pub experience has been lost. It is now forbidden to drive after consuming even a small amount of alcohol, so it has become impossible to visit distant pubs. Beer is anyway available cheaply in supermarkets. It seems that of the more than 50,000 pubs in Britain, as many as 6,000 have closed between 2005 and 2010. To my mind, a Britain without pubs is not Britain at all.

FRIENDS

On my very first day at college, a strikingly good-looking young man came up to me at lunch and introduced himself as Rishad Talyarkhan. He was a Parsi from India, but he was so light-skinned that he could pass for an Englishman. He invited me to his room for coffee.

Rishad was younger than me. He'd had a westernized upbringing in Bombay, and had done the last two years of his schooling at a public school in England. So he immediately became my guru as far as customs and conduct were concerned. If I slipped up amongst my peers, he would correct me discreetly. He was an excellent dancer and painter, and was good at fencing. At the time, he was seeing a woman named Nirmala, who was one of the most dazzlingly beautiful women I have come across in my life. When she visited, Magdalen students would throng Rishad's room for a glimpse of her.

Once when Nirmala was travelling during the holidays, she met a man named Baron Petit, who came from considerable wealth, had Indian roots and lived in Switzerland. She married him. Rishad sank into a deep depression. Many years later, after the Baron had died, Nirmala was living in London and struggling with cancer. It speaks volumes to the kind of man Rishad was that it was he and his wife Natasha who then took care of Nirmala.

The day after I met Rishad, I was examining the notice board at the Porters' Lodge when I saw an Indian student. I went up to him and introduced myself: 'I am Girish Karnad. I'm new here.' He smiled and said his name: 'Kali Banerjee.' I noticed that he pronounced his name as 'Kalyeh Bannejjeh', but I was in no position then to understand the significance of his accent. He was short, and a little thick around the waist. His hair was long and shiny, combed back to his collar. His mouth was gathered into a pout, his head held back, and he looked at you with raised eyebrows, as if he was speaking to you from a height.

As I got to know Kali better, I began to notice how his manner of speaking surprised English students and even discomfited them. 'Where did he get his awful posh accent?' they would say. Kali would purse his lips and beam with joy. With time, I understood that his manner of speaking was a sign of those who had been educated in the most expensive public schools. Not just his speech, his posture and his mannerisms too were of the upper class.

But he had been in England for only a year. Sanjay Ghosh, who had been his fellow student at Presidency College told us, 'Kali had none of these upper-class mannerisms in Calcutta.' Kali must have attended special classes to learn his accent after coming to England. Friends who had attended public school all agreed that his accent never slipped even for a moment. His command over it was such that he might as well have been born with it. Students who came from grammar schools heard him speak with admiration, envy, and not without some contempt.

The stories Kali later told about our first meeting were indicative of his newly acquired persona. Upper-class etiquette deems it uncivilized for a stranger to simply introduce himself. Two people are supposed to talk only after a third has introduced them. According to Kali, this is how we first met: 'I was standing by myself, looking at the notice board, when this stranger fell upon me saying, "I am Girish Karnad." I stood there taken aback. I was too embarrassed to answer, and so I ran off without saying anything.' When etiquette is violated, the custom among the upper classes is to be quietly brusque and turn their backs.

I would laugh and defend his civility: 'Kali, don't exaggerate. You were not at all so rude. You came to my room happily and we chatted.' He would turn to the others listening to the story and say, with raised eyebrows and a pout, 'You can believe either one of us, the choice is yours.' His stiff laugh would then imply: 'Anyone who truly knows me could, of course, never believe Girish.'

Another feature of the upper classes is the double-barrelled surname, such as Prior-Palmer, Rees-Mogg, Douglas-Hamilton. But with democratic winds blowing, it had become common to lose one half of such surnames. So it was a matter of some wonder in the college that every one of Kali's girlfriends came with the heft of a double-barrelled surname. The first was Patricia Hamsworth-Johns. When I was there, it was Geraldine Smith-Parr ('A descendent of Queen Catherine Parr!').

Despite his attitude, Kali never seemed to have any money. He borrowed from us often, and none of us dared ask him to return it. If we did, he would say, nicely, 'Your money is safe. I will return it. But in the meanwhile, how about another five quid?' When we went to a restaurant together, we all knew exactly what was going to happen. 'I have eaten at college, so I won't take anything. Go ahead and order,' he would say, sitting calmly with his arms crossed. Then, after the food had arrived and we were about to start eating, he would say, 'Perhaps I'll have a bite,' and ask a waiter to bring cutlery and an empty plate for him. He would take a little food from each of our plates and make a good meal of it. Then, when the bill came, he would sit there with his arms crossed like he had nothing to do with it.

No matter what the topic of conversation, Kali had the truly impressive ability of steering it towards a book or an essay he had just read, so he could then display his knowledge.

For all this, there was a certain warmth to Kali, and we remained friends even after college.

One evening, Rishad, Kali and I were chatting in my room. We needed a light for our cigarettes and we knocked on the door opposite mine. The name on the door read J.S.M. Keay. A tall, slender fellow opened the door. I don't remember if we got the matches, but as John told us later, he ran to the room of a fellow student the moment we left and announced, 'Three Indians just came to my room!' The two or three of his friends there besieged him with questions: 'Really? What were they like? What happened?' John had come from the safe confines of a well-known public school called Ampleforth. He would later admit: 'The three of you Indians suddenly knocking on my door broadened my world more than joining Oxford did.' John was a student of history. When he was in his room, he played pop songs ceaselessly on his record player. Since there was only a staircase separating our doors, I could hear the music faintly in my room even when our doors were shut. I was then twenty-two. He was eighteen. Thanks to John, I became well versed in the music young people were listening to at the time.

It wasn't only music that was behind his closed door. There was always a girl there too. All his girlfriends had this in common: a round, delicate face, a slender waist, thin legs – altogether a personality that had internalized the fragility of a doll.

Because we both spent two years as neighbours at the top of the staircase, there grew a deep friendship between us. John invited me to his house for Christmas and introduced me to his parents. Later, he came to India with his fiancée. They stayed in Dharwad for three days and met my parents. Then they went to Himachal Pradesh, where they got married.

John went on to write several well-known books on India's history. A book called *The Great Arc* – about how the British measured and mapped the length and breadth of India during the nineteenth century – was a great success. But with *India: A History*, an elegant, comprehensive history of India for the lay reader, he gained a worldwide readership and became the foremost popular historian of India.

When my daughter Shalmali got married in 2009, John visited with his wife Julia. It was forty-nine years since we had first met. Rishad and his wife Natasha were there too. Their presence was a testament to the fact that our friendship remained alive and vibrant despite the separation of oceans and half a century.

At Oxford, with friends

GIRLFRIENDS

The problem of sex constantly troubled me and my Indian peers. It was a belief that had firmly taken root in adolescence that a white woman was some kind of apsara who was well beyond our reach. The white women we had seen in Indian cities – a flash of thigh, a glimpse of cleavage, hair that was brown or red or golden – had filled us with a burning desire to somehow get hold of one. And then, after setting foot in England, we saw couples at street corners, on park benches, at bus stops, locked in embrace, kissing and caressing each other, apparently taunting us for our naïveté and lack of experience.

Oxford had around eight male students to every woman. At Cambridge, it was worse: ten to one. Both had separate colleges for men and women. And (if I remember correctly) women could not be in men's colleges beyond 10 p.m. If this lakshman rekha was crossed and a woman was found in one of the rooms, some colleges had the heartless tradition of expelling the male student. In more lenient colleges, the young man could stay on after paying a fine. Some colleges had installed spikes and broken glass on their compound walls to discourage anyone from scaling the walls at night. Thankfully, Magdalen was not so fiercely conservative and had only taken the half-hearted step of sticking blunt nails into the lamp posts on the street outside so they would not be used as a climbing aid. But with a little practice, the nails could themselves be used as handholds to climb up or down the pole. I had become quite adept at this. I should clarify that girls were not the only reason to sneak into or out of the college at night. Sometimes the dining hall's evening meal would not suffice, and the only way to address a midnight pang of hunger was to go out and surrender to a plate of Britain's famous fish and chips.

Though the number of women students in the universities was low, both cities had several women's institutions unrelated to the university. The importance of English had grown in Europe after the Second World War, and this had given rise to language schools to which flocked young women from countries like Sweden, Denmark, Switzerland, Germany and France. For English girls, there were secretarial classes. For young women from lower-middle-class families, there were schools that taught etiquette. Then there were the secretaries, nurses and schoolteachers who worked in Oxford and

Cambridge, and were always eager to receive an invitation from one of the male students. Some of the students obtained a degree from the university, and while they were at it, a wife from outside the university.

Evening parties organized by students at Oxford began with the arrival of young men and women, introductions, small talk, drinks, dancing, all this under visible conditions. Then the lights would go out one by one, and bodies would gradually draw closer. It didn't take long for the dance floor and the surrounding rooms to be in complete darkness. I would remain a spectator, sipping wine while stuck firmly to my chair. Sometimes, the friend who had invited me would say, 'Girish, why are you just sitting there? Pick up a bird,' and vanish into the dark. I would be disgusted by my own well-mannered helplessness to do so. From the time I was a child, I had been accustomed to behaving in a certain way around women. This behaviour reawakened the instant I was in proximity to a woman, and I would freeze.

After an entire year of struggling with myself, I finally blurted out to a girl sitting next to me at a party: 'May I kiss you?' She said yes. I kissed her and told her, 'You're the first girl I've ever kissed.' She said, in a matter of fact way, 'No one gives it much importance here.' I drew courage from her amiability and asked, 'Will you meet me again?' She agreed, but I never called.

Every Oxbridge college hosts a Commemoration Ball once in three years. It is a grand all-night event held in the third week of June. At this time of the year, there is very little night in Britain. Daylight extends until around 1 a.m., and then the sun rises again in a couple of hours. I remember the ball as a spectacular event with many kinds of food, drinks (though mostly champagne), dancing and entertainment. The grand evening also came at the cost of a grand fortune. The ball provided an invaluable opportunity to make an impression on a young woman. Or, if the woman was already close, to show her what a prominent position she occupied in one's life. To my misfortune, the ball came towards the end of my first year in Oxford. The only young women I knew well at this time were all the girlfriends of my friends, and they already had invitations.

At this time, Rishad was being visited by two of his cousins, Anita and Rita. Rishad's father was Parsi and his mother Bengali. His mother's sister was married to the younger brother of W.H. Auden, and Anita and Rita were her daughters. Anita had a round, smiling face and a cheerful, affectionate disposition. She wrote poetry. She was married (though none of us liked her husband). Her sister Rita was a medical student. She had a narrow face, deep black hair, a slightly long nose and a piercing gaze. A suppressed intensity radiated from her entire being.

Rishad was gracious as ever. He told me repeatedly, 'You don't have to invite her simply because she is my younger sister.' But there wasn't anyone else on the horizon, and so I invited Rita to the Commemoration Ball. Since I hadn't yet had my sherwani stitched, I rented the traditional formal wear for the occasion – a white bow tie and dress coat with tails. Rita wore a flowing black off-shoulder evening gown. She squinted at her surroundings like an enigmatic actress who had stepped out of a Hollywood silent film.

There was not much to say. What little conversation we made struggled along awkwardly. We danced now and then. The silence between us grew until it felt like a large block of ice. We moved from here to there, from there to here, hoping to talk to someone we knew so that the ice might melt a little. The night was spent waiting for dawn. And dawn refused to come.

Forty years later, we met again in London. Rita laughed and said, 'Do you remember? I spent the night reading a book I had found in your room – *Tragic Themes in Western Literature*.' I remembered all too well. And in the intervening forty years, there had occurred two things that had made her something of a tragic heroine herself.

Her uncle Auden had earned a fortune from his poetry. Since he was gay and had no children of his own, his estate was to go to Anita and Rita after he died. He had fallen in love in the United States with a young poet named Chester Kallman. Auden wanted to spend his life with Kallman, who did not want so deep a commitment. Still, Auden, as a mark of his devotion, left everything he had to Kallman. Kallman had no close relatives of his own, and so he made a will leaving Auden's estate to Rita and Anita. Kallman died two years after Auden. But his will had gone missing, and the entire fortune went to a distant relative, a woman whom Kallman did not even know.

The other tragedy had to do with Rita's mental health. She had been a surgeon, but at some point she stopped leaving home and embraced a voluntary house arrest.

Rishad told me about her when I became the director of the Nehru Centre in 2000. 'She refuses to leave home. Why don't you ask her for a meal and see if she accepts?' I called Rita and invited her home. Surprisingly, she accepted at once. It was a small gathering – me, Saras, Rishad, his wife Natasha, and Rita. She spent the evening in good cheer. This was when we reminisced about *Tragic Themes in World Literature* over much laughter. Our connection was limited to the one night of the Commemoration Ball – and it was a night that had brought no joy to either of us. Still, forty years later, it was enough for her to break her house arrest and step outside.

After I returned to India, Rishad called one day and informed me that Rita had died unexpectedly. She had been a mystery to me at our first meeting, and she would forever remain one.

One day in May, I saw an advertisement on the JCR notice board for a group tour. In my first year, I had joined one such tour to Austria, where I had gone skiing at Zürs. But that had been a luxury tour restricted to Oxbridge students. The tour being advertised now was an inexpensive one to Greece. I registered.

In its class composition, this group could not be more different from the group with which I'd travelled to Austria in December. There wasn't a single Oxbridge student. My fellow travellers were all lower-middle-class and aged between twenty and twenty-five, mostly young women who worked as schoolteachers, clerks, shop assistants and secretaries. It was a time when it was still difficult for young women to travel alone or with a few other women friends. A large group provided safety and made a trip like this less expensive for someone from the lower middle class. Since the travel company was paid in advance, there was no fear of unexpected charges either.

I met Helen Burton on the first day of our tour. She was shorter than the other girls, and not all that good-looking, but she had an incisive wit. She had read more widely than the others and was well informed. There was no fear of running out of things to say to her.

Since ours was a low-cost tour, it skipped the more expensive destinations and went to smaller islands such as Skyros, Skiathos and Skopelos. It comes as a surprise to those who have heard of the vibrant civilization of ancient Greece to see just how barren the country is and how harsh the terrain. The islands consist of steep cliffs all around, on which are scattered tiny, square houses with rough, whitewashed walls. Every island has a small church. These churches allowed entry only to those wearing garments that covered the knees – so the girls had to tie long towels around their waists. We had come here to enjoy ourselves by the seaside, but it was hard not to sense something solemn about the dense, unrelenting rock formations. And perhaps a touch of fear and tragedy too.

We marvelled at the marble pillars of the Acropolis. I stood on the vast stage of the amphitheatre where plays by Sophocles and Aeschylus had been performed and felt my spine tingle.

I have no interest in travelling alone, wandering from place to place looking at scenery and monuments. I need company. The trip to Greece proved particularly enjoyable because of Helen's presence. Since everyone on a group tour of this sort is an adult, there is no intrusive moral supervision. Helen joined me in bed on the very first night of the trip as our train hurtled through Europe. A day spent taking in the sights of Greece or lazing on the seashore took on a different quality knowing that the warmth of her body awaited me at night.

But Helen was still a virgin when our group returned to London and dispersed. As Helen explained to me, physical intimacy – not intercourse – between two young people in Britain most commonly took two forms. The first was smooching, where the couple would embrace, kiss, caress, and so on, but this was not carried too far. What one saw couples engaged in on buses, in parks and on the roads was this: smooching. The next phase: necking. This involved a more thorough exploration of each other's bodies, along with the freedoms to press, squeeze, rub and grind. Here, there was the possibility of bodies being partially unclothed, and so this was most conveniently carried out in a private place such as a car or a hotel room. But this was not to end in intercourse. 'Don't think that couples at parties are actually having sex in the dark,' Helen warned me. 'There the main aim of the evening is necking, that's all.'

And so, young women had to decide in advance with whom to attend a party, to what extent they wanted to go, to what extent they may be expected to go, and accordingly configure the level of resistance their underclothes had to offer. There was often some playfulness involved in bras being hard to loosen. A firm knot or a particularly tight hook created the opportunity for laughter even during moments of desire. But matters were more serious where a young woman's virginity might be at stake. Here buckles, belts, hooks and nylons were used to fashion a safe, impenetrable armour.

There were several reasons for this strange morality. Mainly, it was misgivings about sex handed down traditionally to the middle class since the Victorian era. There was the fear that if a young woman has intercourse with her boyfriend, then he begins to hold her in contempt and think of her as easy or cheap. This had been Helen's main concern. Another reason was the ignorance among young men and women about each other. Boys and girls did not have co-education at the school level. There was no frank discussion at school about sex, and absolutely nothing on family planning or contraception.

To buy a condom, one went to the chemist's shop on the pretext of buying toothpaste or shaving cream, took the shopkeeper aside and spoke to him in a low voice. The shopkeeper, too, would hand over the package with a frown or a faint smile to convey that the immoral act about to take place did not have his approval. The entire transaction was fraught with unease and awkwardness.

Helen and I had been clear with each other. As we grew close, I told her that I was not planning to stay on in England after my studies. And even after returning to India, I would not think of marriage until I was certain about my future. To Helen, there was no question of intercourse where marriage was not a possibility. In this respect, it must be said that her generation was monogamous. I, too, had no intention of getting a woman pregnant and turning my future plans upside down. Despite our having shared a bed from time to time for two years, there was no bitterness between us when I left England. The last time I took her to a restaurant, she said, 'Girish, let's not write to each other. This has been a beautiful experience. Let's leave it here.' There is no doubt that my time at Oxford was richer for having met Helen.

Within a year or two of my returning to India, the culture around sex changed completely in the West. The strange conservatism I experienced was replaced by free sex. My time in England did not overlap with it.

LOVERS

Students living in college did not have permission to lock their rooms when they went out because the scouts were opposed to it. Their fear was that students might leave valuables in their locked rooms, and suspicion would fall on the scouts if these valuables went missing. Students were to lock their valuables in their trunks, and leave the rooms themselves unlocked.

And so, one evening when I went to see Kali, the door to his room was open. Kali was not inside, but sitting there was a young man waiting for him. It was evident from his clothes that he was an Oxbridge student. He had a Bengali face, along with the spectacles that seemed obligatory for all Bengalis (except Kali). His name was Sanjay Ghosh. Kali never arrived, so Sanjay and I went to a pub to eat.

Sanjay had taken a first class in physics at Cambridge and was working in Oxford at the research complex at Harwell. But his interests extended beyond research and academics. He had a keen wit that quickly picked out the absurd in an argument, no matter what the subject. His political consciousness was well developed, and had led him to a humanitarian outlook with an affinity for socialist ideas. He was quietly self-assured about India without any hollow nationalism. I liked him at once.

While he was at Cambridge, Sanjay had met a Dutch woman named Seskia, who had come there to learn English. They fell in love and became engaged. Sanjay had rented a small house in Oxford, now that he was working there. Seskia had followed him to Oxford, but since it was not yet common for unmarried couples to live together, she had taken a room elsewhere. She spoke English with a Dutch accent, which gave her an exotic charm. She had brown hair, delicate features, and a dancer's body: altogether a beauty that was distinctly not British. She radiated kindness and was always ready to lend an ear to anyone who needed it.

And there we all were, craving the company of an affable woman who would listen sympathetically to us. To Rishad, Kali and me, Sanjay and Seskia's house became the centre of gravity of our daily lives. We were always welcome there. It became a place for us to find something we sorely missed – the warmth of family.

Seskia had lost her parents early in life, so there was no one pressing her to return to Amsterdam. She had organized her life around Sanjay while she waited for them to be married. But into this harmonious arrangement crashed Sanjay's older sister Neela, who had come to study art. Her emotional outbursts turned their lives and their relationship upside down. I have used this tragic situation in my play *Anju Mallige,* so maybe I should not repeat myself!

Finally, when it seemed like waiting any longer might destroy their relationship, Sanjay and Seskia decided on a registered wedding. Sanjay's father was in poor health in Calcutta, so his mother came alone. After the wedding, she remained in Sanjay's house while the couple went on their honeymoon. The day they were to return to Oxford, Neela jumped into the Cherwell river and killed herself.

Sanjay's mother was sitting alone when Rishad and I went to see her. There was no hint of agitation on her face or in her manner. She spoke with great self-possession and retained her composure when we discussed arrangements. The body was to be kept in the morgue until Sanjay and Seskia returned. It was only when the word 'it' was used to refer to her daughter's remains did she falter. Her eyes welled up with tears.

Sanjay and Seskia's married life began to crumble under the weight of Neela's suicide. They were married now and legally entitled to share a bed, but a deep silence had come between them. Seskia was not close to anyone else in Oxford. Rishad, Kali and I continued to visit their house every evening, but it was me that she looked to for support. I began to feel attracted to her. Her relationship with Sanjay was already fragile, and the thought that it might break because of me was unbearable. I respected Sanjay and was fond of him. At the same time, I was deeply moved by Seskia's tears and pain. It was agonizing to keep our attraction from leading to a physical relationship, but there was no alternative. Both of us had a deep affection for Sanjay. I was not prepared to betray a man whose friendship, whose home, whose wife had become the bedrock of my life at Oxford. Seskia, too, was confident her marriage would revive with time. Still, I had told her, 'If your marriage ends, let me know. I will come and marry you.'

Of all the Western women I had the chance to meet at Oxford, the only one who showed the ability and inclination to blend into Indian life, and the only one I wanted, was Seskia.

I returned to India after my examinations. The next year, I received a greeting card from Sanjay. 'I've had a son,' it said. 'The entire credit for this goes to me.'

Twenty years later, Saras and I met Sanjay and Seskia over dinner in New York. While reminiscing about Oxford I said, 'My love for Seskia was intense and platonic.' Sanjay stared at me silently. Seskia carried on with her meal as if nothing had been said.

Come to think of it, it would be hard for me to describe Ann Duncan as a girlfriend. She visited college because she was seeing a Magdalen student named Robin, a boy with a dull face who wore thick, black-framed glasses, and walked around with his shoulders hunched together as if he were perennially cold. In contrast, Ann stood out for her liveliness. I had not then heard of the disability known as spina bifida, so I did not realize it was the reason she wore calipers on her deformed legs and used crutches. Her head was large in proportion to her body, and perhaps her condition also had something to do with her tendency to laugh excessively.

Ann was a student of French literature and was very bright. Everyone agreed that she was likely to get a first class. She came to me one day after hearing that my friend Krishna Basrur was in Paris. She said, 'I have to visit Paris for research, but I don't have much money. Can I stay at your friend's flat?' I knew how generous Basrur was and agreed on his behalf. College was on break, and I had anyway planned to go to Paris. Ann and I left together.

I had already visited Paris a couple of times and stayed with Basrur. While he was at office, I walked endlessly by the banks of the Seine and along the stately avenues of the city. A seventeenth-century architect named Baron Haussmann had demolished parts of medieval Paris and built this beautiful new city. His work has, to this day, been preserved with pride by the French. The first time I went to Paris, France was struggling to retain control over its colony Algeria. A war was on in Algeria against revolutionaries, and its echoes were being felt in Paris. Bombs would go off in the middle of the night, and the sirens of police vans and ambulances would rouse a frightened city from its sleep. During the day, soldiers stood guard with machine guns behind fortresses of heaped cement bags at the avenue corners. Since Basrur and I could be mistaken for Arabs, walking on the streets meant we had to endure looks of anger and hatred from the French.

One day, Basrur and I were in a café when we learnt that a stranger sitting at another table had left without picking up his suitcase. We ran from there, fearing it was a bomb. Thankfully, it was only a few months before General Charles de Gaulle came to power and withdrew the French army from Algeria. Paris returned to its free and lively self.

The economic growth of France under de Gaulle was evident in Paris when I visited with Ann. I love to walk and can go long distances without stopping to rest. Paris, too, seems made for exploring on foot. This was not possible in Ann's company of course, but then, she knew not only the French language but also the literature, the history, and even lewd jokes. We sat with our legs stretched out on the banks of the Seine, enjoying French wine, tasting various kinds of French cheeses with baguettes, chatting and laughing the days away. Ann did not seem in the least concerned with whatever research she had wanted to do in Paris. I told her about Helen. She laughed and said, 'This fear of sex is the curse of my generation of English girls. French girls have no such anxiety. I'm still a virgin, you know.' I said, 'Me too.' Though she was eager to have sex, Robin wanted to wait until they were married. 'It disgusts me to be a virgin, but Robin has a tremendous regard for my hymen,' she said, and laughed loudly.

Inevitably, we were together the three nights we spent in Paris. Since we were both inexperienced, it was more a clumsy struggle than it was lovemaking, but when we returned to Oxford, it was with the satisfaction that we were no longer virgins.

But I had made a blunder in my eagerness to be an 'experienced man'. Between Ann's unconditional submission and the spell cast by Paris, I had neglected to pay attention to her feelings. It was not long before the consequences were in front of me. Ann left her boyfriend Robin, saying, with candour, 'He was just convenient.' She announced that she was in love with me and proceeded to take over my life at college.

Ann began to turn up at college practically every day. If I wasn't in my room, she would roam around looking for me. Since I was the JCR president, I had a large room to live in. One day, I found myself holding an invitation to a party at my room hosted jointly by Ann Duncan and Girish Karnad. Ann had not said a word about it to me. I was furious, and I shouted at her saying I would not attend the party. 'Will you humiliate me in front of everyone?' she asked, weeping. I was forced to attend the party, and she spent the evening stuck to me in front of everyone.

On another occasion, Ann came to my room while I was studying. Robin entered behind her. I ignored them and continued studying. Ann sat in silence with her back towards him. He sat there glaring at her, looking as if he was about to cry. Neither of them got up for an hour. Finally, I made an excuse saying I had to go to the library, left them in my room and got out.

A friend of Robin's complained to me, 'You're destroying him.' One afternoon, I was in Seskia's house discussing the trouble with her marriage and my own confused role in it, when the doorbell rang. Standing there was Ann. 'I knew I would find you here,' she said, entered and sat down.

I escaped this torture only when I returned to India after my examinations. Ann became a professor of French at Cambridge and was regarded an excellent teacher by her students. Only, it seems she spewed fire at the sight of Indian students. Some twenty years later, I received news that she had taken her own life. When I think back to Ann now, I feel I should have been more careful from the beginning, I should have shown her more understanding. The pain of having treated her so cruelly still bothers me.

THE OXFORD UNION

I can't remember when I first grew infatuated with the Union, but I know that the ambition to be president of the Oxford Union took root many years before I actually went to Oxford. I used to participate in the weekly student assemblies at the Marikamba School in Sirsi, and I knew even then that I had the confidence required for public speaking. I had also experienced the glow of contentment that seemed to fill every part of my body and spill over when members of the audience appreciated my speech.

The Oxford Union was one of the world's most celebrated debating societies, and I longed to fly my flag over it. When I was growing up, it was common among cultured people to follow public discourse in England as if it were personally relevant to them. They read about what was happening, and took pleasure in discussing it. The newspapers carried stories about the brilliance shown in public debates by people like G.K. Chesterton, Bernard Shaw, H.G. Wells, Winston Churchill and others. It was in this cultural context that I must have read about and been inspired by the dazzling oratory, debates, political discussions, and displays of wit and repartee at the Oxford Union.

My father had mentioned to me the best-known debate in the history of the Union. I learnt more about it later. In 1933, the topic moved for debate at the Union was that 'This House will in no circumstances fight for its King and Country'. The motion passed comfortably, and the matter should have ended there. The row started when Randolph Churchill – son of Winston Churchill – rushed to Oxford three weeks later, claiming the vote went against the interests of the country, and asking for the motion to be deleted from the Union's records.

The students of Oxford had passed a resolution amongst themselves. And here was a politician from London – so what if he was a member of the Union, he was still an outsider – who had come to try and change it. The students were incensed. Outside, all over the country, Oxford students were condemned as traitors. Not just that, it had been suggested that the resolution formed the basis for Mussolini's plans in the Second World War. So, the students behind the resolution were even accused of betraying all of Western civilization. The episode became well known as the 'King and Country' debate. It's a different matter that this generation did not hesitate to enter the battlefield when the World War started in 1939.

Naturally, once I reached Oxford I went to the Union's auditorium, where debates were held every Thursday evening and students who were members of the Union could attend. I would go as an audience member and take notes. Everyone there was eager to see the sparks fly when sharp minds took each other on, and the auditorium became packed when well-known speakers participated.

Debates were supervised by four student office-bearers of the Union. The president sat in the middle, to his right and left were the librarian and the treasurer respectively, and in front of them was the secretary, all dressed formally. Elections were held at the end of every term for the four positions. No one directly became the president or the librarian. Only someone who had been elected as treasurer or secretary and discharged that responsibility for a term could aspire to the higher positions.

Every debate at the Union followed a defined format. First, two students spoke for fifteen to twenty minutes each, for and against the motion respectively. This was called the paper speech. Then, two or four prominent figures from public life spoke for fifteen minutes each. The debate was then thrown open to the floor. Any member could raise their hand to draw the president's attention and come forward to speak for three or four minutes.

So, a new student who wanted to make an impression in the Union had to first make such a floor speech. Once he had demonstrated his ability to speak well, the president might invite him to deliver a paper speech. A student had the chance to give only one paper speech in a term. If he impressed the members with that speech, he could stand for elections, and in this way climb up the ladder until, perhaps, he was a candidate for president. My first speech at the Union was a huge success. I contested the elections at the end of the term and became secretary.

This meant I had a foot on the first rung of that ladder. The Union was like a scaled down version of the British parliament. Accordingly, its atmosphere mirrored that of politics and the moral values operating in the world of the Union were ambition, envy, deviousness, treachery, cleverness and eternal vigilance. The main aim of those participating in the Union's activities was to distinguish themselves to the members as unique and special in comparison to other candidates. With this aim in mind, I had a black sherwani stitched. The English office-bearers wore their traditional white ties, and my Indian attire stood out for its distinctiveness.

The other decision I took was even more important. From the day I arrived in England, I had sought to make my spoken English more 'English' and less 'Indian'. I didn't aspire to a superior, upper-class accent like Kali Banerjee's, but I did think it was vital to have an accent that would be regarded as cultured in England. I abandoned all attempts at this after I joined the Union. I realized that the ways of my Kannada tongue made me stand out. Retaining it was the smart thing to do.

Most importantly, if I was going to move up from position to position across four terms and end as president, I would have to make sure that no one tripped me up along the way. And so, it was strategically essential to make a show of my deep concern for others, to go around smiling as if I did not have any airs about me. How well I played the game is evident from the fact that I was elected unopposed to the post of president.

There was another reason for my being elected unopposed. Women did not have the right to be members of the Union until 1962. They could only attend as guests of male members. For several years, there had been attempts to get rid of this outdated rule by putting it to a special vote. But old-timers, those who had become members of the Union thirty or forty years ago, still had the right to vote. The resolution had failed every time in the past, and it failed again when I was librarian. The treasurer at the time, Lawrence Reid, who was going to be my opponent in the election, resigned his post to protest the regressive outcome. I became the fourth Indian president of the Union.

When I was president, there was again a vote. This time, the resolution passed and women obtained the right to be members of the Union. My role was only to conduct the vote in an impartial manner, and I cannot take credit for the result. Still, it was a matter of satisfaction to me that the historic change happened during my term. Some of the older members wrote to say they were resigning in protest. This was expected. I wrote to all of them personally to placate them. This was expected too.

In 1976, the future prime minister of Pakistan, Benazir Bhutto, became the Union's president.

I must mention some of the unforgettable people I met through the Union. There was a debate every Thursday, and at least two of the invited speakers were from outside Oxford. As secretary, it was my duty to receive them at the station, take them to the renowned Randolph Hotel, and then to dinner at the Union, before the debate commenced. The next day, I would accompany them to the station to see them off. As a result, I was in a unique position to learn what impression the Union made on them.

In 1961, an Immigration bill was presented to parliament to control the inflow of Indian, Pakistani and West Indian migrants, who were flooding Britain. One of the MPs leading this initiative was Sir Cyril Osborne. He was

The Oxford Union

invited as a speaker when the immigration bill was debated in the Union. I welcomed Sir Cyril at the station as per custom. When he rose to speak at the debate, liberal students booed him for being racist without listening to him. Whether his argument was right or wrong, I felt an injustice had been done to him.

Sir Cyril was worked up on the way to the station. 'I am absolutely not against migrants. All I am saying is this: today, we bring in the poor from other countries to sweep our roads, to clean our toilets, to drive our buses. But isn't it our responsibility tomorrow to educate their children and make sure they prosper? Who does the menial jobs then? If we say we cannot do them and continue to bring in migrants for the purpose, what happens to them? What happens to us?' He repeated the points he had made during the debate. I don't remember what I said, but he seemed comforted by my sympathetic response. 'Let me know when you're in London,' he told me. 'You can come to parliament as my personal guest. We can eat with the MPs in the members' dining room.' After he reached, there was again a pressing invitation from him to visit parliament.

One of the guest speakers invited during my term as president was Sir Randolph Churchill, whom I have already mentioned in the context of the 'King and Country' debate. Randolph was the son of Winston Churchill, the great wartime prime minister of England, and an intelligent man who could have achieved much. But with such a dominating father, and a mother who neglected her children while tending to her husband's political life, he turned wayward. One evening, he turned up drunk to a debate at the Union and began to behave badly. The students, amidst their laughter, were waiting to see how I would handle the situation. I warned him: 'If the honourable member does not behave himself, I shall have him physically removed from the hall.' When he realized it was not an empty threat, Sir Randolph quietened down.

The next day, he sent word through a student named Jonathan Aitken that, if I could leave at once for London, I could have lunch with Winston Churchill. Unfortunately, I was not in college or in the Union when Jonathan came looking for me. Churchill was one of the leading political figures of the century and someone who had vehemently opposed independence for India. I missed the chance to meet him at his house and have lunch with him.

The bearer of that message, Jonathan, was himself from a prominent political family. His grand-uncle Lord Beaverbrook was the owner of Britain's most popular newspaper, the *Daily Express*. He had been a great support to Winston Churchill during the war and was known to be his friend. Jonathan's father was a managing director in the newspaper company. We were convinced that Jonathan had a bright future in politics and could one day be the leader of the party and ultimately the prime minister. He had all the qualities needed to rise to the top in politics. He was good-looking, charming, polished, ambitious. And ruthless.

But he managed to ruin his future even as he was rising up the ranks in politics. When he was a member of the cabinet, *The Guardian* reported that he had gone on a secret trip to Paris in relation with an arms deal involving Saudi Arabia. Jonathan claimed the accusation was false, that he was in Paris with his wife and daughter on a personal trip, and took the newspaper to court. He even had his young daughter sign a statement corroborating his story. *The Guardian* managed to prove in court that this was all a bundle of lies. Jonathan became notorious for being prepared to use his teenaged daughter for political ends. He ended up serving a prison sentence for perjury and perverting the course of justice. When I met him in 2001, he had become a born-again Christian and was involved in efforts to uplift Dalits in India.

The Cold War between America and Russia was at a particularly fierce juncture when I was at Oxford. Both nations had amassed nuclear weapons and threatened to annihilate the entire world in the event they fought a war. It had become an urgent question for Britain to decide its position on the Cold War face-off. The philosopher Bertrand Russell had taken the stand that Britain had no use for nuclear weapons. They would only draw Russia's attention, so the right thing to do was to give them up entirely. He had started a movement called the Campaign for Nuclear Disarmament (CND) that had become the subject of debate.

Surprisingly, it was Russell who had argued in 1948, after the war, that atomic bombs be used to destroy Russia before they could acquire nuclear weapons. Now, he had taken the opposite stand: giving up nuclear weapons entirely was the only means of self-preservation. From 1958 onwards, activists from various parts of the country would come to London during the Easter weekend in April for a massive gathering in Trafalgar Square.

Their position was that, even if it meant defeat at the hands of Russia, even if it meant having to accept communism, it was preferable to being destroyed: 'We would rather be red than dead.' From Trafalgar Square, the demonstration would walk nearly eighty kilometres to Aldermaston, where the Atomic Weapons Establishment is located. Several people I admired from the arts were part of the movement, including the novelist E.M. Forster, the playwright J.B. Priestley, and the composer Benjamin Britten.

In 1963, as president of the Oxford Union, I was invited to address the gathering at Trafalgar Square. Some 60,000 people were assembled that year. True, it was an opportunity to stand in public alongside a colossus like Bertrand Russell. But I believed that it was up to the citizens of a country to determine what was best for their nation's security. It would be wrong for an outsider to interfere, and so, I declined the invitation and missed meeting Bertrand Russell.

The Union made my time at Oxford memorable beyond anything I could have imagined. Not only did I meet England's politicians, intellectuals and artists, I also had the chance to engage them in close conversation. I gained a rich understanding of Britain's social, cultural and political life. The three years I was at Oxford were also politically significant ones for India: Goa was liberated from the Portuguese, China attacked India. I learnt what impression my country made on Western thinkers – many thought highly of it, some were dismissive – and what could change that picture. One of the three subjects I was studying at Oxford was political science. I'm not sure how much of it I learnt from my textbooks, but I certainly learnt a lot from my experiences at the Union.

TUGHLAQ

As soon as he had published *Yayati*, GB began to insist that I write another play for him. But what was I to write about? *Yayati* had come to me without warning and had practically written itself. I had poured into it everything I had read and internalized about the puranas, about myths and mythologicals, about Greek drama, about French playwrights, and I felt like I had nothing left in me. At one time, I had longed for GB to ask me to write something for him. But now, I dreaded the very sight of a letter from him.

The publication of *Yayati* brought a new dimension to my life at Oxford. I was determined to closely follow the theatre activities happening around me so I could grow into a more adept playwright. This was easier said than done. Plays were ceaselessly being staged at Oxford, and productions headed for London's West End usually came to Oxbridge first. Still, barring a few productions, I did not see a single exciting play in my three years in England.

Until around 1950, Bernard Shaw had ruled the world of British theatre. At the time, it was impossible for anyone writing 'modern' plays to escape the influence of Shaw and his guru Ibsen. In Kannada, too, Sriranga and Kailasam had established a tradition of extended conversations carried out in middle-class living rooms. This had never appealed to me.

After John Osborne's *Look Back in Anger,* critics began to speak of a fresh new breeze blowing through British theatre, one that marked the end of Shaw's era. As far as I could tell, all that was new was that Shaw's upper middle class had been replaced by the working class. British theatre considered the presence of a clothes iron in *Look Back in Anger* as nothing short of revolutionary. But as an outsider, I was completely uninterested in class conflict and this redecoration of the living room. While the themes and the class to which the characters belonged might have changed, British playwrights still continued to treat the interior of the house as their entire world. Perhaps it was the cold, fog and incessant rain of Britain that made it difficult for playwrights to even think of venturing outdoors.

Even though my *Yayati* was puranic, I was keenly aware that it was essentially in the mould of Ibsen. I longed to break the living-room walls and go out into the abundant breeze and sunshine we are blessed with in India for nine months of the year. I wanted to use in my work our forests, hills and streets. All this was conceptually clear to me, but I didn't know how to move towards realizing it in practice.

Among the books I had brought with me to Oxford were the first two volumes of *Nadedu Banda Daari,* an anthology tracing the development of Kannada literature. In it was included Sriranga's play *Kattale Belaku,* which astonished me with a modern sensibility the likes of which I had never before encountered in Kannada. Sriranga had been dismissive of *Yayati,* but I felt that any response from a playwright of such quality deserved to be taken as a compliment.

Kirtinath Kurtakoti's introductions to the works in *Nadedu Banda Daari* opened the door to a world I didn't even know existed. They offered new perspectives and inspiration. I found my attention drawn to a comment about Kannada plays: 'But no one has attempted to use historical material to try and reveal new layers of the truth. Along with resurrecting the past, we need to develop a vision that looks at the past in a new light. We need new works that use the raw material of history. Shaw and Ibsen must be emulated in this respect too, as they have been in other ways. It is a matter of regret that we don't have a single work like *Caesar and Cleopatra* or *Saint Joan*.'

As soon as I read that short paragraph, I thought such a play was worth attempting. I had inherited a love of history from my father. When I was thirteen or fourteen, I had read H.G. Wells's *The Outline of History* and been so inspired that I had embarked on writing a world history of my own. I still have six or seven notebooks filled with notes. Reading history books with a view to finding material for a play would not be a difficult task.

I went to the library and found a textbook of Indian history. I started from Mohenjo-Daro. I read through the Mauryas, the Greeks, the Huns, the Guptas, the Pallavas, the Cholas, and reached the fourteenth century. The material I was looking for was here, waiting for me: the 'mad' reign of Muhammad Tughlaq.

For students of that generation, existentialism was a much-beloved school of thought. It had become popular internationally through the work of French writers like Sartre and Camus. But to me, the main attraction of existentialism lay in its dramatic quality. Camus's *Caligula* was among the plays I was thinking of while writing *Tughlaq*. When I tried reading it recently, I was surprised that a play so mechanical and contrived had ever appealed to me.

Oxford philosophy at the time was mired in linguistic analysis. This school of thinking believed – essentially – that the philosophical problems that confront us can be solved by describing them completely. In contrast, existentialism spoke with concern for the human condition. It addressed, boldly and with great vitality, questions about human existence, fate, our position in the world, and the relationship between god and the individual. It also possessed a moral dimension, in that it allowed us the ability to confront the absurdity of existence, make choices about how to shape our lives, and act accordingly. And so, it was conducive to being a philosophy of action. The philosophers at Oxford – with the exception of Iris Murdoch – were all uninterested in existentialism. As a result, I looked upon them with some disdain.

In the existentialist view, god too is a character. His relationship with man is one of the main problems it explores. When I read about Muhammad Tughlaq, I was immediately drawn to two aspects of his life. The first was that, despite being the most brilliant sultan to sit on the throne of Delhi, he came to be regarded as 'mad' by both his contemporaries and by posterity. The other was that, for nearly five years of his reign, he had forbidden public prayer. I remember my hair standing on end when I read about this. At the time, I considered myself an atheist, and I believed Tughlaq's astonishing move must have arisen from his own atheism. As I learnt more about him, I began to realize that it had its origins in his struggles with religion. It was no simple matter to keep faith in god. It was more of a hard penance.

I had written *Yayati* like a man possessed. It came easily, at one stretch. With *Tughlaq*, it was the very opposite. First, I had to assimilate all the information I had collected in the library. Then, an imagined detail here, an idea there, a flash of insight elsewhere – all these had to be brought together into a definite form.

Take, for example, a sentence in the last scene: 'When it comes to washing away filth, no saint is a match for a dhobi.' I had written it down in my diary when I was in Bombay, two years before I started working on *Tughlaq*. It was this line that made Aziz a dhobi. From there, images involving changes of attire spread through the play like a creeper. Here, it hardly needs to be said, was also the influence of Caroline Spurgeon's essay on *Macbeth*.

I wanted the play to resemble a traditional company natak, and so the pair of characters, Aziz and Aazam, were modelled on the Ramayana's Akara and Makara. But Aziz grew in stature right in front of my eyes, and stood up as an independent character. I wasn't sure what to do with him. Then, my friend Krishna Basrur advised me: 'He must confront the sultan. It is essential they have a face-off.' I decided he was right. But it took another year before I knew what would happen during that confrontation.

All in all, I struggled for around two years to finish *Tughlaq*.

EPILOGUE

I took my examinations in 1963. I had done poorly in one paper – that too, statistics – and this meant I had passed in the upper second class. A viva was conducted to decide if I could be given a first, but I was unsuccessful.

I was sitting in my room in despair after the viva, when my tutor David Worswick paid me a visit. He looked at me questioningly, saw the tears in my eyes and said, 'This is nothing to worry about. All of this will seem trivial in another twenty years.'

Looking back now, I feel I was fortunate to miss a first class. Had I obtained a first, I would certainly have been offered a teaching position at one of the colleges in Oxford, which might have shaken my resolve to return to India. My second-class degree did not allow the dilemma to present itself.

Two months before my examinations, the general manager of OUP India, Roy E. Hawkins, visited Oxford looking for youngsters who had the ability to edit books in English. Since OUP India began operations in 1912, its editors had all been British. Even when Indians became managers, it was in administrative or marketing roles. But in 1962, an Oxford student, Ravi Dayal, had been appointed manager in an editorial capacity. After him, it was my turn now. A good job had sought me out even before the examinations – I accepted at once. Hawkins told me, 'It is not possible for us to pay you as you would be paid by the Tata or Birla companies. If you join us, it will have to be for the intellectual satisfaction.' That was all I wanted.

The reason I call my second-class degree a stroke of good fortune is because India was in the throes of a cultural renaissance. The nation was struggling economically, but the gates were opening on to a wonderfully vibrant era of cinema, theatre, literature and arts. Without knowing anything about the infinite opportunities beckoning from within, I set foot again on Indian soil.

7

MADRAS

PRELUDE

My working life began with an extended nap. I joined my new job by reporting at the London office of OUP, where I was welcomed warmly by Philip Chester, a senior executive who had not only worked in the India branch for several years, but had married an Indian woman as well. He entrusted me to a colleague, who showed me to my independent office and put down a stack of about a dozen files on my table. He said, 'Read these. You will understand the process of publishing books,' and left. I browsed a few files near the top. I was not entirely ignorant of publishing, with my *Yayati* having just been brought out by Manohara Grantha Mala. Anyway, I thought to myself, I had my whole life ahead of me to understand the intricacies of publishing. I adjusted the stack of files in front of me to suit my height, rested my head on my folded arms, and went to sleep.

The ability to fall asleep at will is a boon bestowed upon me by nature. I can even decide how long I want to sleep and wake up exactly on time as if an alarm clock has gone off. My sleep is unaffected by noise around me. Later, when I started working in films, I once managed to sleep through the din of a crowd gathered for the shooting of a village-fair scene. On another occasion, when I was supposed to be unconscious on an operating table, I told the director, 'Do whatever you want, but don't wake me,' and went to sleep. The director moved the table around, changed the lighting, and finished all the shots in the scene before waking me. At the OUP office, there was not even any disturbance. I slept deeply for three hours and woke up in time for lunch. 'It's a good thing I've joined publishing,' I thought to myself.

It was the custom for senior executives at OUP to gather before lunch and spend some time talking over drinks. I knew that upper-class professionals took sherry or beer or cider before lunch, even on working days. Since I had studied economics, I also knew that Britain was struggling financially. I had heard a theory that attributed this to the poor productivity of executives who spent hours drinking and eating on the pretext of business lunches, leaving them in no position to finish the day's work. Now I witnessed this with my own eyes. Thankfully, American work culture took over with time and the practice of prolonged business lunches came to an end.

Among OUP's employees was a young man who belonged to an aristocratic family. He was a member of the House of Lords, but his family had lost their wealth and he had been unable to study at Oxbridge. This meant that he did not have an invitation to the room where lunchtime drinks were had.

My Oxford friend Paul Rayment had put me up in a spare room in his house, so I did not have to pay for my stay in London. When I had been a student, it took considerable effort to go to London, see a play or a film, and rush back to Oxford. Now, Paul and I went to see a play or a film almost every evening. Of all the productions I saw, I only recall one now: *Oh, What a Lovely War!* directed by Joan Littlewood.

It was set during the First World War, and depicted how British and German politicians and generals, first by being confident that the war would be won in three months, and then by being unable to accept that they were losing, had destroyed an entire generation of young men. The uniqueness of the production lay in its documentary format. Littlewood's group had written the play after gathering as research material songs, newspapers, diaries and letters from the period. It was all based on fact; not a single line was imagined. Scenes where British and German troops in their trenches took orders from their superiors to kill each other were accompanied by captions – 'Fifteen thousand lives were lost in this battle. Ten feet of land was gained.' – that sent a shiver through the audience and drove home the futility of war. It remains one of the best theatrical productions I have ever seen.

At OUP, I met Jon Stallworthy, a young poet whose work had been deeply influenced by W.B. Yeats's later poems. He was passionate about literature and English poetry, and he believed that OUP, in addition to publishing scholarly works, also had to create room for new creative writing. Accordingly, he had started the Oxford Poets series to publish young poets. Talking to him about contemporary literature was a revelation – it felt like I was being shown entire landscapes that had been invisible to me at Oxford. He had discovered and published new talents such as Charles Tomlinson and James Kincaid. A.K. Ramanujan's name floated into my head while talking to him, but there was no use mentioning him without having his poems to show. I stayed quiet then, but I immediately wrote to Ramanujan and asked him to send all his poems to Bombay, addressed to me.

After I finished my training period in London, OUP gave me the choice of either flying back to India or sailing first class. I knew that the days of sea travel were coming to an end, so I chose to sail back. Now I remember nothing about the journey, not even the name of the ship.

INTERLUDE: BOMBAY

I was to train at OUP's Bombay office before going to Madras. By the time I reached Bombay, my parents and younger sister Leena had been staying with my brother in Karnatak Buildings for around six months. A groom was being sought for Leena and my elder brother was looking for a bride for himself.

I had returned to India after spending three years at Oxford. Emotionally as well as in everyday matters, I expected a gap to have opened up between me and our society and culture, and I thought I would be incapable of reconciling with our traditional ways. I was astonished to find that this was not the case. I slipped back effortlessly into the system I thought I had given up and dissolved into my family with such ease that I had to wonder if those three years spent abroad were just a dream.

One day, my father's older brother's wife, a woman of eighty, came to see me. 'You've brought us all a good name. At least you've returned without having taken a white woman for your wife. Now if you settle down with a girl from our caste, I can die content,' she said, weeping. I despaired at the thought that no rebellion could stand firm against such tenderness and concern.

Even more surprising to me was that, as a result of having returned to Karnatak Buildings and the heart of Saraswat society, I too gradually began to feel that I might as well get married. Still, I didn't agree to 'see' potential brides the way one looks at vegetables before buying them. (One of my cousins had gained quite a reputation after having seen over twenty girls.) I accepted an invitation to dinner with a good-looking young woman who had done her BA. We went to the cinema. She met with my approval and I was going to say yes, when Aayi said she was not in favour of the match. I was furious. I said, 'If you had objections, why didn't you say something all these days when I was going with her to dinner and the cinema? Do you want me to insult her now, after things have worked out? I can't do that.' Aayi and I stopped talking. Bappa took me aside and counselled me: 'Why hurt your mother? If this is going to be the shruti of your marriage, how will they both coexist? Just say no.' I told Aayi I would listen to her this time, but on the condition that she was not allowed to advise me in future. She agreed happily. I said no to the match on some pretext or the other. Then Aayi promptly forgot her side of the deal and began to indicate which other girls I could meet. I ignored her.

I used to argue, 'Marriage within the caste is wrong', 'The arranged marriage system is barbaric', and so on. I astonished myself by how easily, in a certain frame of mind, I agreed to a traditional marriage.

Leena's marriage was finalized around this time. The groom was a Kenyan Indian, and his relatives in Bombay were looking on his behalf. My older brother Bhalchandra enquired about him with some friends who lived in Kenya. The report came back: 'He is a golden boy.' His name was Sharad Rao, and he had studied law in London. Sharad and Leena didn't even meet each other. There was an exchange of photos and they spoke on the phone. The understanding was that, if they liked each other when they met in person, the wedding would proceed at once; if they didn't, it wouldn't. This unusual arrangement turned our life at home upside down. I lamented: 'We are educated people. How did we manage to promise our beautiful, well-educated sister to someone entirely unknown?' Aayi spent all her time crying.

It is now fifty years since those events. The wedding took place and Leena went to Kenya. She and Sharad have two daughters, and everyone is well and happy. But it still disturbs me to think of that year of anguish and frustration for me, Aayi and my sister Prema, who was in Malaysia. My brother Vasant remained detached from these goings-on. Even while all this was happening, he met an attractive Gauda Saraswat woman who taught sociology – Sunanda. Though Vasant and Leena both got married around the same time, all I can remember is the fraught atmosphere around Leena's wedding. Several episodes from it appear in my play, *Wedding Album*.

I began to distance myself from Saraswat society soon after I left Bombay for Madras. After coming to Madras, I would be invited to lunch almost every Sunday by one Saraswat family or another. When I accepted, along with the food would invariably be an eligible young woman for me to meet. The very next day, I would be set upon by the hosts. 'What do you say?' they would start, and go on for hours together, offering pragmatic counsel such as, 'You're at the right age to get married. If you miss this chance, you may not find someone as good,' or making seemingly compassionate enquiries such as, 'Should you not be thinking of how your parents will be cared for in their old age?' There were times when this took up the entire day. Word reached me that our people had begun to think of me as rude and arrogant because I always refused. Since it is discouraged among Saraswats to openly express anger or dissatisfaction, there is a long-standing tradition of writing anonymous letters to scold, mock or vent one's fury at someone. I began receiving such letters and decided I had had enough. I broke my ties with Saraswat society and that is how it has remained.

SATYADEV DUBEY

In the 1960s, the beautiful and expansive compound of the Bhulabhai Desai Memorial Institute on Warden Road (now Bhulabhai Desai Marg) emerged as the cultural hub of Bombay. Even when I was doing my MA in Bombay (1958–60), I had watched plays there directed by Alkazi, and had been to art exhibitions by then-emerging stars such as Husain, Gaitonde, Raza and Souza. Classical music concerts and dance recitals, both by Indian and international performers, were happening there all the time. Since Alkazi had gone to Delhi as director of the National School of Drama (NSD), his group Theatre Unit was being managed by Satyadev Dubey.

When I was going to England by ship, one of my fellow passengers had been Farida Sonawala, an excellent actress who had worked with Alkazi. She was in Bombay now, and she told me, 'Go to the Bhulabhai terrace and meet Satyadev Dubey.' She had already told Satyadev that I was a playwright.

We did not begin on a good note. Satyadev was brusque, and showed no interest in me or my work. Our conversation was struggling along when he changed the subject suddenly. He pounced on me with pent-up annoyance: 'What do you hope to gain by writing in English? Is it even possible for us to express ourselves with integrity in that foreign language?'

I stammered, 'My plays are not in English. I write in Kannada.'

Satyadev looked as if he had just been slapped. He asked me to read my work, and I read all of *Yayati* from the Kannada copy, translating it into English on the fly. Satyadev sighed when I finished. He said, 'I insulted you, thinking that you write in English. Now I have to make up for it by bringing your play to the stage.' I later learnt that it was not Satyadev's way to simply say, 'I like the play.' Still, he was the very first person to tell me that my plays could be performed on the stage.

Under Alkazi, Theatre Unit had performed only English plays. Satyadev had taken over the reins, swearing that he would only do plays in Indian languages. Now, a Hindi translation of the play was needed, and G.B. Joshi recommended someone in Dharwad named Hundekar for the task. Satyadev grumbled that the translation's Hindi was not conversational, but accepted Hundekar's translation and edited it himself.

But I was an unknown playwright, and Hindi theatre did not yet have the kind of audience in Bombay that English theatre did. Other than the occasional production by Prithvi Theatre, Prithviraj Kapoor's professional company, it was only Indian People's Theatre Association (IPTA) that involved itself with Hindi plays. *Yayati* was produced by Indian National Theatre (INT), and it took four years for it to be performed in Hindi after I first read the play out to Dubey. Of the seven characters in the play, four were played by actors from the Marathi stage. Amrish Puri played Yayati; Satyadev was Puru. In spite of Satyadev only having directed minor farces until then, the production was a big success. Later, Sunila Pradhan, who played the

Amrish Puri and Tarla Mehta in Satyadev Dubey's production of *Yayati* (1967)

role of Devayani, told me, 'Once the play was successful, Satyadev as usual quarrelled with INT and the shows ended.'

Still, through Satyadev I had developed what I can call a kinship with living theatre. He acted as well as wrote plays, but where he truly shone was as a director. I grew through arguing and fighting with him.

One day in 1968, Vinod Doshi, managing director of the Walchand Hirachand business empire, and his wife Saryu came to watch one of Satyadev's plays. Vinod was mad about theatre. (He had given the Marathi stage director Arvind Deshpande a job in his company and told him, 'It's enough if you're doing plays. You don't have to bother about office.') He was thrilled after watching *Yayati* and asked Satyadev if he needed any support. Satyadev immediately said, 'Neither I nor Arvind Deshpande have a place where we can teach theatre. It will be a huge help if you can find us some such place.' Vinod at once handed over the ground floor of Walchand Terrace, a beautiful building in Bombay's Tardeo, to Satyadev and Arvind. For the next three and a half years, this place became the laboratory of creative theatre in Bombay. All day long, it buzzed with the commotion of theatre people; in the evening, drinks and discussion; at night, a row of mattresses laid out in the auditorium for theatre persons who needed a place to sleep. One night, I had been drinking with Vijay Tendulkar, and I fell asleep beside him in the middle of an argument. When I woke up in the morning, Tendulkar was gone, but sleeping next to me on the other side was Badal Sircar, who had arrived in the middle of the night! My play *Anju Mallige* is dedicated to the memory of Walchand Terrace.

OUP

OUP's India branch started in 1912. In the early 1930s, Roy E. Hawkins became the general manager and firmly established OUP – and himself – as a force in Indian publishing. For the next four decades, Hawkins dominated the field of English language publishing in India. He was called Hawk – a name that captured the affection, fear and faith he inspired in the Indian book business. Whether it was in printing or in administration, he was renowned for having a hawk's eye for details and defects.

OUP India's head office was in Bombay, with regional offices in Madras and Calcutta. Each of the regional offices had a manager and an assistant manager. The managers were almost always Englishmen, many of whom had spent years working in India and had a good understanding of the country. Indian managers mainly looked after marketing, with the actual editing of books reserved for Englishmen. This was based on the reasoning that English was a second language for Indians, and they lacked sufficient command over it to be editors. The first Indian to break this tradition, and someone who transformed OUP, was Ravi Dayal, who was ahead of me by a year in Oxford. He had joined OUP two years before me and was assistant manager at Madras. I was to finish my training in Bombay and replace him there.

Though he was the general manager, Hawkins had not taken an independent office for himself. He sat in a vast room, with the Bombay office manager's desk to his left and mine in front. There was a sense of parity in the office, with employees of different ranks working in the same room. Hawkins was invariably courteous, but I was kept alert by the knowledge that his sharp gaze was always on me. Proofs of new publications were given simultaneously to Hawkins, me and anyone else who was undergoing training. We made our edits independently, after which Hawkins gathered all of us around him and reviewed our work side by side. He would say, 'Ideally, all the proofs should have the same edits. But that is a rare occurrence.' Still, under Hawkins's guidance, the India branch developed a rigorous approach to editing.

The man who joined as manager or assistant manager – women were not allowed to reach those positions yet – had to take charge of every aspect of publishing: editing manuscripts, getting them ready for printing, reading and correcting proofs, dealing with the printer, designing book covers and publicity material, dealing with sellers and agents, keeping track of stocks, discussing our schemes with members of textbook committees, and planning the future of textbooks published by OUP India. But our main responsibility, in addition to all this, was to sell books that had come from London.

OUP's parent organization at the time was Clarendon Press in Oxford. It only published scholarly works and was entirely indifferent to sales. OUP's function was to provide a financial foundation for Clarendon's academic publishing, and so OUP had branches all around the world, mainly in commonwealth countries. OUP's London office existed to make money for Clarendon Press, and OUP India existed to make money for the London office. Since two-thirds of our earnings came from local publishing, our operations did not need financial assistance from London. So, even though we were controlled from London, we were in a sense free to operate independently. To work in the India branch of OUP was to get a good understanding of how the British East India Company must have operated in the eighteenth and nineteenth centuries!

THE STRIDERS

By the time I joined OUP in Bombay, Raman (A.K. Ramanujan) had sent a typescript of his poems there addressed to me. I showed it to Hawkins and asked, 'Shall I send it on to Jon Stallworthy in London?' He looked through the poems, grimacing every time he turned over a page. 'Why should these be called poems?' he asked. 'They look like prose that has been cut up and pasted lengthwise to resemble poems.' I insisted: 'Let's send them and see what happens.'

Hawkins was firm in his instructions: 'All right. If you're going to send them to London, do so by sea mail and not airmail. And don't send it on behalf of the office. Make sure to mention that it's your personal recommendation.'

Ramanujan happened to visit India around this time. I explained what had happened and told him, 'OUP doesn't have any great standing as a publisher of poetry. Your poems will be much better received if Faber and Faber were to bring out the collection.' He said, 'It's enough for me to see the poems in print. It's all the same to me who the publisher is. I would have paid the airmail charges myself, had I known!' He was terribly anxious to hear what Stallworthy would say.

Stallworthy wrote back: 'Ramanujan is already a good poet, and potentially a very good one ... His rhythms are sure but relaxed in the approved American style of the moment; his voice, however, is his own and India's.' He went on to say that he felt there weren't enough strong poems yet for a collection and asked to see more.

OUP London published Ramanujan's collection *The Striders*. My reputation in the office soared as a result. Within six months of joining, I had discovered a new writer and got him published through London. Such a thing was unheard of in the India office.

Ramanujan wrote to me: 'This is one of the few events in my life that has made me personally happy!' (Raman hardly ever used the word 'happy' while speaking of himself.)

In November 1966, Raman's collection was chosen by the Poetry Book Society in London as one of their recommendations. I was eager to pass the news on to journalists. Hawkins said, 'Why should we chase them with the news? Let them learn of it and get in touch if they want.' But he didn't specify how he thought they would hear of it. I, too, didn't ask. I had already strutted about enough following the success of *The Striders*. It was unusual for an experienced publisher like Hawkins to be reticent about such a significant honour to the organization. I assumed he was not entirely pleased with the success of a book he had rejected, and let it be. But as a result of our silence, Ramanujan did not gain the recognition he deserved in India as a poet. He got his due seven years later, after Penguin published his *Speaking of Siva* to a marvellous response.

The publication of *The Striders* proved useful to Raman in an unexpected way. He was teaching at the Department of South Asian Languages and Civilizations at the University of Chicago. To gain tenure and make his position permanent, it was essential for him to have a scholarly book to his name. But Raman hadn't published any such book. The university was anxious to have him tenured as soon as possible, so they deemed *The Striders* sufficient for their purposes and gave him tenure.

Ramanujan's stature at the University of Chicago was such that they had agreed to let him stay in India for six months of the year. Some of this time was spent in Madras. He was then establishing himself as an unrivalled translator into English of ancient and medieval Tamil poetry. In *Speaking of Siva,* he had announced his talents by translating Kannada vachanas. Now, he went on to translate Sangam poetry in *Poems of Love and War,* and Alvar poetry in *Hymns for the Drowning,* and astonished the world with the quality of ancient Tamil poetry. Not only the translations, his introductions to the poems, too, were written with a rare depth of feeling.

Life brimmed with vitality when Raman visited. Except when he was working, he needed constant company and conversation. S.G. Vasudev, Lakshmi Krishnamurty and I were only too happy to provide this service. It was customary to spend the entire night talking over smuggled whisky and then going to Woodlands Drive-In for a breakfast of idli and vada. This was not restricted to weekends either. Once, G.B. Joshi and Kirtinath Kurtakoti both happened to be in Madras at the same time as Raman. That time spent with all three of them together is among the richest memories I have: literary discussion, jokes and sparkling conversation through the night and day. I still thrill when I think of it.

Since Ramanujan's opinions were well argued and clearly expressed, we were always eager to hear what he had to say. When he visited Madras in 1965, I was editing the manuscript of *Tughlaq*. Like *Yayati, Tughlaq* too was an intense, tragic play. But with *Tughlaq,* I had also tried to introduce elements of comedy, and I was not sure how it worked as a whole. Raman read it and at once said, 'This is a more mature play than *Yayati*. We simply do not have anything else like it.' He also wrote to Kirti and GB saying so. I grew more confident about the play.

OUP MADRAS

I worked in Bombay for two months, then went to Madras and occupied the assistant manager's chair just vacated by Ravi Dayal. The manager in the Madras office was Stewart Melluish. Since I have already mentioned the East India Company in connection with OUP, I can also say that Stewart would have fit right into the Company.

He must have been seven or eight years older than me, but he looked at least twenty years older. He was broad-shouldered with a heavy step, and he had dull, brown-red hair that reached his collar at the back. Having just returned from Oxford, what stood out to me at once was his plummy voice and affected upper-class accent. I laughed to myself at the thought that a mode of speech which was on its way out in England was thriving here. To myself, because he was a terribly sensitive man who would have been insulted by even the hint of a smile. He tended to be deeply wounded at the mere suspicion that someone might be making fun of him. It was not just his accent that made him a character from a century past. Like the British pioneers who came to India in the eighteenth and nineteenth centuries, thoroughly studied the land's culture, history, environment and society, and wrote gazetteers that are invaluable even today, he too had come into his own in India. He had explored the area around Madras and researched its geography, botany and ornithology. He was well acquainted with historical relics found in the region. In the office, too, he was knowledgeable about every aspect of printing, and was an expert in typefaces and page layouts. He also acted capably in a play I directed – Pinter's *The Caretaker*.

At the same time, he took pride in being arbitrarily brusque with people. The British upper classes have a weakness for whimsical behaviour, and he was no different. He once recounted an episode that illustrates this.

The Madras office did not have separate rooms for the manager and assistant manager. A partition had been installed down the middle of a long hall to fashion two offices. This partition was a hardboard screen mounted on three-foot high legs. So, while the manager and assistant manager could not see each other, the lower section of the partition was open.

Stewart had just then arrived from England and joined OUP as assistant manager. One day, after a disagreement with the manager, an Anglo-Indian named Dabras, he was sitting alone in his office in a rage. After everyone had left for the day, Stewart decided there was only one way to vent his anger. He had to become a tiger that tore Dabras apart and ate him up. Accordingly, Stewart got off his chair, sank to the floor and let out a roar. He entered Dabras's office on all fours through the gap below the partition and, gnashing his teeth, moved towards Dabras's chair. He then noticed that a bewildered Dabras, working late that day, was still in his chair. Stewart stopped roaring and reversed into his office. Neither he nor Dabras brought up the matter afterwards.

I was Stewart's assistant manager for seven years. If those seven years absolutely had to be spent taking orders from someone, then I consider myself fortunate to have had Stewart as my manager. We did have conflicts and differences of opinion, and we had more or less stopped talking a couple of months before he married a Malayali woman and returned to England. Still, there is no doubt that I learnt much from him.

My job at OUP was comfortable. Unlike in other foreign organizations at the time, there was no contempt directed towards Indians here. Since all the managers and assistant managers were from Oxbridge backgrounds, even where there wasn't actual camaraderie, there was at least parity. The office paid part of my house rent. And I had been given a Herald car for my personal use.

What a fine specimen the two-doored Herald was! It was a car for young people, and something of a wonder back then, because it was possible to execute a sharp U-turn even on a narrow street. It had front seats with generous legroom (even if the rear seats were cramped), and a long window to rest one's elbow on while driving. I drove it from Madras to Dharwad every year. Compared to the Fiat and the Ambassador, the Herald vanished relatively soon from the market. But unlike those cars, the Herald, with its sleek design, managed to embody the speed and spirit of youth.

Over time, I started losing interest at work. The main reason for this was our completely uninspired publishing catalogue. Though our showroom had books of significance published by Clarendon Press and OUP London, our office was engaged solely in making money by publishing books to teach English as a second language: supplementary readers, simplified versions of English novels, such as *Robinson Crusoe Retold* or *Treasure Island Simplified*. There was absolutely no opportunity for intellectual excitement. We had universities in India that must have been producing new work in the sciences and the humanities, but our office was oblivious. The best known among Oxford's books on Indian history was one written by an ICS official named Vincent A. Smith in 1918. The only scientific book on Indian music was by the musicologist A.H. Fox Strangways, written in 1914. The pinnacle of scholarship as far as the India branch was concerned was the messy Indian philosophy propounded by Sarvepalli Radhakrishnan.

To give a specific example, when I visited Dharwad in 1964, I met the well-known sociologist Prof. T.N. Madan at Karnatak University. He showed me a textbook written by him that was being used at Harvard University. I asked, 'Why not allow OUP to publish your next book?' Madan laughed and said, 'I had sent this book to OUP. They returned it saying it was unfit to publish.'

OUP Madras: With Charles Lewis, Ravi Dayal, and the future literary agent Martin Pick

Hawkins retired in 1970, and the OUP office moved to Delhi. Ravi Dayal, who was well connected with scholars working in Indian universities, became general manager. He got in touch with people like Ashis Nandy, Sudhir Kakkar, Romila Thapar, Irfan Habib, Veena Das and others, and published their work. He brought OUP India on par with OUP London, but by then, I was no longer working there. Though Ravi and I were colleagues, I did not recognize his intellectual courage and dynamism at the time. It never occurred to me that the constant friction between him and Hawkins was, in fact, a sign of his dedication to publishing.

The year I left OUP, Alyque Padamsee and Theatre Group staged *Tughlaq* in English in Bombay. The main role was played by a hulking model named Kabir Bedi. Indeed, everything about the production was larger than life, with little scope for subtlety or nuance. The exquisite fortress gates that opened and closed onstage – sets were by the famous sculptor Pilloo Pochkhanawala – were a witness to the hollow beauty of the production. Nevertheless, it was a success. Alyque was a leading light of the advertising world, and he worked his magic to promote *Tughlaq* across the country.

Ravi got in touch and asked if OUP could publish *Tughlaq* in English. I refused. 'Who will buy the English translation of a Kannada play?' I asked him. When Ravi insisted, I said, 'As a former employee of OUP, I veto the project.' Ravi laughed and said, smoking a beedi as always, 'Maybe that's why you are a former employee.' He published *Tughlaq,* and it went on to sell lakhs of copies.

This was a time when universities were coming up across India, and there was a scarcity of Indian plays that could be studied in English. In fact, there were none that were suitable for use as a course text. This had never occurred to me, but Ravi had identified the gap.

When I went to Pakistan in 2007, I was astonished to learn that the English department of Lahore University was using my plays as textbooks. Prof. Shaista Sirajuddin told me, 'When I finish teaching English playwrights like Tom Stoppard and turn to *Tughlaq* and *Naga-Mandala,* I can clearly see the students' interest and enthusiasm shoot up.' The students of this department, along with students from the National Academy of Performing Arts, enacted scenes from my plays in English and in their own translations from English to Urdu. I then remembered Ravi with gratitude.

ENTER KARANTH

As the seven-year term of my agreement with OUP neared its end, I started finding it unbearable to work in an office, and began to question why I had committed myself to this servitude. I didn't know what to do next, but then, the future was not a very serious problem. I had no family responsibilities. My elder brother was in Bombay with his family, my sisters were busy with their own lives, and my parents were living in a house that my brother-in-law had bought in Dharwad's Saraswatpur. Increasingly, the thought that gnawed at me was, 'Why am I not making use of this freedom?' Thankfully, Aayi felt the same way too, and had been after me for a while: 'Put an end to this office work and do something meaningful.' There was also the fact that my standing in Indian theatre had begun to change rapidly.

The reason for that change was a stranger who, without warning, stepped into my office in 1965. He had a pencil moustache, a gentle face, and a manner that was polite to a fault. But when it came to discussing the subject of theatre, he was dazzling in his perspicacity. The newspaper editor and cultural figure Y.N. Krishnamurthy (YNK to everyone) had already told me about him in Bangalore: B.V. Karanth. He worked as a Hindi teacher in Delhi, but he had been a student at NSD and had kept alive his relationship with the school.

Karanth, along with Nemi Chandra Jain, had translated Sriranga's play *Kelu Janamejaya* into Hindi. Alkazi, who was the director of NSD at the time, took it up with a view to staging it. He was unable to see any substance in the play and entrusted it to his student Mohan Maharishi. The Maharishi-directed *Suno Janamejaya* came as a jolt to the world of Delhi theatre. I doubt many people until then had even heard of a language called Kannada, but now, their eyes turned towards Kannada plays. Maharishi's fellow student Om Shivpuri began nagging Karanth to find him a Kannada play. Karanth had told him about *Tughlaq*, and had come to Madras, on his way to Delhi, to discuss the matter with me. Karanth also wanted my permission to direct *Tughlaq* for the Kannada Bharati organization in Delhi. Opposite my office on Mount Road (now Anna Salai) was a new restaurant called Kwality that had set out to try and make Punjabi food our national cuisine. We went there

With B.V. Karanth

for lunch. The conversation we started that day remained ongoing as long as Karanth was alive.

India and Pakistan fought a three-week war beginning 1 September 1965, during which life came to a standstill. Delhi was shrouded in darkness. Karanth sat with a candle and an Urdu dictionary, and used this time to translate *Tughlaq* into Urdu.

I felt no anger when Alkazi told me at the All India Writers' Conference in 1965: 'We are chopping your play into bits and rejoining it.' Instead, I rejoiced at the knowledge that it would be staged in Delhi.

Om Shivpuri brought *Tughlaq* to the stage in 1966, and I went to Delhi to watch it at Alkazi's invitation. I was delighted to find that the play had electrified Delhi's theatre world. Newspapers were full of mentions of *Tughlaq*, and for the first time, I experienced the fame I had madly craved since I was a child. Later, in 1972, Alkazi would himself direct *Tughlaq* in the majestic setting of Delhi's Purana Qila with Manohar Singh in the lead. By then, *Tughlaq* had acquired such a reputation for itself that I could barely think of it as my play.

IN SEARCH OF A NEW FORM

In 1968, a Calcutta-based organization called Anamika Kala Sangam organized a wide-ranging seminar on Indian theatre. The secretary of the Sangeet Natak Akademi in Delhi at the time was a man of great enthusiasm and initiative named Suresh Awasthi. I cannot think of another secretary in the fifty years of the Akademi's existence who worked as hard as he did. He maintained a personal relationship with every theatre person, every folk and theatre group, and was dedicated to rejuvenating traditional forms. Awasthi invited me to Calcutta as the Akademi's guest. Also there for the seminar was the Hindi playwright Mohan Rakesh, widely known for his *Ashadh Ka Ek Din*. Before leaving for Calcutta, I had heard Karanth speak highly of an emerging Bengali playwright named Badal Sircar and his play *Ebong Indrajit*, so I was eager to meet him. As soon as I reached Calcutta, I rushed to see Badal's play *Kobi Kahini*, in which he was acting along with his wife. It lacked form, and felt like a play put up by college students.

Manohar Singh in *Tughlaq* at the Purana Qila, Delhi (1972)

One evening, Mohan Rakesh and I went to see a popular Bengali musical. The production had been well received, but Rakesh and I could not control our laughter at some of its absurdities. Finally Rakesh said, 'Do you know why we are laughing so much, Girish? It's because we know the future of Indian theatre is in our hands.'

But the reason that visit to Calcutta became unforgettable was because of a theatre group called Shoubhanik and their production of *Ebong Indrajit.* Though the playwright was clearly influenced by Ionesco, and though I didn't understand parts of the play because it was in Bengali, I was exhilarated by how the play had used mime, improvisation and music to depict the desires and anxieties of contemporary life.

Badal Sircar did not like the production. 'They have ruined my play,' he raged. But I returned to Madras replaying every moment of it in my mind. Anamika Kala Sangam was then led by Pratibha Agarwal and Shyamanand Jalan, with both of whom I developed a close and enduring friendship. Pratibha had translated the play into Hindi as *Evam Indrajit,* and I brought the text with me to Madras. I decided to translate it into English and have the Madras Players perform it under my direction.

According to my agreement with OUP, I was to go to London for two months after completing seven years at the company. I had informed OUP that I would be leaving the firm after my contract period. Philip Chester wrote asking me not to leave; Stewart was returning to London, and I would succeed him as manager. I did not agree, but still, as per our agreement, OUP sent me to London.

My experience of London theatre had proved indifferent during my Oxford years (1960–63), but it improved considerably with subsequent visits. So much so that the spirit of London theatre is for me represented by a deeply moving incident that occurred when I was passing through the city in 1986 and decided to try my luck with *Guys and Dolls,* which was running to full houses at the National Theatre. I cannot remember if it was the last day of the run or whether it was the last show in which an American star was playing the lead, but critics had raved not only about his performance but the entire production.

I joined the queue for the returns at the box office. These are tickets booked in advance but resold at the last minute since those who bought them were unable to attend the show. It was a long line, and we were informed that if a single ticket was returned, it would naturally go to the next person queuing up, but if two came up for resale, they would go to the next couple. So, when the woman in front of me suggested that we should pretend to be a couple in case two tickets were returned when our turn came, I happily agreed. As we moved slowly towards the box office, we chatted about our likes and dislikes in theatre, shared our opinions on other actors and films, and began to seem quite convincing as a couple. Along with this was an intense shared anticipation that only those addicted to theatre can appreciate. During our conversation, I must have mentioned that I was not a Londoner but only passing through Britain.

As it happened, the last ticket to be returned was a single, and with that return the evening's house was full. I congratulated the woman and turned to leave when she burst out, 'No, you take the ticket. I don't want it.' I protested that since she was ahead of me in line, the ticket was hers by right. 'But you have come from India,' she argued, and began to march off. I followed her, pointing out that it was the last seat in the last show, and there was no possibility of her getting another chance. At this point, the person at the box office bellowed that we should make up our minds or he would give the ticket to the person next in line. I hurriedly paid for the ticket and turned to argue further with the woman, but she had vanished. I could not even thank her.

The play was directed by Richard Eyre and the production was hailed for its innovative use of incandescent lights to recreate 42nd Street and Broadway. But nothing registered that evening except the unknown woman's generosity.

That, however, was much later. Returning to my visit in 1969, I took the opportunity to watch a large number of plays and films, and they proved equally generous in the influence they had on my own work as a playwright. I marvelled at how John Barton had taken *Troilus and Cressida*, considered one of Shakespeare's weaker plays, and reimagined it into a spectacular production about the depravity of glorifying war.

But the production that truly stunned me was *Canterbury Tales*, adapted for stage by Nevill Coghill, who was a renowned English don during my time at Oxford, and Martin Starkie. They brought the fourteenth-century English poet Chaucer's stories to the stage accompanied by traditional music, and without any attempt at being 'proper', because there is no shortage of bawdy situations and crude humour in Chaucer's stories.

Back then, the London stage had a Lord Chancellor for its moral supervision, and he would flash his scissors at the merest hint of anything that was 'indecent' or 'obscene'. Chaucer's humour borders on the 'obscene', but since he is regarded as the father of English literature, he could be brought to the stage with a boldness that would not be possible with contemporary plays.

The aspect of the production that made a powerful impression on me was the sets. Inspired by medieval art, the stage contained a flat world without any depth or perspective. The art director had tried to recreate the beauty of that era's woodcut blocks. If a scene had people eating at a round table, the stage would have, instead of a real table, a circular piece of hanging fabric with the meal's contents drawn on it. Some actors would stand around it, some would kneel, and some would sit on the floor to conjure up the scene of people sitting at the table. If someone was to be depicted as sleeping, the bed would be positioned upright on the stage, and the actor would slide behind a bedsheet attached to the bed. Two actors standing behind the sheet and grappling with each other denoted sex. The production had found a new and inspiring way of using traditional elements, and even as I was watching, I began to think, 'Why shouldn't we, too, experiment imaginatively with our traditions?' That thought stayed with me and gathered force.

My *Yayati* and *Tughlaq* had both used the conventional division of plays into scenes. But with *Evam Indrajit,* Badal Sircar had abandoned the system of scenes and found a way to make the play's action flow unchecked. Now, *Canterbury Tales* had used traditional elements on stage to create an entirely new theatre experience. I wanted to use these technical elements to further my own expression, but I was struggling to find a way to do so.

I returned from London to learn that the film *Samskara,* with which I had been deeply involved before leaving, had not been approved by the censor board. The stage retreated from my attention and film-making took its place for a while.

B.V. Karanth visited Madras for a few days as I was getting ready to leave OUP. While talking to him one day, I narrated the story of Thomas Mann's novella *The Transposed Heads*. The original story is from the *Kathasaritasagara* and is in the form of a riddle: If two men's heads are interchanged, then who is who? Would a man be identified by his head or his body? Thomas Mann had taken the riddle and its traditional answer – 'the head is the superior part, the body inferior; the head identifies the person' – and worked it ironically into a novella.

When I said the story would make a good film, Karanth immediately said, 'Why a film? It would make an even better play.' I was startled by how evidently true this was. Why not bring together the ideas from my London visit and everything that Karanth and I had been discussing – music, masks, dance, mime – to write a play?

'And this will be the next play you write,' was Karanth's prophecy. It came true. Once I started writing it, it flowed steadily and was finished in two weeks. It was published in English in the magazine *Enact*, brought out from Delhi with Rajinder Pal as editor. At this time, Karanth and I were involved in jointly directing the film *Vamsha Vriksha*, and the play's title – *Hayavadana* – came from Karanth too. It won the Bharatiya Natya Sangh's Kamaladevi Chattopadhyay Award that year.

A.K. Ramanujan read *Hayavadana* in *Enact* and responded with great enthusiasm. Not only did he write me a letter praising the play, he had students at the South Asia department of the University of Chicago perform it. The first production of *Hayavadana* was directed by a student named Gwendolyn Dietmann.

Later, I wondered if I had gone too far in acknowledging my debt to Thomas Mann. A theatre director named Erin Mee, who had planned several shows of *Hayavadana* in New York under the title *Divided Together*, had publicized it as 'Based on Thomas Mann's *The Transposed Heads*'. Soon, there was an objection from a representative of Mann's estate. She wanted the shows cancelled because the estate's permission had not been obtained. Erin called me and I faxed her the permission given to me by Mann's wife Katia Mann. The estate's representative then argued that Mrs Mann did not have the authority to give permission. I suggested to Erin that she invite the representative to sit in on the rehearsals. The estate agreed that *Hayavadana* and Mann's story were only distantly related. They disappeared after asking us not to use Mann's name on the publicity material. The New York shows turned out to be a great success.

THE WORLD OUTSIDE: GB, KIRTI, YNK

Not learning Tamil was the biggest blunder I made while living in Madras, and it is something I still regret. In seven years I could have gained excellent command over the language.

During my first year in Madras, I found a teacher and practised reading and writing for a month. But what he was teaching me was senthamizh – the literary form of the language. I was new to Tamil Nadu, and saw no connection between what I was learning and the world I was living in. I stopped the lessons. What I should have done was first learn the spoken language that surrounded me. It is not very difficult for a Kannadiga, and I was renting the ground floor of a house owned by an Iyer family that treated me as one of their own. All I learnt from them was the 'zh' sound, which has disappeared from modern Kannada.

The arguments that were going on all around me, with some English thrown in even; street fights; haggling in the shops; crying children being cajoled; breathless torrents of words from DMK leaders wherever one was in 'Chennai'; the mischief and teasing in Tamil film songs – I remained a stranger to these riches despite living in Madras for seven years.

In 1965, when I was in Madras, Hindi was due to become the sole official language in India, a prospect which antagonized even those who had nothing against Hindi. In 1967, the DMK, which was at the forefront of protests against Hindi in Tamil Nadu, surprised itself by deposing the Congress and coming to power.

Before I left Madras, I stayed in the Woodlands Hotel for a month while I tied up loose ends at office. The staff there did not speak a word of English, but I was surprised to find that I could understand everything they were saying. And without trying, I had absorbed enough Tamil to talk about everyday matters. I can't describe the anguish I felt then at the lost opportunity.

But because I had not learnt Tamil, and because of the monotony at OUP, I firmly linked my consciousness to two centres outside Madras: the Manohara Grantha Mala atta in Dharwad, and YNK, whom I met regularly in Bangalore.

I had three weeks of leave every year at OUP, and they had provided a car for my use. I was new to this part of southern India, and while I could have taken in the sights of Tamil Nadu, Kerala and Andhra Pradesh, I had absolutely no interest in travelling alone. So, I would rush off to Dharwad as soon as I got leave. Thankfully, Bangalore was on the way.

Aayi and Bappa were pleased that I spent every holiday with them. I too was happy to be home, but there was also the intellectual stimulation that I got at the atta, which had become something of an addiction.

Having grown up in Sirsi, my Kannada fell somewhere between Havyaka and Gauda Saraswat usage. But after living in Dharwad's Saraswatpur where there was no trace of Kannada, moving around in the English-speaking company of Krishna Basrur and Aurora, and going to Oxford, my Kannada was in complete disarray. This is not evident in *Yayati* because Kirti edited its dialogue, but the first edition of *Tughlaq* gives my weakness away.

One day, I told a joke in Kannada to my friend Ashok Kulkarni, who laughed more than necessary and said, 'The joke is good, but your Kannada is terrible.' It came as a wake-up call. If my friends were saying this, then what might my critics say, especially given that the overnight success of my plays was bound to have generated envy and resentment? From that day, the atta became my classroom.

While G.B. Joshi had a charisma that drew people to him, the conversation at the atta was all left to Kirti. For a while, I didn't participate in these conversations. I only listened, constantly alert to new words, sayings, ideas and information. Often, I returned home, took a notebook and wrote down what I had learnt that day.

Around this time, GB and Kirti started publishing a magazine called *Manvantara*. One of the issues was dedicated to drama, and the essays on Sanskrit plays that Kirti wrote for it are undoubtedly among the best works of criticism produced in India. They led me to take an interest in Sanskrit. GB and Kirti asked me to write about plays such as Sriranga's *Harijanwara* and Masti Venkatesh Iyengar's *Kakana Kote*. They organized seminars on emerging literature. In a sense, they compelled me to become aware of my cultural history and the playwrights who had come before me.

All GB wanted was to be surrounded by writers, and to this end, he was prepared to tolerate writers from all generations. In those days, consuming alcohol was frowned upon, so there were times when Yashwant Chittal, Shantinath Desai and I went to the atta at night. We could drink there without being seen by disapproving eyes, have dinner and spend the night. GB and Kirti did not drink, but they never had trouble keeping up with our rising spirits.

Once, in Bombay, Chittal, GB, his son Ramakant and I went to a restaurant. The next day, Ramakant told me, 'You should have seen my father's face when you were eating fish.' Apparently, GB had never seen anyone eat fish or meat before.

GB's charm lay in his eccentricity, and there are hundreds of stories that can be told about him. Kirti glowed with a quiet brilliance that was manifested in his composure, sensitivity and profound intellectualism, but in spite of having spent a great deal of time in his company, I can hardly think of any memorable episodes involving him.

Madras to Dharwad is a distance of around eight hundred kilometres. I never covered it in a single stretch, preferring to spend at least one night in Bangalore on my way there and back.

My very first visit to Bangalore was unforgettable. Within a few months of my joining OUP in Madras, Ramanujan invited me to his younger brother's wedding in Bangalore. I thought the wedding was a good pretext to visit the city, and I set off in the evening after work in my Herald with Stewart Melluish's driver, a young man named Jayaram. We were supposed to have reached in five and a half hours, but we hadn't accounted for the poor condition of the tyres, and after mending puncture upon puncture, we reached Malleshwaram at one in the morning.

Neither of us knew Bangalore, and Malleshwaram was lifeless at that time, without a light visible anywhere. Needless to say, there were no signs to help us identify the roads, nor did we see a single hotel. We decided to look for the wedding hall, and ended up driving up and down the slopes of Malleshwaram until we spotted a light in the distance, charged towards it like riders in one of Galaganatha's historical novels, and knocked on the door. An elderly man opened it. When we asked for directions, he said, 'Aiyo, where will you go searching at this time of the night? I'll lay out mats for you both. Sleep here, have coffee in the morning, and then go looking for your wedding hall.' That was all we wanted. We rested there and reached the wedding hall the next morning. This experience was typical of Bangalore's culture before it became a metropolis, and I can say that my first glimpse of Bangalore was not very different from that of its founder Kempegowda, who is said to have been fed boiled beans by a stranger after he lost his way.

I met Y.N. Krishnamurthy at the wedding hall. As GB and Kirti were in Dharwad, YNK in Bangalore would go on to be a guiding light to me. But the two experiences could not be more different.

In Dharwad, my life was centred around the Manohara Grantha Mala atta and sometimes GB's house. In Bangalore, I would stay at YNK's house, but YNK, apart from the time he spent at office, was continually on the move. A typical day might find him having breakfast at Vidyarthi Bhavan near his house in Gandhi Bazaar. And then he might be seen near his office – he was on the editorial board of the *Prajavani* newspaper – at a bar run by a man named Yati on the first floor of the building that now houses Cauvery Emporium. At other times of the day, he would be at the Press Club in Cubbon Park or at Century Club. He would roam across this intellectual zone of the city, meeting new poets, writers, publishers, journalists. If YNK liked a book or play or poem, his appreciation would not stop at mere words. It would spill over into other forms.

YNK read *Yayati* and liked it. He asked me to send a copy to Kamala Subramaniam (Bapsi) who lived in Madras. Bapsi was the writer T.P. Kailasam's daughter, and she told me, 'If you've created a character like Puru, it must mean that you, too, have a famous father.' Bapsi's husband was an ENT surgeon, well known across the country, but she was the centre of her household, which revolved around her like the planets of a solar system. She was a large woman, and she was to be found in her expansive bedroom, sitting on a cot, back against the wall, with her big family gathered around her. Guests were welcome to join the group. The conversation overflowed

With Ramakant Joshi, YNK and B.V. Karanth

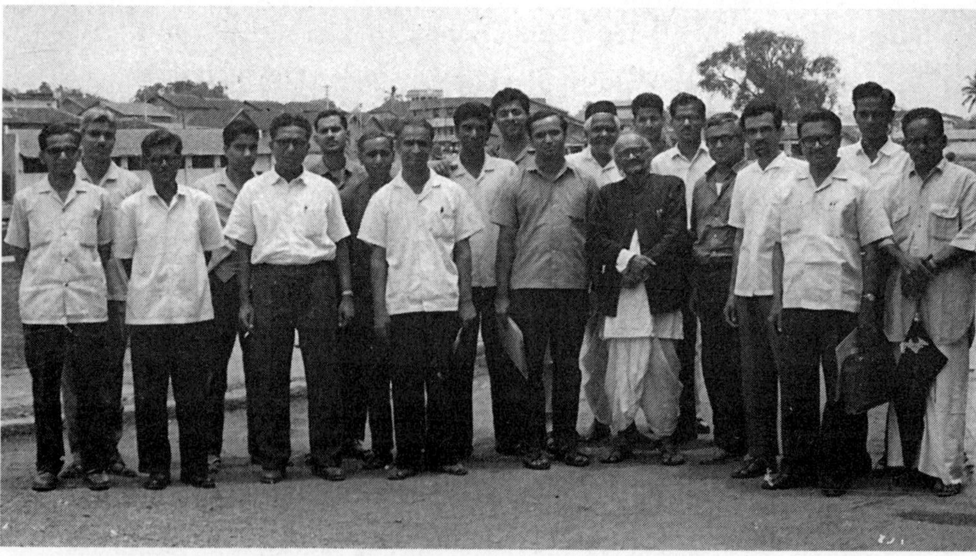

With Bendre and others at a literary gathering, Manohara Gratha Mala (1968)

with life: from light-hearted talk, to discussing films and literature, to the latest Madras Players' production. When Dr Subramaniam entered the room, he would sit smiling in a corner without saying much. I remember that when Bapsi's *Mahabharata* was published by Bhartiya Vidya Bhavan, she said, 'You know, the surprising thing is that both Girish and I studied mathematics.' I heard Dr Subramaniam mutter under his breath: 'You snobs.' Bapsi did not discuss her father very much, but one day she said, cheerful as usual, 'Do you know, these days even my mother speaks of him with reverence?' That said it all.

One day, when she went to get a tooth extracted, the bleeding would not stop, and it was discovered she had leukaemia. She died from the mishap. Her son later said that his father lost all interest in living after she died, and he, too, died soon after.

YNK was thrilled when he read the manuscript of *Tughlaq*. He wrote to me praising it, calling it 'great'. When I was in Bangalore next, he got together the theatre group Ravi Kalavidaru and had me read the play to them. (He cursed them later when they brought up all sorts of deficiencies in the play and said they could not perform it.) He got together Lankesh, Nissar, Simha and a few other youngsters in a garret in Gandhi Bazaar, and had me read the play again. He introduced me to the Urdu writer and editor Riyaz.

Later, YNK's enthusiasm knew no bounds when Simha started staging *Tughlaq*, and Karanth began directing *Hayavadana* in Kannada. When some of us got together and ventured into the film world with *Samskara*, he was with us all along the way as guide, adviser and critic.

CHOLAMANDAL

Two institutions in Madras literally brought colour to my life. The first was Madras's School of Arts, and the other, Cholamandal Artists' Village.

It was through YNK that I met S.G. Vasudev, who was from Bangalore and studying at the School of Arts. Vasudev took me to the school and introduced me to his fellow students. The period was one of great exuberance in the history of Indian art, with discussions raging about what constituted Indian identity, with new experiments constantly being attempted. At the forefront of this exploration was the principal of the

School of Arts, K.M. Panikkar. He was working towards a manifesto for visual arts that freed itself from the influence of Western forms and drew inspiration from Indian roots.

Panikkar noticed that art students were going different ways after graduating, and earning a living by working in offices or at jobs unrelated to art. Instead of dissipating their creative energies like this, Panikkar dreamed, they could come together to form an arts village where they would support themselves by selling art and handicrafts. Panikkar transformed that dream into an extraordinarily successful reality. He started the Cholamandal Artists' Village by the seashore some twenty kilometres south of Madras. It is still thriving and is a role model for other artistic groups.

S.G. Vasudev, Arnawaz Driver, V. Viswanadhan, K. Ramanujam, Rani Pooviah, P.V. Janakiram and S. Nandagopal were all either students or teachers at the School of Arts. I became one among them and took part in the discussions they were having. I tried to disseminate the philosophy underlying Cholamandal by writing for *The Indian Express* as an art critic. I understood from within the search for direction, the conflicts and the experiments ongoing in the world of Indian art. If I could relate to Cholamandal's quest, it was because I too was engaged in something similar in the realm of theatre. I did not want to simply repeat the success of *Tughlaq*. It was a matter of great concern for me to find out what our traditional forms had to offer, and how I could use them for my own expression.

Vasudev was not content with being only a painter. He was also interested in drama and literature, and I introduced him to the members of Madras Players. Later, when A.K. Ramanujan visited, Vasudev responded enthusiastically to his poems and his translations of Sangam poetry. Because YNK and I were great admirers of Gopalakrishna Adiga, Vasudev too developed an interest in Adiga's poetry. He didn't stop at reading, discussion and appreciation – he made Kannada writing his own, and interpreted it through his sketches.

Before him, K.K. Hebbar had responded similarly to Shivaram Karanth's work, but Vasudev did not limit himself to one or two writers: he took on the entire field of Kannada literature with his art. He did the cover art for Manohara Grantha Mala books, and when OUP published *Tughlaq*, he designed the cover and won an award for it. He worked with me as art director on films such as *Samskara* and *Vamsha Vriksha*. He organized play readings and concerts at Cholamandal. Vasudev ended up broadening the outlook of writers he associated with. He took that age-old lament of prose writers – 'Oh, we don't understand modern art' – and banished it, at least where Kannada was concerned.

When Vasudev and Arnawaz got married, it was in the face of opposition from Arnawaz's Parsi family. At their wedding in Bangalore, it was I who stood in for her older brother and gave away the bride.

MADRAS PLAYERS

When I joined OUP Madras, my senior Ravi Dayal introduced me to Ashok and Malti Nehru. Ashok was the son of the well-known diplomat B.K. Nehru and was related to Jawaharlal Nehru, so he was welcome in the higher echelons of Madras society. It was through him that I met Balasaraswati and Subbulakshmi, and grew close to Ammu Swaminathan, who was the mother of Captain Lakshmi and Mrinalini Sarabhai. But the main benefit of knowing Malti and Ashok turned out to be entry to the amateur theatre group Madras Players. Since no one in the group knew Tamil, it only did English plays, and so had the support of the British Council. Since the atmosphere those days was relatively easy-going, the Players even had officials from the British Council and USIS participating in its plays. Madras also had the Madras Amateur Dramatic Society, a group of expats who performed light comedies. Indians were not allowed to join, and in any case, we thought their comedies silly.

When I got to know Ashok and Malti in 1965, the Madras Players were putting up American playwright Tennessee Williams's *The Night of the Iguana*, directed by S.V. Krishnamurty, with Ashok as the male lead and Snehalata Reddy as the female lead. I was given the small part of a truck driver, with brief entrances at the beginning and end of the play. In those days, Madras's Santhome Beach was not as densely inhabited as it is today, and Krishnamurty had the sets put up by the seashore to wonderfully recreate the ambience of Mexico. Some five hundred people must have seen the two shows.

The members of the Madras Players were restricted to the cultured, affluent upper classes. Krishnamurty's wife Lakshmi had studied at Cambridge, his father had been the governor of Madras, and his father-in-law was an Indian Civil Service officer who had been governor of the Reserve Bank. Pattabhirama Reddy's father owned mica mines, and the rumour was that his father had transferred ownership of the mines to his grandchildren since he disapproved of Pattabhi having married Sneha, who was a dancer. Pattabhi was a modern poet in Telugu, as well as a film producer. Sneha's voice had musical possibilities, her walk a dancer's grace, and her expressions could convey subtle shades of feeling.

Then there was Ammu Mathew, a tall, dark-skinned, beautiful woman who taught physics at the Women's Christian College and had been at Cambridge with Lakshmi. She was the younger sister of Abu Abraham, who had become well known after drawing cartoons for London's *Observer* newspaper. Though Ammu didn't know how to act or direct, she had an extraordinary love for theatre and was a woman of great discipline.

It was important to get along with the others culturally and in matters of decorum. Otherwise, even good actors found themselves quietly cast out from the Madras Players. YNK used to tease me: 'Girish is the poorest member of Madras Players. He has only one car.' After two years, Ashok was transferred to Delhi and the Nehru couple moved from Madras, which left the Reddy and Krishnamurty couples as the backbone of the Players. In all three couples, the men had immense love and respect for their wives, and in turn, the women were extremely protective when it came to the reputations of their husbands. This sometimes led to friction within the group, but that is an unavoidable part of amateur theatre.

Since none of us knew Tamil, we had absolutely no contact with Tamil theatre. We all had contempt for plays like Cho Ramaswamy's *Tughlaq*, seemingly performed without any rehearsals. But during my last two years in Madras, two actresses who knew Tamil – Vishalam Ekambaram and Bhagirathi Narayanan – joined the Players. Vishalam's English diction was particularly pleasing, and when television came to Madras, she was entrusted with reading the English news.

The reason I am naming these people here is because, in addition to productions of the Madras Players, they were also later part of the film *Samskara*. The film would not have been possible without their discipline, resolve and dedication.

We usually performed two plays a year. We could not give more time than that, since we all had jobs or ran businesses. We used to perform at Madras's most beautiful venue, the Museum Theatre, which meant the audience could not be larger than two hundred and fifty. And it was only possible for us to perform two shows of each production. Still, our dedication to theatre was such that we rehearsed for three to four weeks during which everyone gave up their other commitments and involved themselves with every aspect of the production – acting, prompting, sets, costumes, publicity. This experience proved useful to me because the shortcomings that are inevitable with amateur productions helped me learn the discipline required for theatre.

It was during my time with the Madras Players that I understood how a playwright can use sentences effectively from the perspective of action in a play. I had been involved in public speaking from the time I was in Sirsi, and so, was well versed in the rhythm of language on stage. In Madras, through memorizing lines by accomplished playwrights and performing them, I realized how the rhythm of speech in a play is different. I learnt that the way an actor breathes through words is different from the way an orator does. The plays we were performing were in English, but this knowledge could be applied to Kannada plays as well. Later, because translators might not be aware of these nuances, I translated my own plays into English.

In those seven years, the playwright who, for me, emerged as the greatest next to Shakespeare – for his sensitivity to the human condition, his technical brilliance, his character development – was Anton Chekhov. In 1969, Ammu Mathew staged *The Cherry Orchard* at the Women's Christian College. The characters were all played by girls aged between sixteen and eighteen. Ammu was not a good director, so I took up the responsibility, and since the girls were young and inexperienced, I had to tease apart Chekhov's subtleties strand by strand and explain it to them. In doing so, I got to know Chekhov much better. The same year, I had a part in *Uncle Vanya*, directed by Stewart Melluish for the Madras Players. Not only did Stewart play the male lead, he also fell in love with the Malayali girl playing the female lead, as a result of which the play lost its way. Still, it gave me the chance to go deep into the play and study the marvellous workings of Chekhov's artistry.

With Ammu Mathew and other Madras Players

With Vishalam Ekambaram in the Madras Players' staging of *Uncle Vanya* (1968)

In that moment of dissonance – when someone else is directing, and the actor sitting there waiting for his entrance is getting worked up thinking, 'Oh no, that's not how it should be!' – a good play can sometimes reveal unexpected possibilities, offer up meanings contained deep within it. Such moments came up from time to time when I was with the Madras Players.

A YOUNG MAN IN MADRAS

I lived in Madras from my twenty-fifth year to my thirty-second. I had a good salary, a car and a house, and my association with the Madras Players and my Oxbridge background saw to it that there were plenty of attractive young women around me.

Madras was under prohibition the seven years I was there. When I arrived, drinking was rare in the middle class, especially so in Brahmin families. By the time I left, it was quite common to find some 'social drinking' going on in the evenings. As drinking gained popularity, it became harder and harder to find alcohol. But I was working at OUP, and from time to time we had visitors from England and other countries who were eligible for a liquor permit. As soon as they arrived, we would whisk them off to the excise office, have them write out in the appropriate bureaucratese that there was danger to their health if they failed to consume alcohol, get a signature, take them to Spencer's, and buy the quota of bottles allotted to them. It can be said that true independence from foreign rule arrived in the state only with the lifting of prohibition.

I met Saraswathy Ganapathy at a party, within a few months of coming to Madras. There was a deep attraction between us from the moment we met. It didn't take me long to decide that if I was going to marry any of the women on my horizon it would have to be her.

Like my own mother, Saraswathy's mother Nurgesh Mugaseth, too, had rebelled against tradition, endured the painful consequences of doing so, and after a struggle, had managed to live life on her own terms. Nurgesh was Parsi, and while in medical college, she had fallen in love with a fellow student from Kodagu named Kodandera Ganapathy. Both families were opposed to the relationship, but the two got married anyway.

In 1942, with the Second World War raging, Ganapathy found a job with the Indian Medical Service. He was posted to the North-West Frontier Province, where he fell ill and died. Nurgesh, who was pregnant at the time, returned to Madras and joined government service as a doctor.

Since Nurgesh had married a Hindu, the Parsi clergy of Madras ordained that she had lost the right to offer prayers at the fire temple. Nurgesh confronted them, and argued that being Parsi was something she had inherited from her father. How then could she be banished from the religion of her birth simply because she had married a Hindu? She threatened to drag the priests to court, and they, fearful of the commotion this would cause, backed down and withdrew their objections.

Though she had defied Parsi orthodoxy, Nurgesh continued in some ways to be a fiercely traditional Parsi. Saraswathy would offer to drive her to the fire temple when their driver was not around. Nurgesh, having just taken a bath in preparation for worship, would be in a state of ritual purity. She would sternly warn Saraswathy to keep her distance lest she touch Nurgesh and defile her. In her will, Nurgesh had asked for prayers to be held for her soul in the fire temple, and listed the names of people to be taken during those prayers. Along with her parents, she had included the name of her husband and written, in parentheses, 'No need to mention to the priests that he was Hindu.'

Nurgesh's Kodava in-laws had broken ties with her, and so Saraswathy was raised among Parsis. Still, she made sure that she did not entirely lose connection with her father's side of the family. In medical college, she chose to stay in a hostel room with three girls from Kodagu so she could learn their ways. She studied Kodava culture, and grew close to her grandparents and cousins. Years later, when Saraswathy and I were finally married, the politician A.K. Subbaiah caught sight of me in a Mangalore hotel lobby and thundered: 'Welcome to the son-in-law of Coorg!' Saraswathy was overjoyed when I told her about it.

But that day was a long time away. Even after being together in Madras for six months, we were not prepared to think of marriage. Saraswathy intended to go to the United States to continue her medical career. That was where her future seemed to lie, and I was not ready to move there. Nor did I know with any certainty what I would do in India. In my indecision, there lay possibilities, a certain kind of freedom. I was not prepared to have them curtailed by the responsibility of a wife and children.

She was there, I was here. We met occasionally, when we could, and for almost fifteen years, our relationship went on in this manner. I did not expect her to be faithful to me during this period. That would have been foolish, given the atmosphere of free sex that prevailed in the United States in the 1960s and '70s.

But in India, things still worked traditionally, and it was generally expected that a physical relationship would lead to marriage. I did not want that sort of commitment, and so, for several years after coming to Madras, I did not allow myself any opportunity to have a physical relationship. This period was one of the darkest in my life. I found myself gloomy and withdrawn for weeks at a stretch because of my self-imposed celibacy. There were times when I wondered why I shouldn't kill myself. I had always thought of myself as being – physically, mentally – an entirely normal person, so I was alarmed by the self-destructive state I had been driven to by sexual frustration. Eventually, it was my own play that released me from the agony.

When Satyadev Dubey began to stage performances of *Yayati*, I thought, 'Why spend all that time and money going to Bombay,' and remained in Madras. Then I got a telephone call from an unknown woman. She was from Madras, but had been in Bombay for some reason, and had happened to watch a show of *Yayati*. 'It's fantastic,' she told me. 'It would be an unforgivable crime to miss it.'

So, on the praise and persuasion of a stranger, I travelled to Bombay and watched the play. She was right. What a blunder it would have been to miss it, I thought to myself. When I returned, I called her on the phone to thank her. She was a married woman from an affluent family. Her husband owned a business, and she too ran a small business of her own. She said, 'In all of modern Indian literature, I haven't seen female sexuality depicted as you have done with the characters of Sharmishtha and Chitralekha.'

We became friends, and within a year, lovers. The relationship saved me from the crushing despondency that had taken hold of me. With this release, I felt inspired and invigorated.

When it came to writing plays, I had been entirely unproductive since coming to Madras. It can hardly be a coincidence that I wrote *Hayavadana* within a few months of embarking upon this relationship. The poems I wrote to my lover became songs in the play. (After the relationship ended, I never could write poems again.) She once said to me, 'Do you know how much trouble it causes when a lover steps into a marriage? During sex, the tongue is confused about whether to take the husband's name or the lover's.' This influenced how I developed *Hayavadana*. I wrote the play, translated it into English and placed it in her lap. She was thrilled, and said, 'I never thought my body would receive such an offering.'

I did not want to marry. Her marriage was companionable enough and she did not want to disrupt it. So we continued to see each other, discreetly and without complications. She gently undid the knots of sexual anxiety and awkwardness that had formed in me from those eight or nine years of deprivation. We took care never to be seen together in public, and our relationship remained a secret even from my friends in Madras.

What had started with *Yayati* transformed without my knowledge into the crucible for *Hittina Hunja* (published in English as *Bali: The Sacrifice*).

My flat on New Boag Road was barely five minutes away from my office. I came home for lunch every day, and she would visit me on her lunch break. One day, we had finished making love and were chatting when the doorbell rang. I opened the door to her husband. He entered and sat down without a word. His face was expressionless and he did not seem angry. For a few minutes, there was a deep silence in which even our breathing was audible. She said, 'I'm getting late for office,' and left. He, too, got up and left with her.

This sequence of events began to repeat itself again and again, but he would never interrupt us – he always arrived after we were finished and were presentable. He would sit down without speaking, and quietly leave when she did. She explained later, 'He was afraid that I was going to leave him for you. When I assured him that I had no such intention, he stopped with all the needless drama.' I couldn't begin to imagine the turmoil in his mind. Where would he wait while I was with her? How did he decide when it was time to enter the house?

I started writing *Hittina Hunja* around 1968. The events recounted above happened in 1969–70. Though it appears that reality took after the play, it was more complicated. Even while I was trying to understand Yashodhara's agony

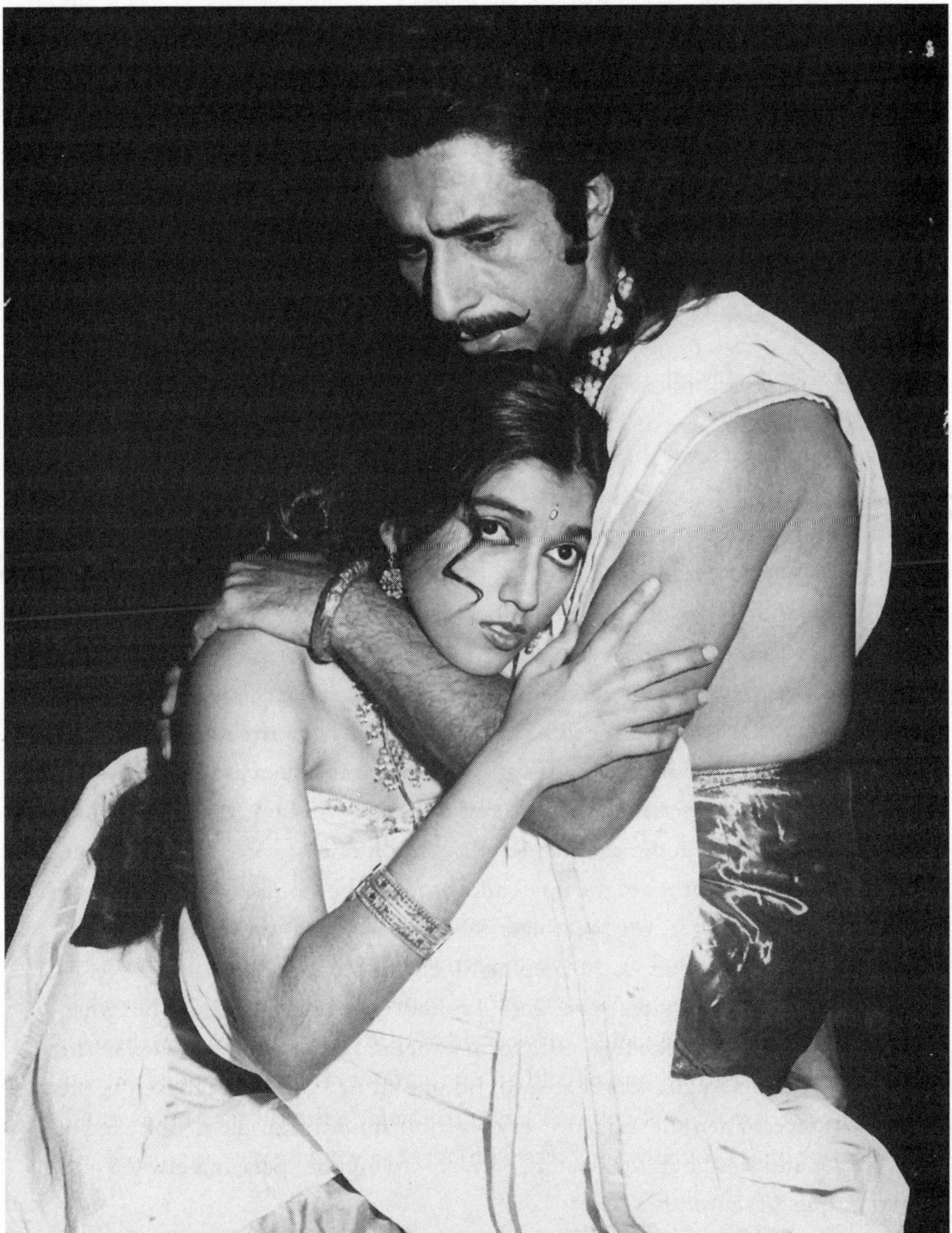

Naseeruddin Shah and Ratna Pathak Shah in *Bali* (1984)

in the play, in real life I was in the position of Ashtavanka. My characters and I were reflecting one another like the infinite chain of reflections one sees in a barbershop when two mirrors face each other. I certainly can't say that this made writing the play any easier. I edited *Hittina Hunja* repeatedly, and unable to change it any further, I let go only in 2001. It was staged in London as *Bali*. I am still not satisfied with it.

BALA

My account of Madras would be incomplete if I didn't recall a truly great artist I met there.

Madras had few vehicles back then, so there was hardly any traffic on the roads, making it straightforward to go from one part of the city to another. There was also no television at the time. The result was that Madras was throbbing with vitality when it came to the arts. Some of the best musicians, dancers and artists of the twentieth century had made their homes there, and they found an audience easily. Almost every week, I heard a singer or instrumentalist who was a musical giant, I saw legendary dancers.

But of them all, I can think of just one for whom the only applicable adjective was 'divine': Balasaraswati. She must have been around forty-five then. She was a bit stout and appeared to have a wheezing problem. When she danced, it was in the sari that devadasis traditionally wore, but tied higher, and without any other make-up or adornment. She would dance for around ten minutes and become breathless. While she caught her breath, she stood with her hands on her waist, keeping time with her foot.

But what ten minutes those were! I cannot stand exaggeration – but when Bala danced, it felt like the entire form of her dance remained etched in the air. While this might sound absurd, I don't know how else to describe the experience. When she moved, every position, mudra and adavu took a life of its own and was liberated from her limbs, carving the space in between into an exquisite sculpture.

Bala spoke Tamil; my Tamil was poor, but I could follow what was being said. Her younger brother was the mridangam player Ranganathan. His student (and, later, his wife) Edwina and I used to drive together in my car to a teacher with whom we studied the theory of Kathakali. It was through Ranga and Edwina that I grew close to Bala.

Ranga asked me one day: 'Will you marry Bala's daughter Lakshmi?' I had heard that Bala had not wanted Lakshmi to suffer as she had by becoming a dancer, and so had not taught Lakshmi Bharatanatyam. Whatever it was, I might have been tempted to become the son-in-law of such an eminence, but Saraswathy was already in my life and I said no.

An unforgettable incident I witnessed in Madras involved Bala and the singer M.S. Subbulakshmi. Bala was by birth a devadasi, and she spoke about her devadasi heritage with pride. Like Bala, Subbulakshmi was also a devadasi by birth. They had been friends when they were young, and there was even a rumour about the existence of a photograph in which the two of them were smoking a cigarette. T. Sadasivam, a Congress leader, married Subbulakshmi. He was the editor of *Kalki* magazine, a friend of C. Rajagopalachari, and a man who was at the forefront of Brahmin society. With his encouragement, Subbulakshmi left her devadasi roots behind and became a perfect mamiyar – she turned into a role model for the Brahmin women of Tamil Nadu when it came to wearing a sari, carrying oneself well, and speaking Tamil. (But Ramanujan used to say: 'If you listen carefully when she is singing, there are no mahapranas [aspirated consonants].')

Ashok and Malti had been invited to a wedding at Sadasivam's house, and I accompanied them. Subbulakshmi and Sadasivam welcomed us at the door. Soon after, Balasaraswati arrived. Subbulakshmi joined her palms in a namaste and said, 'Vaango.' Please come. Bala bowed slightly, returned the namaste and said, 'Vanden.' I have come. Subbulakshmi bowed deeper with a namaste. Bala bowed even deeper. This went on for a while. Then they both stood straight, looked at each other, and burst out laughing. They embraced each other. In those few moments that the two artists were face to face, I saw manifested physically the internal conflict that ran through their lives.

I never met Subbulakshmi. I only listened to her and saw her from a distance. But her flawless beauty, the Brahmin-ness in her that could never put a foot wrong, the care with which she sang every alapa, arohana, avarohana and gamaka exactly the same way each time as if she were afraid of some rash spontaneity, and most of all, a personality that seemed pieced together from facets – they hinted at something there that was false or insecure.

Bala was not like that. Her anger, anguish, intensity, her exquisite art, were out in the open for the world to see.

Some years after I left Madras, Narayan Menon, director of Bombay's National Centre for the Performing Arts (NCPA) produced a documentary film on Balasaraswati. Bala's condition for participating in the film was that it had to be directed by Satyajit Ray. Ray agreed and asked for a sum of one lakh. Bala insisted that she, too, be paid a lakh.

Today, that film bears witness to the clash of egos between two great artists. It is a fine example of how not to make a film about an artist. As Bala dances in the sand in front of the temples of Mahabalipuram, her sari keeps billowing in the sea breeze like a sail. When the soundtrack has the line 'He showed his mother the three worlds in his mouth', the visuals have Bala milking a cow. The film even finds a way to make the laughable assertion that the name Bharata comes from the initial sounds of bhava, raga and tala. Ray ignored every suggestion Bala had and did as his own genius indicated. Later, Bala would explode every time the film was mentioned. Still, when she died, this was the film broadcast on Doordarshan.

HAYAVADANA

My job at OUP ended in 1970. Three months before that, Narayan Menon, who was also the director of Bombay's Homi Bhabha Fellowships Council, met me and suggested I apply for the fellowship, and I duly put in an application. I had chosen folk theatre as the area of my study, and when I appeared in front of the interview panel, which included Alkazi, I said, 'Everyone says that we must use our traditional theatre forms and their devices in contemporary theatre, but no one has actually done so. With this end in mind, I want to travel across India and study various theatre traditions.' Alkazi asked, 'After you finish your study, do you plan to write a research paper?' I said, 'No. Research takes a different mentality. I want to effectively use elements from traditional theatre, not set out to be a researcher and get bogged down in documentation, photographs, equipment and so on.' I got the fellowship. I would be paid 25,000 rupees a month for two years, and if I went abroad, they were prepared to give me foreign currency.

The funny thing was that, even before I got the Homi Bhabha Fellowship, I had written a play that made use of traditional theatre elements: *Hayavadana.* I had read it out to Dubey and Karanth, and they had liked it. Since I had already finished the project I was supposed to undertake at the end of the fellowship, I spent the duration travelling around India without any pressure on me. I started work on the film *Vamsha Vriksha.*

The next year, I was invited by the US State Department to spend a month in New York. It was a city full of vitality where theatre and cinema were concerned. It was also an expensive city, and the State Department had booked me into an exorbitant hotel called the Barbizon-Plaza. Saraswathy, who was in New York at the time, arranged for me to stay somewhere else. I saw films by Kurosawa, Ozu, Fellini and Antonioni. And Saraswathy kept me company whenever she could.

In 1972, Karanth directed *Hayavadana* in Delhi for the theatre group Dishantar. Only a day before, Satyadev Dubey had staged *Hayavadana* in Bombay with Amrish Puri, Sunila Pradhan and Amol Palekar. The reception to both was overwhelming enough to be termed explosive. In Delhi, Shanta Gandhi, who had herself directed traditional plays like *Jasma Odan,* welcomed *Hayavadana* as the very first modern play to use elements of traditional theatre, especially music and dance. Suresh Awasthi, secretary of the Sangeet Natak Akademi, described it as 'the theatre of roots', and proclaimed: 'This is the return of the *Natyashastra.*' When Satyadev staged *Hayavadana* in Delhi, Prime Minister Indira Gandhi saw it and expressed her appreciation. I won the Sangeet Natak Akademi Award that year.

In Bombay, Vijay Tendulkar saw Satyadev's *Hayavadana* and said to me: 'I too want to use folk forms in a play. I'll sit down to write at once.' He wrote *Ghashiram Kotwal* in 1972. Habib Tanvir saw Karanth's *Hayavadana* in Delhi and said, 'I felt like doing this play as soon as I read it in *Enact.* Some moments in it – the scene with Padmini singing a lullaby, for example – are reminiscent of García Lorca. But Karanth had already announced that he was going to direct it and I did not want to enter into any kind of competition with him.' Habib wrote *Charandas Chor* and staged it in 1974. Both *Ghashiram Kotwal* and *Charandas Chor* are held to be milestones in the history of Indian theatre, but neither Tendulkar nor Tanvir ever accepted that the two works were inspired by *Hayavadana.*

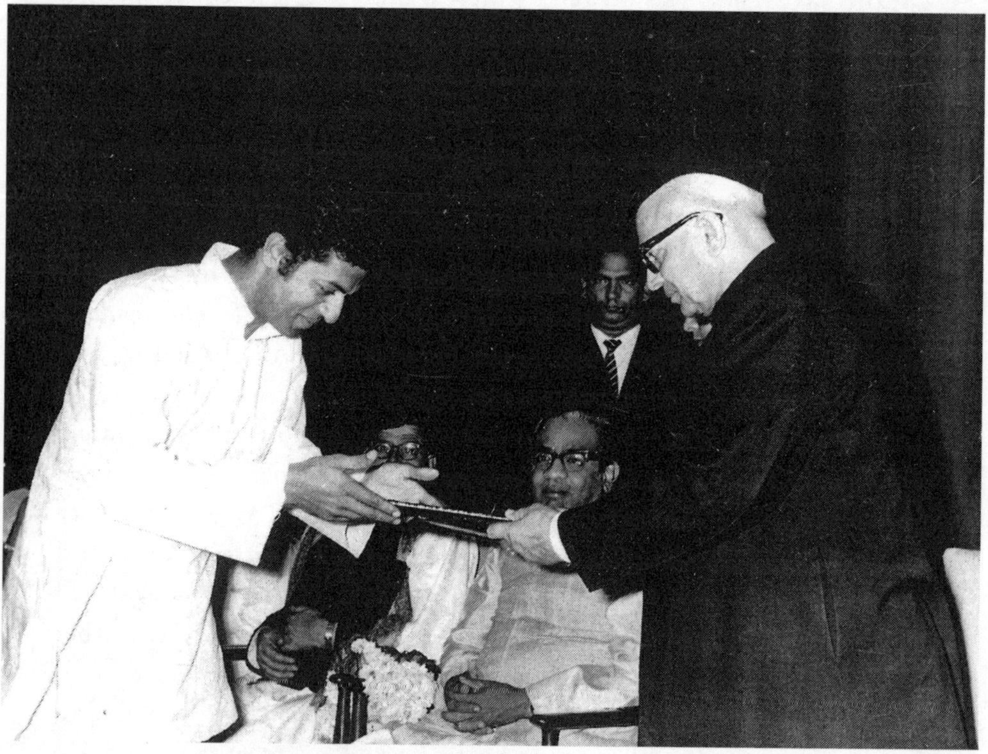

Receiving the Sangeet Natak Akademi Award from the vice president of India, Gopal Swarup Pathak (1972)

8

SRINGERI

Samskara

In May 1965, the Kannada Sahitya Parishat's annual meet was held at Karwar. With his college closed for the summer, Kirtinath Kurtakoti was visiting Dharwad, where he was staying with G.B. Joshi. It was decided that I would go there and we would all leave together for Karwar.

I had joined OUP's Madras office as assistant manager in 1964. My plan was to meet professors and library officials at the university in Dharwad, and having finished with official work, proceed to Karwar in a relaxed frame of mind. Accordingly, I left for Dharwad in the car the office had provided for my use.

When I reached Bangalore, YNK, who had said he would join me, backed out. He dropped the writer Sumatheendra Nadig in my lap and asked me to take him instead. All I remember of the drive to Dharwad is that Nadig entertained me by reading out obscene folk songs that his grandfather had collected.

Since Bappa and Aayi were in Bombay, our house in Dharwad was locked. Nadig went to stay at GB's house. I went to meet Prof. K.J. Shah at the Karnatak University campus. He said he was about to leave for Bombay – his house would be empty, and I could stay there if I wanted. He gave me the keys and left for the station.

That day, Kirti handed me a manuscript that had been submitted to Manohara Grantha Mala. It was U.R. Ananthamurthy's *Samskara*. I read it that night at Shah's house, and could not sleep after I finished it. My reaction was hardly surprising, considering that it would jolt the entire Kannada literary world when it was published. But my staying awake that night was not solely from the excitement of having read a great novel. Just as turning a kaleidoscope changes the relationship between the bits of coloured glass inside and creates a new pattern, my reading *Samskara* had fundamentally changed the way I saw the Kannada landscape.

The novel is set in an agrahara, a closed-off Brahmin settlement. It begins with the sudden death of Naranappa after returning from a nearby town. Naranappa, while being of Brahmin birth, has seemingly violated every tenet of living like one. While he was alive, he drank, he ate meat, he abandoned his wife and lived with a Shudra mistress named Chandri, and he did all this in a conspicuous, taunting fashion. Now, the problem the agrahara residents face is about his final samskara, his last rites. He has no sons to perform them, and since he was a Brahmin, they can only be performed by another Brahmin. None of the agrahara's Brahmins want to be involved lest his many sins be transferred to them, but then, neither are they allowed to eat, bathe or offer prayers while the corpse lies in the agrahara. They turn to Praneshacharya for a solution. Praneshacharya is the spiritual light of the agrahara and everything that Naranappa was not. He has studied the scriptures in Varanasi, and is renowned for his scholarship and wisdom. He has married a bedridden woman named Bhagirathi and cared for her while remaining celibate. While he searches his texts for an answer, the corpse lies rotting. Hunger is weakening the Brahmins and the ominous piling up of dead rats in the agrahara suggests that Naranappa has brought with him the plague that has been spreading through the region. Unable to deal with the intrusion of the larger world, the Brahmins' way of life is literally killing them. In desperation, Praneshacharya prays to Maruti for a sign, but none is forthcoming. Overwhelmed, he has a spiritual breakdown. He has sex with Chandri and goes on to break the moral codes he so fiercely upheld. It is as if he has transformed into Naranappa. He wanders around in a frenzy and runs into a garrulous stranger named Putta, who shows him the sights of life at play – a cockfight, deformed beggars, a temple festival, a prostitute's house. It is as if Praneshacharya is seeing the world for the first time.

I knew nothing about the places that Ananthamurthy had described. I had heard about agraharas, and I had seen villages in the Malnad region reserved for specific castes, but I had thought of them as remnants of a distant past and not deemed them as being of any importance. Now, not only had Ananthamurthy wonderfully recreated this world, he had also used it to great effect. The novel described the most minute details of life in an agrahara, its customs, the surrounding landscape, its human conflicts, values that seemed to operate entirely in another dimension, perspectives I simply could not grasp. I grew disoriented as I read on. The novel did not operate only in the realm of events and factual details. It went beyond them and shook me at a level that is difficult to describe. It dragged me to a place of spiritual angst that lay beyond any particular societal framework.

To tell the truth, for the first time in my life a contemporary writer had made me jealous. Ramanujan always used to say: 'Translation is a way to take an excellent work written by someone else and make it one's own. A good translation is impossible without being jealous of the original.' Suddenly, I understood what he meant. This book should have been written by me, but somehow, this undeserving fellow named Ananthamurthy had gone ahead and written it before I could. Now I had to make it mine, but it was not clear right away how I could do that.

I had no interest then in the art of film-making. I had seen good films by European directors when I was at Oxford. France's New Wave was making a big splash. Italy had given Fellini and Antonioni to cinema. But somehow, I was not attracted to the medium.

From Dharwad, GB, Kirti, Ramakant, Sumatheendra and I went to Karwar for the Sahitya Parishat's annual meet. We had lost our way in Karwar when we saw some young men standing in a group and asked them how to reach the Kannada sammelana. One of them pointed his finger and we went in that direction. There was an explosion of laughter behind us, and we learnt why in some time when we ended up at the seashore. That was when we realized just how much the Kannada sammelana had antagonized the Marathi-speaking people of Karwar.

By the time the sammelana ended and I dropped the Dharwad contingent off at the atta and drove to Bangalore, a new idea had taken shape in my mind: to make a film based on *Samskara*. The spectacular setting of the novel alone demanded a film, not to speak of its other merits. It was all I spoke about when I met YNK in Bangalore, and as always, YNK was ready to be part of the venture.

A few months after I reached Madras, the Players began rehearsals for the play, *Six Characters in Search of an Author*. All through the rehearsals, I went on about *Samskara* to anyone who would listen. The only one of them who had actually read the novel was S.G. Vasudev, who, being an artist with a keen interest in drama and literature, was immediately excited by the idea of turning it into a film. But to the rest of them, the very idea of making a film must have seemed strange and impractical. The only person among the Madras Players who knew anything about films was Pattabhirama Reddy.

Pattabhi and his wife Sneha had deep political convictions. They were disciples of Ram Manohar Lohia, and proclaimed themselves to be socialists. That year, when the socialist politician Shantaveri Gopala Gowda came to Bangalore, Pattabhi hosted a party at his house. That was the only time I met Gowda. He asked Pattabhi, 'Why don't you produce a film based on *Samskara*?' With the guru having spoken, Pattabhi was ready at once.

Sneha was a remarkably beautiful woman and one of the best actresses I have come across in my life. She was a person of great sensitivity who, when she set out to understand a character, explored depths that were barely visible to others. Playing the part of a maid in Ionesco's one-act play *The Lesson*, the ripples of fear she was able to evoke in the audience was comparable to anything a professional actress could have managed. There was a strangely mysterious aura around her past – her name before marriage had been Joyce, she was partly of Bengali descent, which was something she cherished, and she was supposed to have learnt flamenco in Spain. She spoke perfect English, and in an enchanting voice.

Pattabhi was soft-spoken and always smiling. He was tall and, going by photographs, had been handsome when he was young, but had now begun to put on weight. Pattabhi had brought modernism to Telugu poetry, and he was constantly engaged in trying to prove Fermat's Last Theorem. He had also produced a few Telugu films that had not been very successful. For all this, it could not be said that he was on familiar terms with hard work. Pattabhi was completely devoted to his wife, and we used to talk affectionately among ourselves that one could see love for Sneha gush forth from his eyes every time he looked at her.

Sneha wanted to be a film heroine. She was said to have gone to Gemini Studios in Madras to pursue this ambition, but things had not worked out and she had returned. Pattabhi's attempts at making her a film star had not been successful either. The *Samskara* film project, therefore, came as a convenient means to fulfil that desire.

Vasudev and I had decided that *Samskara* had to be a film of exceptional quality, and we had spent a great deal of time discussing the best possible cast. Among the actresses then working in Kannada films, we felt that Kalpana alone had the skill and the earthy personality required to take on the role of Chandri. (Later, when we heard stories about Kalpana's behaviour with film-makers, we thought ourselves fortunate not to have asked her.) Once it became clear that Pattabhi was going to produce the film, the role was inevitably reserved for Sneha.

At the time, the novel had not yet been translated into English. Pattabhi and Sneha knew nothing about *Samskara* beyond my enthusiasm for it and Gopala Gowda's endorsement. There was not enough time to translate it formally, but I had acquired the skill of translating on the fly – I could hold a Kannada book in front of me and read it out in English. So, it was decided that I would do an English reading of *Samskara*. The Madras Players gathered at Pattabhi's house and settled on a mat. I read the novel out twice. Everyone was blown away by its brilliance. Pattabhi committed to producing the film, and a new banner called Rama Manohara Chitra was registered. But it was when Pattabhi said he would direct the film himself that Vasudev and I looked at each other with raised eyebrows. In the five years we had known him, Pattabhi had not once shown any interest in direction. A director needs a well-defined vision of the world and the ability to take firm decisions, but Pattabhi had a soft personality. It was only when he asked Vasudev to be the art director that I felt somewhat hopeful about the project, because *Samskara* was very close to Vasudev's heart.

Pattabhi, a film distributor named Surendranath, Vasudev, YNK and a cinematographer from Madras all went together to Sringeri and visited nearby agraharas. Vasudev shortlisted some of them as being suitable for shooting the film, but the cinematographer began trying to convince Pattabhi against outdoor shooting and in favour of putting up sets in a studio. This annoyed Vasudev. Satyajit Ray's *Pather Panchali* had influenced us so much that we had begun to believe that an art film could only be shot outdoors. (It was only several years later that we learnt that *Pather Panchali* had been filmed on a studio set.)

An accidental meeting at this time was instrumental in taking the project to an entirely different level. A young Australian cinematographer, Tom Cowan, had come to India to meet Satyajit Ray. Like so many wanderers who came to Madras, he found his way to Cholamandal Artists' Village. There he met Vasudev, who brought him to my house, and we talked endlessly about *Samskara.* Tom left for Calcutta saying he would return after meeting Ray. Later he told me, 'I have been a part of many such projects. There's always a lot of excitement at the beginning, but it fades away. I had expected that it would happen here too, but I returned from Calcutta to see the project was still going strong.' He screened his documentaries for us after having them brought through the Australian embassy. He was ready to come to Malnad with us. I told him, 'You have come to see India. You will not earn much by doing the cinematography for this film, but the India you will see here cannot be found anywhere else.'

An account of the making of *Samskara* would be incomplete without mentioning the colourful E. Surendranath. As mentioned earlier, most of the people involved with the making of *Samskara* were members of the Madras Players. They were sophisticated, highly educated people who were strongly influenced by English culture. Like me, some had even lived in England for a while. It was not possible to gain entry to the Madras Players unless one was refined and proper in social settings, and the most important prerequisite was the ability to speak perfect English.

Into this picture entered the Telugu film distributor Surendranath. Apparently, Pattabhi had, once upon a time, warned him against getting

The *Samskara* team: Singeetam Srinivasa Rao, Tom Cowan, U.R. Ananthamurthy, me, Sneha, Pattabhi, Kanakanahalli Gopi and S.G. Vasudev involved with a film project and saved him from burning his fingers. This had earned him Surendranath's undying loyalty, and he had now invested in *Samskara*. This meant that Surendranath became a fixture at our parties despite his ways being those of the commercial film industry. Sneha found his behaviour crude and contemptible: talking loudly when drunk, laughing uproariously, dancing when the mood took him, speaking in broken English, telling jokes that skirted close to the obscene. Sneha made no effort to disguise her contempt either. It was Pattabhi who saw to it that matters between them did not deteriorate.

Once when Pattabhi, Surendranath and I were drinking, Pattabhi got up and went to the bathroom. Surendranath grabbed my hand. He said, 'Look at him, Girish, just look. His father is a crorepati who owns mica mines. But this man goes around with his shaving kit in a plastic bag. In a plastic bag! What can I say?' He wiped the tears from his eyes, and continued, 'He's a good man. A saint. He saved me in a situation where anyone else would have betrayed me. He saved me.' Surendranath began to weep. 'It is my responsibility to take care of him. You are a gentleman. You work for art, not for money. I believe in you,' he said, took both my hands in his, and fervently kissed the back of my right hand. I was completely at a loss. If he remembered the next day what he had done while drunk, I thought, he was sure to hold the one-sidedness of this interaction against me. So, after some fifteen minutes, I too grasped his hands in mine. Talking to him while overcome with emotion, I kissed the back of his right hand and settled our account.

The film project began to gain momentum. Since the novel had not yet been translated into English, I asked Pattabhi if I should attempt to write the screenplay, and he agreed. Ever since I returned from Karwar, I had immersed myself in studying the film medium. A friend named S. Gopali, who had trained at NSD, had given me books on the technical aspects of both drama and cinema, among them a book written by Karel Reisz and Gavin Millar called *The Technique of Film Editing*. As I read the book, I felt as if the medium was giving up its secrets to me. It took scenes from different films, broke them down into their constituent shots, explained why the camera was where it was in those shots, and demonstrated how the shots had been stitched together into scenes. All this along with the accompanying dialogue. After reading the book, I was confident that I could make a film. (It was only later that I realized that film-making was not quite as simple as that.)

The first two parts of the novel unfold in a manner not very different from a screenplay. Scenes are described from an external perspective, and it was relatively simple for me to adapt these – I even picked up most of the dialogue directly from the novel. But in the third part of the novel, the narrative enters Praneshacharya's internal world, and depicting the workings of his mind visually proved to be a significant challenge. Still, I wrote the screenplay, and it was used as the basis for filming.

Writing the screenplay had proved a satisfying experience, and now I longed to direct films. I had no interest in acting, and had told Pattabhi, 'I don't want Praneshacharya's role. I will instead work with you and gain experience in directing.' But Pattabhi had seen me on stage and knew my capabilities as an actor. In any case, who else could we ask? Pattabhi's experience with professional actors in the Telugu film industry had not been satisfactory, and anyway, we could not afford a professional actor. Perhaps Pattabhi took some special satisfaction in Sneha working with an actor who had the Oxford stamp. Whatever it was, he insisted I take Praneshacharya's role, and I certainly cannot say that his decision caused me any great anguish.

YNK swung into action in Bangalore. One of his major contributions to *Samskara* was introducing us to Kanakanahalli Gopi. Gopi had been interested in theatre and films for quite some time, and had worked as M.V. Krishnaswamy's associate director. He was a lively character, liked by everyone, and more importantly, he was a proper Madhva, with close connections to Madhva mutths. Since no one else on the directorial side knew anything about Madhva customs, Gopi was invaluable in helping us achieve realistic detail in religious observances, gait, posture, gestures and so on. Had Gopi not been by my side, I would have found it extremely difficult to play Praneshacharya. For example, I am used to walking tall and straight, like a cultured city-dweller. To play a traditional Brahmin, I had to learn to walk more loosely, with slack shoulders and a slight hunch. Gopi was director and adviser when it came to such details. In a scene where Praneshacharya eats a banana, I peeled it halfway as usual and bit off the top. Gopi said, 'Not like that. First take the banana in your left hand. Use the right to strip the peel off completely and throw it. Then take the peeled fruit in your right hand and eat it. That is the traditional way.' I am indebted to Gopi for this and the many other nuances he brought to my performance. It was Gopi, along with Vasudev, who went to shops selling used clothes, and bought dhotis, saris and blouse pieces for the entire cast at a cost of less than a thousand rupees.

In addition to Gopi, YNK introduced us to all the amateur actors to be found in Bangalore. These were pre-television days, and stage actors did not mind coming all the way from Bangalore, waiting patiently until they were needed, and returning after playing a small part. Among them were Dasharathi Dikshit, B.S. Ramarao, C.R. Simha, Kokanath, and U.K. Jayadev. G.V. Shivanand put us in touch with retired actors from the Gubbi theatre company. Since Pattabhi did not know Kannada, it was impossible for him to talk to the actors, get them to read lines and assign roles. Nor was he interested in doing so. I selected the actors and he accepted them all.

Our main problem was finding actresses. Only two amateur actresses from Bangalore came forward willingly to be part of the film: Vasudev's elder sister Goda Ramkumar, and Bhargavi Narayan, wife of the actor and make-up artist Belavadi Nanjundaiah Narayana, popularly known as Makeup Nani. The other actresses were all willing to act on stage but reacted with horror at the very mention of film. Finally, it was actresses from the Madras Players who came forward: Vishalam Ekambaram, Rani Burra, Ammu Mathew; Lakshmi Krishnamurty, who volunteered to play the part of the shaven-headed Lakshmidevamma; Yamuna Prabhu, who played the prostitute Padmavati and stunned the Kannada film world with the way she used just her eyes to invite Praneshacharya in.

Around this time, *Samskara* was published in abridged form in the magazine *Kasturi*. With this, a story that had been limited to the readers of Manohara Grantha Mala was now being discussed in every household in Karnataka. A reader wrote a letter to the editor saying that if a corpse was lying unclaimed in this way, 'I would perform the last rites in the name of humanity. Even if I did not know who it was, I would not have to fear taking on any sin.'

Apparently, there was a mantra that ensured this. He called the central premise of the book 'a house of sand' and blew it away. We decided to ignore this and went on with our work on the film.

In the middle of 1969, Pattabhi, Vasudev, Tom and I went to Agumbe and camped at the inspection bungalow. We wanted to finalize exterior locations for filming and give Tom a chance to become familiar with the environment he would be working in. After visiting a couple of agraharas, we came to Vaikunthapura. Pattabhi said, 'I have seen this location already,' and chose not to enter. Since his zamindari culture could not tolerate much physical effort, the rest of us stepped into Vaikunthapura.

Every director knows that finding the right location is as thrilling as falling in love at first sight. I cannot describe my exhilaration on seeing the agrahara. It seemed to have been made for *Samskara* – Vaikunthapura had not changed for at least one hundred and fifty to two hundred years (except for the poles that accompanied the arrival of electricity), but this only made filming there easier for us. The pillars were of wood, the walls were made of mud. Cow dung-swept yards in front of the houses. Thatched roofs. Not a trace of cement or concrete. Some of the agrahara's men were moving about in dhotis and short-sleeved tunics; others had only their sacred threads across their bare torsos, a tuft of hair at the back of their heads, and vibhuti across their foreheads. It felt as if they were all waiting for shooting to begin.

But the popularity of *Kasturi* had worked against us. The people of Vaikunthapura, who had earlier given a warm welcome to Vasudev and the others, were now wary. A man named Shastri sat me down on the platform outside a house and explained: 'There has been an uproar after the novel appeared in *Kasturi*. It is being seen as a work that mocks sanatana dharma. We fall under the Sringeri mutth. One of us was almost ostracized once for arranging a drama performance and had to seek atonement. Your story has to do with Madhva society. We are Smartas and have no objection to the film. But we are not prepared to incur the wrath of the mutth. So, if you get permission directly from the mutth, you can go ahead and shoot the film here without any worries.'

This meant that there was more running around to be done. That night, Pattabhi shed tears of dismay at the bungalow. He had completely failed to understand the concerns of the agrahara's residents and thought they were being unreasonable. Tom said to me, 'If there's a problem with this agrahara, can't we shoot the film in one of the other villages identified by Vasudev?' I did not think so. First, there was no assurance that the same problem would not arise in any other agrahara. And more importantly, the other agraharas were somewhat haphazard, made up of a few lanes with houses scattered here and there. Vaikunthapura, in contrast, was clearly defined.

A single lane ran straight from the base of a hill to its top, with ten or eleven houses on either side. At the upper end of the lane, as if it was supervising daily life in the agrahara, was a temple enclosed by walls. I said to Tom, 'We can cover the temple entrance with a screen and treat it as the front door of Naranappa's house. Then we can convey the idea of Naranappa's rotting corpse dominating the entire village. Every time there's a long shot of the agrahara, with the camera at the lower end of the lane, the door will keep the viewer continuously aware of the corpse lying behind it. Houses on either side with their doors closed. A forlorn street in the middle. And at the top, frightening the whole village, this reminder of Naranappa's remains. This way, we can visually establish the complex interconnections of *Samskara*.' Tom liked the idea.

We began to pursue the mutth. We went to the Shankar mutth in Bangalore after learning that the Sringeri swami was staying there. I wrote out a summary of the story that was slightly tweaked so it would not be unflattering to sanatana dharma. In the novel, it is Naranappa's Muslim friends who come under cover of darkness, take his body away and cremate it. I knew this would never be acceptable to the mutth. I changed the story so that it is Praneshacharya who returns to the agrahara to cremate Naranappa, and handed the note to a functionary at the mutth. Who knows if anyone read the note or not, but he finally said, 'Very nice. We have no objection to your shooting the film. Wonderful landscape! Use it as you like.' We were free to begin filming.

We kept it hidden that we were using the temple as the house in which Naranappa's corpse was lying. Otherwise the agrahara residents might themselves have objected.

As discussions about the film progressed, tensions flared up amongst us. One of the major reasons was the Reddy couple's preconception that an art film had to resemble a Bengali film. As if to prove that she had Bengali antecedents, Sneha insisted on pronouncing 'samskara' as 'shonshkar'. (I even made fun of her a few times, saying, 'What is that? I've never heard the word before.') Pattabhi had studied at Santiniketan. They both were keen that our film, even if it was in Kannada, should feel like a Bengali film.

One day, Pattabhi beckoned to me as if he wanted to discuss a major problem. 'Girish, in the film Praneshacharya waits in front of a Maruti idol for a sign. Don't you think this is ridiculous? If we replace the Maruti idol with a Devi, it can bring some depth and beauty to the scene.' I panicked and tried to explain: 'No, no! For Madhvas, Maruti is the prana deva, who infuses life into the universe. In these parts, the Devi is usually worshipped by Dalits.' Pattabhi argued, 'But will the viewers know all that? I feel we should have a Devi.' I went to YNK in a daze. In his usual style of spitting out half his words and swallowing the other half, YNK said, 'No, no, that will be stupid. The film will become a laughing stock,' and eased the Devi out of the film.

Pattabhi sent for a young man named Singeetam Srinivasa Rao to assist him with direction. He was a Madhva and had some experience in the film industry, both of which made him potentially very useful. But he did not know Kannada. His addition would mean that our entire directorial team – Pattabhi, Singeetam and Tom – had absolutely no Kannada between them. I kicked up a fuss about this, but Pattabhi reassured me by saying that his skill and experience would be an asset.

Around this time, a journalist and photographer named Raghavendra Rao wrote about the *Samskara* film project in the *Kannada Prabha* newspaper and added fuel to the already burning fire. Rao met us all together at Pattabhi's house, interviewed us, took photographs and wrote his article. Like all such articles, its purpose was to generate curiosity and interest about the project among the public, but it ended up causing trouble within our unit.

I had won the national Sangeet Natak Akademi Award. S.G. Vasudev had won the national Lalit Kala Akademi Award. Kannada readers were already familiar with our names. Tom Cowan was the very first international cinematographer to work in Kannada films, an aspect bound to generate interest. But Pattabhirama Reddy was an unknown Telugu film producer and there was nothing more to say about him. This state of affairs was reflected in the article. Vasudev and I received more prominence than we should have, and Pattabhi, who had shouldered the burden of the venture, was sidelined.

This disturbed Sneha more than it did Pattabhi. From this moment on, a Kannada versus Telugu conflict began in the unit.

The day-to-day sources of friction usually originated in the fact that none of us had much experience making a feature film. Minor issues that are an unavoidable part of shooting a film were perceived as enormous calamities. When something went wrong, instead of trying to set it right, we began to ask who was to blame. We had enthusiasm, but no experience, and this resulted in overblown grievances. When we could not understand a problem, the very existence of the problem felt like a shortcoming. The result of all this was vicious backbiting.

The only one among us who had some experience of film-making was Tom. He had worked as a cinematographer on documentaries for the Commonwealth Film Unit. I told Tom, 'It's true that there's tension and conflict among us right now. But it will disappear magically once we start shooting.' Tom said gravely, 'All film units have these troubles. But the unfortunate thing is that they don't get better after shooting starts, they become worse.' His prediction came true, and more severely than we could have imagined. The major share of credit for the *Samskara* project not collapsing midway has to go to Tom.

The dates for shooting were finalized. I took two years' worth of annual leave all together and set aside six weeks for shooting. Pattabhi, Vasudev, Tom and I left in my two-door Herald. Of the three models of cars available in the market then, the Herald was the most delicate. The Ambassador was ideal for rough and long journeys, the Fiat was popular as a taxi for use within the city, and the Herald was an appropriate car for executives to go to office, or for a couple to drive to a party in the evening with their kids secure in the doorless back seat. By using it as a film production vehicle, it has to be said that I committed an unforgivable violence on that car.

We went to Sringeri and stayed in the mutth's guest house. But when the women arrived, we gave it over to them and moved to three or four houses we had rented in the town. Sneha settled into one of the guest-house rooms, and Pattabhi joined her after the other women left. At some point, the mutth officials began to insist that they vacate the room, but they refused to do so until shooting was complete. This led to friction with the mutth and soured that relationship.

The house in which we men lived took me back to Sirsi: the row of mattresses on the floor, the morning line for the faraway toilets in the backyard, the warm bathroom with water that was heated on a wood fire and smelled of cow dung.

The food supplied by the contractor we had hired proved unsatisfactory, so we arranged for an eating house called Mallika Bhavan to supply us meals. I saw here for the first time a graph that I noticed in future shoots too. In the beginning, the plate is sumptuously full. Then, as the days go by, items begin to vanish one by one until the meal is reduced to rice, rasam and watery buttermilk. This whittling down of meals is a sign that the producer has not paid the hotel bill. As soon as the bill is paid, the plate cheerfully fills up again with rice, rasam, vegetables, chutney, sandige, papad, thick curd. The practised eye can take one look at the plate and tell what is going on with the film's budget.

After we had all settled down in Sringeri, I told Pattabhi, 'The heart of the novel's action takes place in three dramatic interactions. Most importantly, Praneshacharya with the Brahmins. Then, Praneshacharya with Naranappa. And lastly, Praneshacharya with Putta. We have two days before we start shooting. Why don't I get the actors to rehearse the main scenes?' Pattabhi agreed. For two evenings, I got the actors together as if we were rehearsing a play. I introduced the characters to them, got them to practise their lines. I gave them each character's shruti.

The arguments started again as soon as we began shooting. In the scene set on the veranda in front of Praneshacharya's house, Singeetam, Tom and Pattabhi had decided who should sit where without consulting me. In my opinion, they had placed the Brahmins in a way that was inconsistent with their characters. According to this arrangement, Lakshmanacharya and Gundacharya (Garudacharya in the novel) were made to sit facing each other next to the main pillars of the veranda, as if they were rams ready to butt heads in battle. Durgabhatta was to sit leaning against the wall with his back to Chandri. This meant that if he had to look in her direction, he had to turn his head in a way that was clearly visible to everyone. Chandri herself was to sit conspicuously in the street, as if she wanted to attract everyone's attention.

I tried to explain to Pattabhi, Tom and Singeetam that this arrangement of characters simply did not make sense. Gundacharya had experience with courts and government offices, and it seemed fitting that he would take the lead among the group, sit at the front and make his arguments. But Lakshmana was married to Naranappa's younger sister. He was fearful that the responsibility of performing Naranappa's last rites would fall on him, and so he was intent on showing, right from the beginning, that there was no close connection between him and the dead man. Accordingly, he had to be sitting away from the centre of the group, half turned away from the discussion. Only later, when Chandri placed all her gold in front of Praneshacharya, did it make sense for him to draw closer in an attempt to stake his claim. A direct confrontation could begin at this point.

Durgabhatta was a Smarta. He was interested in the discussion only as a spectator, and would naturally choose to be slightly away from the thick of the action. Besides, he wanted to leer at Chandri. He would not choose to sit in a place where he would draw attention to himself by turning repeatedly to look at her. He must be positioned in a convenient corner, such that Chandri is in his direct line of sight, and he only has to raise his eyes to see her.

Dasacharya is easily susceptible to hunger. Instead of having him sit in the middle of the veranda, he must be shown as being in some agony, supporting himself against the wall.

Most objectionable of all to me was having Chandri sit in the middle of the street. She was a woman who had stayed confined to Naranappa's house while he was alive. She knew that the Brahmins would begin to undress her with their eyes as soon as she was seen outside. Instead of displaying herself in the open like this, she should instead be in a lane between two houses, or hidden from view by a wall, but close enough to hear the discussion. She should show herself only when she comes forward with her ornaments.

I argued that it was possible to decide who should sit where based entirely on how Ananthamurthy had developed his characters. But Singeetam was following the conventions of commercial cinema: Gunda and Lakshmana were competitors, and if they sat opposite each other, he could turn the camera from one face to the other in a flash pan when Chandri took off her ornaments and put them on offer. That flash pan was the key shot of the scene, and so everyone had to sit accordingly.

I did not say much. Pattabhi and Singeetam knew nothing about the novel or about Madhva customs. Their scene composition was filled with clichés. We had set out to make a first-rate art film, but now I began to have serious misgivings about what we would accomplish in the end.

Pattabhi's method of 'direction' became clear right from the first day. When it was Sneha's shot he would sit next to the camera with his entire being summoned into his intently hunched body. His eyes did not leave his wife for even an instant. But when Sneha's scene was finished, Pattabhi would leave the direction to Singeetam and Tom, and vanish. Tom would compose shots as it suited him. Singeetam would diligently take care of technical aspects like scene entry from the right or left, and so on.

The first day of shooting. A scene with Praneshacharya and his wife Bhagirathi, played by Goda Ramkumar. As the first scene of the novel takes shape beautifully, the sound technician begins to shout, 'Cut! Cut! Someone is snoring!' The person deep in sleep on the nearby veranda: the director. When the film was finished and Vasudev was writing out the opening credits, he drew at the bottom of the slide for 'Director' the form of a sleeping man.

Another incident served to further vitiate the atmosphere. This time, I was in the wrong. I was sitting in a corner chatting with someone when Gopi came running. He said, 'They're shooting a scene, but there's absolutely no connection between what you taught the actors and what Singeetam is asking them to do. The actors are all confused.' I got up at once, went to where the shot was being filmed, and told the actors what they were supposed to do.

This was a grave mistake. Instead of correcting the actors directly, I should have told Singeetam about what I had previously discussed with the actors. It is disorienting for an actor to be advised by two or three people all at once. Be it on stage or while shooting a film, directorial advice must always come through the specified person. Not only had I confused the actors, I had also challenged the director's authority.

It must have been because of endless provocations such as this that, one evening, Singeetam jumped up in anger during a discussion and stalked about the room shouting, 'I have had enough of being insulted. I will leave. I cannot take this any more.' Apparently, Pattabhi got up and caught hold of him. He sat Singeetam down and comforted him. I heard of the incident from Esther Ananthamurthy (Ananthamurthy's wife, who played a small role in the film) some forty years later!

In response to this mistake of mine, Pattabhi committed an even bigger blunder. I might have barged in during filming without thinking, but there is no doubt that the theatrics that evening were premeditated. And I have no doubt that it happened at Sneha's instigation. She believed that Pattabhi was incapable of protecting his dignity, and that the responsibility for doing so rested with her. So, whenever there was the slightest possibility of a blow to his honour, her gentleness vanished to be replaced by aggression. She must have chided Pattabhi, saying that if Vasudev and I were not put in our places, the shooting was bound to falter.

That evening, Pattabhi gathered the unit in a room at the mutth's guest house. He, Vasudev, Singeetam, Tom, Gopi, a production manager named Santanam and I sat down and began drinking. Outside on the balcony, Sneha was with the women of the unit, leaning on the railing, looking at the sky, making small talk, as if she knew nothing about what was going to happen.

Pattabhi had drunk quite a lot. Though he was smiling as always, he was also shaking as if he were afraid. There was a good reason for this. If Vasudev and I got up and left for Madras, the *Samskara* story would end there. My Herald was standing outside, and it was the matter of a moment for us to leave Sringeri.

'There is no doubt that the quality of the film is improving as a result of both your interventions,' Pattabhi said, smiling ingratiatingly and trembling. 'But we are also losing time because of them. Since we have a tight shooting schedule, there is no time for discussion.'

I said, 'Pattabhi, you know that I had no interest in playing the lead role. I had told you that I wanted to help with the direction. What is important to us is that we make a film like *Pather Panchali* that is acknowledged as a world-class masterpiece.'

'I agree,' Pattabhi said. 'I know that if the two of you don't involve yourselves with the shooting, the film might end up twenty-five per cent worse. But we have no choice.'

He was not wrong. On such a tight budget, the slightest delay could prove disastrous. I know this better now than I did then, but still, it was not beyond my comprehension. Pattabhi went on in this vein for a while. Finally, Vasudev brought up what was bothering us both: 'Pattabhi, the three of us started this project: you, Girish and me. If you have a problem with the two of us, then you could have spoken to us separately. We want to successfully complete the film too. Why call everyone and question us? Why insult us in front of them all?'

Pattabhi grew alarmed. 'No, no, don't get me wrong. Not an insult at all. I only called everyone because it is a matter concerning the entire unit,' he rushed to explain. Clearly, he had realized his blunder, but it was too late – the situation had already got out of hand. I went as far as to take an oath that I would never forgive him.

After the group dispersed, Vasudev and I pondered our course of action. Vasudev said, 'If you are going to leave for Madras, I will come with you.'

Lakshmi Krishnamurty was an old friend of Sneha's. They had worked together for many years in the Madras Players. Lakshmi said, 'I came here with great enthusiasm, thinking it was a venture we were all embarking on together. I had tears of frustration in my eyes when Sneha was chatting on the balcony. We didn't know what was going on inside, but I had not expected something like this.'

Leaving midway through the shooting was not an option open to us. We had made a hue and cry about how we were making an art film. Now, if we fought among ourselves and parted without finishing the project, I was certain that such an attempt would not be possible again in Kannada. Whatever happened, it was essential that we completed the film.

At the same time, I decided the matter would not, and could not, end here. Looking back now, I feel I was not understanding enough of Pattabhi's constraints. In trying to get back at him, I might have ended up needlessly hurting the film. Had Vasudev and I been more patient and cooperative, plenty of time and money could have been saved.

To give an example, we needed Yakshagana dancers for a particular scene. K.V. Subbanna happened to be visiting Sringeri that day, and we were talking in the afternoon when Yakshagana music and dialogue started emanating from the director's camp. Subbanna was taken aback. 'Yakshagana in the middle of the day? What, are they filming talamaddale?' he asked. Talamaddale has the music, songs and improvisation of Yakshagana, but without the make-up, costumes and movement. 'No,' I said. 'The Yakshagana performance is going to be filmed in the evening. But the camera's sound interferes with the dialogue, so they're recording the dialogue separately now. They say they will record the visuals of the performers in the evening and synchronize their lip movements with the audio.' Subbanna looked at me as if I was crazy. 'How is that possible? Their words will be completely different in the evening,' he said. 'Yes. I know that, but they don't. They haven't asked me, and I won't tell them,' I said. They recorded the dialogue for about an hour and a half. In the evening, they found it was all of no use because Yakshagana performers do not repeat their lines, they come up with new dialogue every time. But the realization came only after much time and money had been wasted.

Anyway, after that unfortunate meeting, the unit found itself sharply divided into 'our' camp (Vasudev's and mine) and 'their' camp (Pattabhi and Sneha's). Every evening, after the day's shooting was done, Vasudev, Gopi and I would jump into my car and go to Koppa. There we would go to a liquor store, buy half a bottle of rum, have a few drinks each, and return chatting to Sringeri at night. There were no bars in Sringeri at the time. Lakshmi, Rani Burra and Vishalam, too, would join us sometimes, and YNK when he was around. The car would struggle up the slopes, but we were in no hurry whatsoever. When Lakshmi and Vishalam started accompanying us on the drive to Koppa, Sneha became isolated in the unit.

Sneha was an excellent actress. Chandri's character has fine shades of feeling, a deep humanity, resilience in the face of tragedy, and along with all these, the simple goodness of a village woman. Because Sneha pronounced words with a distinctly English accent, I had reduced Chandri's dialogue in the screenplay to only three or four lines. This gave Sneha plenty of opportunity for expressive acting, but with her being isolated in the unit, there was no one to guide her. She had no idea about the internal life of a village woman in Karnataka, and so she fell back on the 'Bengali' acting that she was familiar with. Instead of the earthiness that Chandri should have exuded, Sneha began raising her eyebrows delicately, looking into the distance and then lowering her eyes – delicately – to the ground while her lips trembled. Her portrayal of Chandri fit right into the Bengali films of Calcutta's New Talkies.

When Lakshmi saw the film, she was full of remorse. She said, 'I was right there. Sneha would have listened if I had told her. She always tries to understand a role thoroughly, but I didn't help her. I didn't sit with her and analyse the character. I didn't point out the unconvincing parts of her performance and help her get rid of them.'

The actor who was completely destroyed by the divided unit was Lankesh. I had asked him to play Naranappa because he had a somewhat gruff demeanour, but behind Naranappa's coarse exterior lies a thoughtful, liberal-minded reformer. The scene where Naranappa confronts Praneshacharya is the only one where this duality has a chance to express itself. I had some idea that Lankesh may not be a very good actor, but I had thought we could rehearse the scene together, even change the screenplay if required, until we perfected what was the foundational conflict of the film.

But Lankesh arrived at the location, took one look at the division in the unit and joined the Pattabhi camp. The rivalry and resentment he had always nurtured towards me could have fuelled his acting. Instead, it was invested in opposing me as part of our camp politics: 'Girish is too anglicized', 'He does not know Malnad', 'He does not know Kannada'. He distanced himself from me, and though I called him repeatedly for rehearsals, he never turned up.

Lankesh was unprepared when he arrived for shooting the crucial scene. And he had had a few drinks already (which might not have been a good idea, even though Naranappa is drinking in the scene). Lankesh struggled helplessly during filming. I was unresponsive and left him to his plight. In these circumstances, there was no opportunity to explore the complex relationship between the two characters. Lankesh's acting became an object of ridicule in the film. It must have reached Lankesh's ears that I was going around saying, 'It was only while acting with Naranappa's corpse that I felt any sign of a living connection.' I had meant for it to reach him.

When we came to Sringeri, we had not yet identified an actor to play the character of Putta. I had asked B.V. Karanth to play the part, but he could not since an opportunity to travel abroad had come his way. Ananthamurthy gave us the name of the person in Thirthahalli on whom he had based the character, but I did not find him suitable. Without knowing what to do, I made a trunk call to YNK, who said, 'There are still some good actors left here. Pattabhi did not even speak to them.' Vasudev and I went to Bangalore. I asked an actor named B.R. Jayaram to come to National College and read for Putta's part. Even before he had read two lines, I knew I had found our Putta.

All of Putta's scenes involved him talking to me as we walked, and in between our shots, Jayaram and I would discuss the scenes to come. Singeetam did not like this, but I knew that if Putta's character was ruined, the entire film would collapse. I need not have worried. It was a joy to work with an actor as responsive as Jayaram. The slightest suggestion to him was enough. He would find a way to weave it into the character and use it in his performance. Since we were almost finished with the shooting and had run out of money, we could not get the retakes we wanted. Despite this, Jayaram brought great liveliness to the film. I had given up smoking for six months in preparation for Praneshacharya's role. The habit rekindled in Putta's company.

Whether it is the stage or the screen, an actor benefits enormously from discussion and constructive criticism, and Jayaram's Putta is a testament to this. In contrast, I received no direction at all despite mine being the lead role, with Praneshacharya appearing in almost every shot of the film. Inevitably, there were shortcomings in my performance. A.K. Ramanujan said to me after seeing the film, 'What is this? Why does Praneshacharya behave so formally even with those who are close to him? Not once does he scratch his head or face, or yawn with his mouth open. Why this sophisticated behaviour among familiar people?' Similarly, when it came to language: 'Praneshacharya pronounces the word as "coffee" instead of "kaapi"!' It is because he was so acutely perceptive that he remained a lifelong guru to me.

The funny thing was that when I told people before we started shooting that I was going to play Praneshacharya, the near universal reaction was disbelief. GB said, 'The way you carry yourself is completely influenced by

With 'Putta' – B.R. Jayaram – during the shooting of *Samskara*

the West. You can never be convincing as a traditional priest.' So, the best compliment to my acting came when Gopi was showing a group photo of the unit to Kirti, telling him who had played which part. Kirti pointed at Praneshacharya in the photo and asked: 'Who is this?'

After *Samskara,* I have played the part of a traditional Brahmin at least a dozen times (and mostly in Telugu films). The money I couldn't make from *Samskara* I earned from those films. Even while working on my most popular film, the Hindi *Swami,* the director Basu Chatterjee said to me, 'It's enough if you manage to express the maturity that you conveyed in *Samskara.*'

A single example is enough to show how savage the atmosphere had turned because of all the conflicts and tensions in the unit. One day, we were all sitting idly on the veranda of a house when Sneha suddenly said to Vishalam in an overly sweet voice: 'Vishalam, they say you're a good dancer. Why don't you dance down from one end of the agrahara to the other?' Not having the courage to attack me, Sneha had picked on Vishalam, who was sitting quietly. And all this, just for having joined our camp.

Vishalam was helpless in the face of such aggression. She teared up. I, too, was taken aback by Sneha's viciousness, and could not speak for a minute. Then I shouted, 'I'll go and tell Pattabhi that he should organize a performance of Sneha dancing for the people of the agrahara. They have seen Bharatanatyam but not flamenco. They say you're a flamenco expert?' Sneha began to weep as if I had raked up a long-buried secret of hers. I felt better after having retaliated.

The conflict in the unit did not abate as shooting progressed, but thankfully, we did not have the time for such childish displays of cruelty. The surprising thing was that while we Indians – who had originally set out to make the film – were busy clawing at each other, it was the outsider, Tom Cowan, who refused to be distracted and carried on with work. If we are talking about the film *Samskara* to this day, the credit must go to Tom. It was he who brought some stability to the filming while ego clashes were causing it to flounder.

Tom's cinematography gave the film an ultra-modern form. In those days, no one knew of the new styles of cinematography that are now practised by graduates of the film institutes in Poona, Bangalore or Madras. The only cinematographers in the film industry were those who had worked as someone's assistant and inherited the ancient ways of the guru. Tom brought not just new techniques to the film, but a new aesthetic too.

Tom employed a modern style of shooting that was particular to India: bounce lighting as in Satyajit Ray's films, the largely handheld Arriflex camera, twenty to twenty-two shots a day. At the time, the Indian government had stopped importing Kodak film and replaced it with ORWO negative film from Eastern Europe. There was an outcry in the industry about the poor quality of ORWO film. Tom did a couple of tests with the ORWO negative and it met with his approval. He was able to deliver good results with it. Tom ensured that *Samskara* stood out among films made in that decade for its extraordinary visual quality.

Tom's experience, dedication and friendliness allowed him to keep his balance between the two groups that had formed in the unit. Once, when he said he would come to Koppa with us, I told him there was no room in the car. He did not take offence. He made sure he could talk freely with us; at the same time, he was close to Pattabhi and Sneha. Especially Sneha, towards whom he showed extraordinary tenderness. Besides, Sneha was always in agreement with the opinions of white people, and so our camp thought it fortunate that Tom was white. During the last week of shooting, he (and Singeetam) were down with diarrhoea, but his commitment was such that work did not stop.

We had treated Singeetam as an outcaste during the shooting of *Samskara.* But judging from the way he later became an important director, he too must have applied himself creatively. Tom always spoke warmly about working with him, but we did not see the significance of his contribution at the time.

After filming *Samskara* and returning to Australia, Tom became a director himself. *The Office Picnic* and a few other films directed by him were shown at international film festivals. Still, *Samskara* was a unique experience in his life. And, all things considered, the real architect of *Samskara* was Tom Cowan.

Of the ten or eleven households in the agrahara, only one remained aloof from us. It was also not on speaking terms with the others, and though the agrahara had a water pump, it was the women of this house alone who descended the hundred or so steps into the gorge to fetch water from the river.

We spent three weeks at the agrahara, during which its residents tolerated us with good-natured affection. This was mainly because our cast was courteous and well-mannered, and in addition, when Sneha made the effort, she could live up to her name and radiate charm and friendliness. But it was Tom who grew close to everyone. An old widow – her head shaven, committed to living in ritual purity – would take him into her kitchen and give him tea. Her son would shake his head in wonder and say, 'My mother is very fond of your Tom.' The day we finished shooting, the entire agrahara came to our vehicles to see us off. Sneha's face was wet with tears.

Before departing, we thought we should meet the Sringeri swami to take leave and seek his blessings. Pattabhi, Gopi, Vasudev and I went to the mutth and stood in line for his darshan. Before the swami arrived, a functionary of the mutth came to ask about us, and made us stand to one side on hearing that we were the film people. Gopi and I immediately understood that he was putting us in the line meant for people of lower status.

The swami arrived, and after speaking to his followers, came to where Pattabhi was standing with a plate containing a coconut, fruits and flowers. Pattabhi said, 'We are the film people. We have come after finishing shooting for the film.' The swami looked incensed even as Pattabhi spoke. He glared at us as if we had done something terrible, turned around and left without saying a word, his retinue vanishing behind him. Poor Pattabhi did not know what to do. I told him, 'Keep the offerings on the ground here. Whether they accept it or not is up to them.' He placed the plate on the ground and we left the mutth. Gopi said with surprise, 'What anger for a sanyasi!' I told him I did my best not to go anywhere near people who wear ochre.

There was much amazement in Bangalore when we returned after shooting the film. Apparently, we had become the object of gossip in Gandhinagar, where the Kannada film industry is concentrated, and the consensus seemed to be that we were amateurs who drank and fought amongst ourselves every day.

Tom returned to Australia and sent a young man named Steven Carthew to do the editing. But Steven lacked Tom's affability and nobody liked him. His work was not well received either. Everything he edited had to be cut again by a local editor and rejoined. Rajeev Taranath, whom Ananthamurthy had suggested as music director, composed a beautiful soundtrack for the film. The first print of the film was prepared after music and sound mixing, and it was screened for the unit and a few others.

As soon as the film ended, Surendranath, who was sitting next to me, cried out, 'Sri Venkataramana Govinda ... Go-o-vinda!' I didn't add my voice to his call, but my reaction to the film was not very different. The journalist Raghavendra Rao laid out his grievances: 'What is the difference between the rushes and the finished film? There's some of Rajeev's music here and there, but there is no sound anywhere. The wheels of a moving bullock cart are silent. People's footsteps are silent. There are no birds. Why are so many parts of the film without sound?' Pattabhi said there was no money to add sound. But later, when I started directing films myself, I realized that sound design did not require much money. Until *Ondanondu Kaladalli* (1978), I used to add background sounds myself, along with others in the directorial team. No, the real problem was that Pattabhi lacked the drive needed to do all this. He came from an affluent, landowning family and was used to a life of leisure. We already had plenty of experience with this side of his nature.

We were all dejected after the screening and concluded that the film *Samskara* was not worth showing to anyone. It had possessed the potential to be a film as important as *Pather Panchali*, so to see it fizzle out like this was frustrating.

Ramanujan visited Madras at this time. A special screening was arranged for him. I didn't know how to face Ramanujan after the film ended, but he seemed excited. 'It's very good,' he said. 'Quite a lot of the novel's nuances have made it to the film.' I was astonished and thrilled by his reaction. Pattabhi and Sneha broke out into smiles. We had all been looking at the rushes since the first day of shooting and, I suppose, repeated viewing had made us indifferent to the film. It brought hope and courage to find that the film had appealed to someone who saw it for the first time, and that too someone as sensitive as Ramanujan.

There is a postscript to this story. After *Samskara* had made it through all its troubles and was finally in the theatres, Pattabhi printed a brochure in which Ramanujan was quoted as saying, 'If I had seen this film abroad, I would have danced in the streets of Chicago.' When Ramanujan came to

Bangalore, he went with Gopi to see Pattabhi and Sneha. As Gopi recounted, Ramanujan told Pattabhi, 'I was surprised to see this quote attributed to me. I did not say anything of the sort.' Pattabhi got up and went to the bathroom. Sneha tried to justify it by saying, 'There are no words to express how much confidence we gained because you liked the film. It's you who reassured us.' Ramanujan replied, 'If you had asked me, I would have written a couple of lines in my own words.'

Some months after finishing shooting for *Samskara* and returning to Madras, I went to London for six weeks on behalf of OUP. When I stopped at the Bombay office on my way back, the first news I heard was that the Censor Board had banned *Samskara*.

I immediately called the chairman of the Censor Board and asked him what the problem was. He said, 'The board is of the opinion that the film is anti-Brahmin.' I told him, 'The novel is written by a Brahmin. The publisher is a Brahmin, I am a Brahmin. The art director and assistant director are Brahmins, as are most of the cast. Given all this, how is it possible for the film to be anti-Brahmin?' He said, 'We didn't know that.' I asked, 'Do you need to know the caste of those involved with a film before issuing the censor's certificate?' He laughed. I said, 'Well, you know now. So please revoke the ban.' But the matter was not in his hands any more. He said, 'The file has gone to the ministry in Delhi on appeal. They will decide.'

Apparently, the Madras office of the Censor Board, finding themselves at a loss after seeing the film, had sent it to the Bombay office, which refused the film a certificate. Pattabhi and Surendranath tried to keep the matter quiet when they received the order from the censors. They were worried that the film would gain notoriety within the industry. Raghavendra Rao, the journalist who had written about *Samskara* first, broke the news to much consternation in the Kannada film world. A film being banned was an extremely rare occurrence back then, and it became a subject of discussion across the state.

Surendranath came to me lamenting that all this would bring the film a bad name. 'I am finished,' he wailed like a tragic hero. Actually, the term 'tragic hero' was an apt one for Surendranath, because right from the beginning of the project he had not understood the film in the slightest. He had become entangled in the project out of devotion towards Pattabhi, but all he got from Sneha was contempt for his unpolished ways. The others, like me, found him a bit of a clown, though we didn't say so openly.

The fate of *Samskara* was to be decided in Delhi by a tribunal constituted by the Information and Broadcasting Ministry. One of its members was Burra Venkatappaiah, father of Rani Burra and Lakshmi Krishnamurty, but he was an ICS officer who at one point had been governor of the Reserve Bank, and not the sort of person to be influenced simply because two of his daughters were in the film. The tribunal saw the film and discussed it before rescinding the ban. They decided it was sufficient if two adjectives were cut from the film's dialogue – 'Shudra' from 'Shudra woman' and 'cattle' from 'cattle meat' – and gave the film an 'A' certificate.

By then, the banned film had aroused curiosity all across Karnataka, and when it finally released, it was successful beyond our expectations. But I don't think it was popular solely for its novel theme or its reputation as a banned film. My hunch is that the provocatively filmed sex scene between Chandri and Praneshacharya also attracted viewers in hordes. Until then, Indian films only depicted sex symbolically. When a couple came close to one another, the camera, as if overcome by shyness, would turn its eye elsewhere. But in *Samskara,* the act begins with an embrace and goes on to bodies pressed together, caressing each other, tossing and turning on the ground. The way the scene is shot – in extreme close-up – confuses the viewer about what exactly is on screen: Is that a shoulder muscle being squeezed or a buttock cheek? Is that frantically seeking hand finding the cleft of an armpit or something else? With this scene being the climax of Chandri's story arc, Sneha poured into her breathing, her eyes, her caresses, all the intensity and desire she could summon. Never before had a woman's sexuality been so openly depicted in Indian cinema. D.H. Lawrence, one of Ananthamurthy's literary gurus, would surely have approved. Tom's inspiration for this scene had come from the French and Italian films of the time.

The funny thing is that Sneha and I were not even on talking terms when this passionate scene was filmed. After each shot ended, we would detach ourselves and sit far apart as if we did not know each other.

Not only did the film do well at the box office, it also won that year's Swarna Kamal – the National Award for best feature film. A film banned by the government receiving the Swarna Kamal from the same government! What made us even happier was that *Samskara* had won over Satyajit Ray's *Pratidwandi.* It was an offering to our guru.

Some months after the film came out, I met Surendranath. 'How are you?' I asked. 'Thanks to *Samskara* I am very happy,' he said, theatrically raising both his arms and laughing heartily. I drew away, lest he decide to embrace me. Apparently, the film in its entirety had cost 95,000 rupees to make. He had earned back that money and was overjoyed now that he was turning a profit.

Though the film was a great success, Vasudev and I had resolved that none of the credit should go to Pattabhi. So, we started saying to anyone who asked, 'Pattabhi doesn't know the first thing about direction. He didn't do any directing, all he did was sleep.' While this was true, it was also in a sense an unfair thing to say given that we were in full possession of the facts when we agreed to shoot for the film. The important thing was that *Samskara* might never have been made if it were not for Pattabhi taking on the responsibility of producing it. He had arranged for funds to ensure that we finished making the film. I did not understand at the time just how demanding this was. Maybe we should have been more understanding of the pressures upon him. As a result of our campaign against him, Pattabhi did not receive any praise for the film even after it won accolades at the national level. Every speech he gave started with the words, 'I am Pattabhirama Reddy. You don't know it, but I am the director of *Samskara*.' His daughter Nandana told me that this was a source of pain to him until the end of his life.

Ramanujan went on to translate the novel *Samskara* into English. He also championed it in South Asian Studies departments in the United States as if it were the only novel to depict a living Hindu culture. As a result of his promotion, *Samskara* enjoyed an extended phase of popularity in American universities, accompanied by interest in the film. Though most non-Kannada cinephiles have by now forgotten the film, there is still demand for the film's DVD among American students. As one student said, 'This must be the only film that is alive because of its book!'

Samskara was received rapturously across India. And because of it, Kannada cinema received unprecedented recognition on the national stage. Mrinal Sen sent me a telegram praising the film and the performances in it. When I met Alkazi, he said, 'The film's direction and acting both stirred my heart.' Raj Kapoor sent word: 'Direct a film for me.' (I decided that not taking him up on the offer was the smart thing to do.)

I met Satyajit Ray after *Vamsha Vriksha* was shown at a film festival in Calcutta. He invited me and the actress Sharada home for tea. He said, 'There's a brilliance to the first part of the film that is absent in the latter part.' He did not seem to have particularly liked my acting either.

After the success of *Samskara,* Kannada saw a wave of art films. In addition to Karanth and me, several writers without the slightest aptitude for film-making tried their hand at direction. Not only did they burn their fingers, they also hurt the cause of art films. But it is a matter of happiness that from all these chaotic efforts Kannada managed to get at least one capable film director: Girish Kasaravalli.

The novel *Samskara* led me to film-making, and the film *Samskara* led me along the path to becoming a professional actor and director. But to the end, I could never get from films the satisfaction I got from theatre.

In 1970, to be eligible for the Karnataka government's film subsidy, a film had to be at least one hundred minutes long. Since we did not have sufficient material from the shooting, we had to include all kinds of unnecessary shots to stretch the film's length. And because we had no funds, we had ignored the entire dimension of sound. Once the film was successful and had earned money, the unnecessary shots should have been removed, the film cleaned up and tightened, and the sound improved before sending it to international film festivals. But Pattabhi could not be bothered.

In 1975, the prime minister Indira Gandhi declared a nationwide state of emergency and imprisoned all political leaders who opposed her. Among her main detractors was the Samajwadi Party's George Fernandes, who gave the police the slip and vanished. Pattabhi and Sneha were close friends of George Fernandes, and were taken to the police station for questioning – and along with them, their children Nandana and Konarak too. Pattabhi and the children were allowed to go, but Sneha endured seven months in jail.

Between giants: With Raj Kapoor and Satyajit Ray

With Mrinal Sen

Sneha suffered from severe asthma, and any anxious situation, including the moments before her entrance in a play, would give her breathlessness. (But it would vanish the instant she stepped on stage.) I have heard of several occasions when she thrashed around on the ground, unable to breathe. She did not receive adequate treatment while she was imprisoned, and is said to have had a few terrifying asthma attacks in jail. One day, soon after she returned home from jail, she suffered an attack and died. When I went to meet Pattabhi, he, despite everything, greeted me with a smile. He said, 'Such a fine actress, but she chose the wrong moment to exit the stage.'

Pattabhi went on to direct three more Kannada films: *Chanda Marutha* (1977) in protest against the Emergency, *Sringara Masa* (1984) and *Devara Kaadu* (1993). None of them were particularly successful. He died in 2006 in his daughter Nandana's house.

The other day, I learnt from Nandana that Pattabhi had given the original negative of *Samskara* to someone, and it is untraceable. So, the primary source of the film is now lost.

9

OLD MYSORE

New Wave

VAMSHA VRIKSHA

After my seven-year contract with OUP ended in 1970, I left Madras and came to Dharwad. Before leaving, I had been awarded the Homi Bhabha Fellowship which gave me the means to travel around the country to study Indian folk forms. I put together my provident fund from OUP and the money I saved from the fellowship, and bought a house in Dharwad's Saraswatpur.

But my decision to put down roots in Dharwad never materialized. When I was still in Madras, Karanth had written: 'G.V. Iyer is planning to make a film based on S.L. Bhyrappa's novel *Vamsha Vriksha*. He has been asking me to direct it. Will you join me?' I had developed a deep interest in the film medium after writing the screenplay for *Samskara* and acting in it. My desire to direct a film was still unfulfilled, so I wrote back to Karanth saying, 'I will be your assistant director.' Karanth said, 'Not assistant director, but co-director. We can direct the film jointly.' I agreed. Since Bhyrappa was in Delhi at the time, G.V. Iyer, Karanth and I went there to speak to him. I returned to Dharwad, after which Karanth went quiet for two or three months.

Vamsha Vriksha was a much-beloved novel of the era. It had at its heart the conflict between Katyayini, a widow who remarries and endures great hardships, and her father-in-law Shrotri, an embodiment of the shining ideals of the Hindu tradition. Every middle-class household in Karnataka had shed tears at the story, and *Vamsha Vriksha* was much sought after in the Kannada film world. Giants such as Puttanna Kanagal and Siddalingaiah had been eager to make a film based on the novel, but Bhyrappa had not consented.

Right around this time, G.V. Iyer re-entered Karanth's life. I say re-entered because when Karanth was in the Gubbi theatre company, G.V. Iyer and his wife had looked after young Karanth like he was their son. 'There have been times when Iyer and his wife were too hard up to cook at home, but they sent for two rice plates from a hotel and shared them with me,' Karanth would often say.

After he left the Gubbi company, Iyer took up film-making. He worked with the film-maker B.R. Panthulu for a while, then directed films independently without much success. After the spectacular failure of his film *Chowkada Deepa* – viewers had apparently been so enraged that they had ripped up seat cushions in the theatres – he had fled his creditors and sought refuge in Karanth's house in Delhi. While he was there, he read *Vamsha Vriksha,* was inspired like every other film-maker, and went to Bhyrappa to seek permission to adapt it for the screen. Bhyrappa is supposed to have said, 'I will agree if Karanth will direct.' This did not go down well with Iyer, who said, 'But Karanth has absolutely no experience in film-making.' Bhyrappa apparently told him, 'Even Karanth's failures are more artistic than others' successes.' This was the winding road by which I came to *Vamsha Vriksha.*

After several weeks of silence, Karanth suddenly materialized at the Manohara Grantha Mala atta. 'All right, when do we start shooting?' he asked. I got irritated. I told him, 'Karanth, we don't have a script, we haven't done any casting, we don't know what the budget is, we haven't decided where we are going to shoot. What do you mean "when do we start shooting"?' He seemed mystified and said, 'Oh, I see. It never occurred to me. I thought this is like a play too – we just start...' He disappeared once again.

Karanth's wandering ways were mainly a result of his financial condition. It had become a way of life for him, beginning in childhood when he had run away from home to join the Gubbi theatre company. Later, he went to Varanasi and did an MA in Hindi, studied at NSD in Delhi, and worked as a Hindi schoolteacher in the city. He married Prema, and when they did not have children, he encouraged her to join NSD as a student.

At this time, the realization was dawning across India that it took a technically trained person to direct a play. But the only place where such training could be obtained was NSD, and not enough students of direction had graduated yet. Karanth was one of the first students of NSD. So, Suresh Awasthi, secretary of the Sangeet Natak Akademi, had created opportunities across India for Karanth to conduct workshops on direction, and to direct plays with local theatre groups and impart training. The kind of service Karanth did to Indian theatre in that period, travelling across the country by himself, was unique in that it had not been done by anyone before, and it did not need doing afterwards. But as a consequence of his itinerant life, those close to Karanth always had to be prepared for the possibility of his vanishing suddenly.

Around this time, S.G. Vasudev – art director for *Samskara* and now for *Vamsha Vriksha* – got married in Bangalore. I attended the wedding and went to Coonoor, where my friend Ashok Kulkarni was living. I installed myself at his house and wrote the screenplay for *Vamsha Vriksha*. I returned to Dharwad and waited for Karanth.

Both novels – *Samskara* and *Vamsha Vriksha* – were similar in some aspects and had attracted much attention, so the literary world was full of discussions comparing the two. I had appreciated *Vamsha Vriksha* for its richly detailed portrayal of family life, its layered analysis of human conflicts, and its depiction of the barely perceptible cruelties, aggressions and sensitivities that flicker into and out of existence in the course of daily life. Since the book was very long, it became necessary to leave out parts of it while writing the screenplay. But *Vamsha Vriksha* did not possess the intellectual depth of *Samskara*, and when it came to discussing Hindu dharma or Indian history, the book was disappointingly simplistic. So much so that it caused one to wonder if Bhyrappa was truly a professor of philosophy. While I had liked *Samskara* more, I can say that I enjoyed the process of writing the screenplay for *Vamsha Vriksha*.

One day, I travelled to Bangalore to catch a flight to Calcutta, where I was to participate in a seminar. I alighted from the train, and waiting for me on the platform was the pair of Karanth and Iyer. I never left for Calcutta, and it was three or four months before I returned to Dharwad. Iyer said, 'The owner of Premier Studios, M.S. Basavarajaiah has agreed to finance *Vamsha Vriksha*. We have to start shooting right now.' He took us to NMH Hotel in Basavanagudi and shoved us into a room as if it were a prison cell.

From then on, Iyer attached himself to Karanth and me until the film was made. He had an extra bed installed in our room and stayed with us. He ate with us. He kept us under such close surveillance that it was impossible for the two of us to talk in confidence. When we absolutely had to, we took an autorickshaw somewhere and made it our private chamber. To this day, I have not been able to completely understand this aspect of Iyer's behaviour. Perhaps he had experienced so much deceit, betrayal and tragedy at a young age that he had lost the capacity to trust others, and feared we were always plotting and conspiring against him. Whatever it was, I found his constant presence suffocating.

Several well-wishers from the film world had warned us: 'Don't trust Iyer.' Since Kanakanahalli Gopi, who had worked with me on *Samskara*, was close to several people in Gandhinagar, we were constantly getting reports about all the people Iyer had cheated. We had asked Iyer to play the part of Shrotri's father. In the book, when this character realizes that it is impossible for him to have children of his own, he finds a man to impregnate his wife and has him stay at home. He unceremoniously throws out the man once his wife conceives. After seeing the film, Gubbi Veeranna's daughter Malatamma congratulated us: 'Well done! You found the most appropriate actor for the role.'

We soon saw with our own eyes the fast and loose ways in which Iyer made his way around the bylanes of Gandhinagar's financial world. One day, Iyer was in a private meeting in a distributor's office while Karanth, Gopi and I sat in the waiting room. A man rushed in from outside and, without even glancing at us, barged into the office. For a while we heard raised voices from within. Then the man emerged, with Iyer's collar firmly grasped in one hand. Even as Iyer made feeble attempts to placate him, the man berated him:

'Come with me, I will show you. Let's see how you escape today ... ' The man disappeared, dragging Iyer behind him. We sat there stunned. Our dreams of becoming Kannada's Satyajit Rays were vanishing in front of our eyes.

After a while, the man and Iyer materialized again. The hand that had gripped Iyer's collar was now wrapped affectionately around him, caressing his shoulder. The man's other hand was holding Iyer's right hand and pressing it to his chest. He said to Iyer in front of us in the waiting room, 'Aiyo, forgive me! I made a mistake. This wretched temper of mine ... I will fall at your feet if you want,' and so on, all the while groaning in profound regret, repeatedly joining his palms in entreaty. Iyer, as if he was forgiving a boy who didn't know better, said sagely, 'Fine, fine. You can leave now.' Without looking at either us or the man retreating with his palms still joined, Iyer went back into the office in a manner that suggested that what had happened was not of the slightest importance.

We asked him about it later. 'I told him: "This film has to be made if I am to return your money. It is being made by none other than Basavarajaiah. You can call him and check if you like. But if the monkey behaviour you just displayed scares those two boys and makes them leave, the film will not be made. You will not see your money, either in this life or the next. You've made a big blunder, now go correct it in front of them." You saw the rest,' he said, laughing.

As he grew more comfortable with me, he recounted several brazen exploits from his past. He told me, frankly and cheerfully, about the people he had cheated and how he had gone about it, the times he had got away and the times he hadn't. He nodded happily when I told him, 'You should write all this down.' He began to write his autobiography for the film magazine *Menaka,* edited by V.N. Subba Rao, and he did not shy away from revealing his questionable dealings. One day, YNK told him, 'There's no need, Iyer. Stop all this now,' and he just stopped. Because of this film, Iyer found a moral compass in the form of YNK.

We had asked Bhaskar Chandavarkar, who was teaching music at Poona's film institute to be our music director. Through him, we found our cinematographer Sharief, who had been a gold medallist at the institute. Along with him came our associate cinematographer S. Ramachandra, who ended up being a lifelong collaborator.

The house in Nanjangud we had settled on as the setting for Shrotri's house belonged to orthodox Brahmins. Karanth and I thought they might not be comfortable with a Muslim cinematographer walking around their house, so we renamed Sharief as 'Guru'. Not once did any of us slip up and call him anything other than Guru during the shooting. After we had finished shooting, the family invited us to a meal that Guru was unable to attend. The head of the family asked, 'How come Sharief is not here?' It turned out they knew the cinematographer's real name all along, after having read an article about the film in the *Prajavani* newspaper.

My mother had insisted that we get an actor from Bombay named Venkatarao Talgeri to play the role of Shrotri. I did not show much interest – he was from our community, and I did not want any favouritism. But Aayi summoned him to Bangalore without asking me. Iyer took one look at him, said 'Aha!' in appreciation, and approved Aayi's choice.

It was more difficult finding someone to play Katyayini. In those days, girls from middle-class families would make a face as soon as you mentioned acting in films. 'No, no, not films' was a refrain I had become tired of hearing ever since we began casting for *Samskara*. In addition, we heard that Kalpana, who was then widely regarded as the finest actress in Kannada cinema, had taunted us by saying, 'Who else is there to play Katyayini? The part is sure to come to me eventually.' This annoyed Karanth and me further.

One day, a young woman named L.V. Sharada came and met us at YNK's house. Karanth and I were elated as soon as we saw her, but when she said, 'You must meet my father and seek his consent,' we both thought, 'Oh god! Not again.' But there was no way out.

Sharada's father was L.S. Venkaji Rao, a man of considerable standing in society and a politician of renown. Despite this, he had no airs, and welcomed us warmly at his house. He had read *Vamsha Vriksha,* and he told us, 'I know the novel very well. The story moved me so much that I took to bed with a fever after I read it.' But when it came to the subject of Sharada acting in the film, he was firm: 'No, it's not possible.' Karanth's face fell. I engaged in some further small talk out of politeness. When I looked at Karanth after a while, he was nodding off, as if now that there was no point talking any more, he might as well catch up on his sleep. I was burning up inside, but I continued to exchange pleasantries with Venkaji Rao. He, being a politician, launched into a commentary about our cultural life and at one point said, 'It is our society's misfortune that its middle class does not support courageous artists such as yourself.' I immediately replied, 'Then why do you say no to us?' For a moment, Venkaji Rao was taken aback. He sheepishly said, 'You have caught me out,' and agreed to let Sharada be part of the film. The women of the house, who had gathered there for tea, broke into smiles. Maybe they were eager to see her act, or maybe they knew how eager she was to act.

We later realized that both Talgeri and Sharada were even better actors than we had reckoned.

After watching the film, in which Katyayini endures widowhood, goes through a miscarriage and eventually dies, Sharada's mother was reported to have burst into tears and said, 'Aiyo, they didn't spare my daughter anything.' Surprisingly, it took me many years to realize that this story, in which a widow with a son marries again, resembled my own mother's life.

Though the character of Prithvi in *Vamsha Vriksha* is a minor one, the actor's story is worth recounting. Kanakanahalli Gopi was once in a restaurant without the change to pay for his tea, when a young man from National College, Sampath Kumar, offered to pay. Gopi told him to go to YNK's house and meet me: 'Girish Karnad is looking for a young man to play a part in the film. Come without fail.'

The next day, I was alone in YNK's house, working on something, when a young man of around eighteen came and sat down. It was Sampath Kumar. He was tall, extremely handsome, and fit to be a film hero. He carried himself with great self-confidence.

'Do you have any experience of acting?' I asked.

'Oh, yes. I play the lead role in all the plays in National College.'

'Have you ever acted in a film?'

'I haven't completed any films yet, but I have signed three or four. I'm playing the hero in a Hindi film opposite Mala Sinha.'

'You're going to be acting with such a big star! But she must be much older than you.'

'Oh, you haven't seen her. She looks like she's eighteen. We're about to start shooting for one film, and I've been offered two others,' he said with considerable swagger.

'When is the shooting?'

'The outdoor is next month. Song picturization in Ooty, but we might go to Kashmir as well.'

'Oh. That means we will not get you. We are planning to start shooting in another fifteen days. It's a pity.'

Sampath Kumar froze. He said in a low voice, 'I didn't get who you are.'

'My name is Girish Karnad,' I said.

Sampath Kumar's haughtiness crumbled in an instant. He surrendered in a flood of words that tumbled over each other: 'Aiyo, I didn't realize who you were! Forgive me, sir. There's still time for my Hindi shooting. Mala Sinha is a very busy actress. She's not available for another eight months it seems. You have nothing to worry about, sir. I am free. I will come whenever you need me. I'll stay for as long as you want.' He had thought I was another aspiring actor there for the role, and everything he had said was to sap my confidence.

Sampath Kumar appeared as 'Kumar' in the title credits. Puttanna Kanagal saw him in *Vamsha Vriksha* and cast him as the lead in *Naagarahaavu*. Kanagal named him Vishnuvardhan, and he went on to become one of the biggest stars in Kannada cinema. When we acted together in *Nee Bareda Kadambari*, he came clean about his pretence during our first meeting and laughed heartily at his naïveté. But when he gave interviews to the press, he always gave credit to Kanagal: 'It was Puttanna Kanagal who discovered my talent.'

Years later, Vishnuvardhan invited me home to talk about making a film based on my play *Taledanda*. His large drawing room had walls that were completely covered with posters and memorabilia from his various films. A plasma screen television played one of his films. Everywhere you looked, there was Vishnuvardhan's face. Right in the middle of all this, just like in a cinema set, was a staircase with shiny gold banisters leading to the floor above. After we had finished talking, Vishnuvardhan said, 'I have everything, Girish. Except happiness.' His wife, Bharati, was sitting right in front of him. I wanted to say, 'Break these walls and put in a couple of large windows to let in fresh air. Happiness will come on its own.' But I didn't.

Another person who was keen on having a part in *Vamsha Vriksha* was G.V. Iyer's second wife, Saroja. Iyer had been indicating from the beginning that we should use her in the film, but he did not seem enthusiastic when I said we could give her the role of the domestic worker Lakshmi. When we chose Uma Shivakumar for this role, Iyer shrugged and laughed bitterly, as if he wanted to convey, 'What say could I possibly have when you're both so obstinate?' We were about to finish shooting the scenes set in Shrotri's house in Nanjangud and leave for Mysore to film scenes of Prof. Sadashiva Rao's family life when Iyer began to get anxious: 'We must give Saroja a role.' But we had already decided on Goda Ramkumar to play the professor's wife Nagalakshmi.

Goda was an enormously talented actress. Even when she had only a few scenes, she was capable of using them to convey a character's travails with nuance. Neither Karanth nor I wanted to take the risk of giving the part to someone like Saroja, who had absolutely no acting experience.

We came to Mysore after finishing shooting in Nanjangud. Accommodation for the entire unit had been arranged at Adinath Lodge. Inevitably, Iyer was expected to stay at his wife's house in Mysore, away from Karanth and me. As a result, his antics took on a new form. Though we all met every day for shooting, Iyer began to write imploring letters to Karanth, saying that if Saroja was not given a part, his life would be in danger. What had been an annoyance in spoken form became excruciating in writing. Iyer began to lament: 'I have borrowed money from Saroja's brothers, and I can't repay them. They say they will let me be if I give Saroja a part. Otherwise, they are threatening to kill me.' Karanth and I decided to sort the issue out with Saroja herself, and went to her house after making sure that Iyer was away. I waited outside in the autorickshaw. After some twenty minutes, Iyer rushed there in another auto. He glared at me and ran into the house. Karanth had finished talking with Saroja in the meanwhile. He emerged and told me, 'Iyer has not told Saroja that we don't want her. He's been reassuring her every day that the role is hers. She started crying when I told her we would not give her that role.' I said, 'If she had her mind set so firmly on playing a part, then we could have given her Lakshmi. It's not a very difficult part.' Karanth explained, 'Oh, Saroja doesn't want to play the part of a domestic worker. She wants to play a virtuous Brahmin woman.'

After this visit, Iyer took Karanth aside and, as usual, created an enormous scene. Karanth and I had already agreed on what to tell Iyer, and Karanth laid out the threat: 'If we give Saroja that part, Girish has said he will quit the film.' I was not only the co-director, I was also playing the lead role of

Raja Rao. Iyer was helpless and he did not bring up Saroja again. Her brothers, too, seemed to have vanished. But after *Vamsha Vriksha* was released, Iyer directed (from behind the scenes) Anant Nag's debut film *Sankalpa,* and he used Saroja in one of the main roles. The film was a failure. 'How was Sarojamma's acting?' I asked him later. He winked and laughed.

Karanth and I had decided to direct the film together, something we knew wasn't an easy task. Thankfully, we complemented each other well – what one of us lacked in experience or ability, the other was usually able to provide. Of course, there were minor differences and annoyances, but for the most part, we consulted each other and were in agreement on various aspects of the film-making process.

One day, Karanth said, 'When I meet a man who knows more than me, I keep quiet and learn from him. I have the confidence that I can do better than him in the future.' Though he didn't say so explicitly, I understood at once that his words referred to me. I had no argument with what he was saying – my attitude in life was the same. But within a decade, Karanth had lost this competitive fire and become complacent. That was the beginning of his decline.

I had studied all the books I could find on film-making. Besides, I had some practical exposure to the art by virtue of having been part of *Samskara*. This was all new to Karanth, but he was an expert at working with actors to draw from them the response required by the director. It was during the making of *Vamsha Vriksha* that I learnt from him how to interweave the gestures and expressions of actors with their larger movements while composing a scene. Once a scene had been composed, I would take care of its division into shots, and Karanth would manage the actors.

I also did not know as well as Karanth the nuances of how the members of a traditional Hindu family behave with each other – when they speak, when they remain silent, how they stand, where they sit, and so on. He had moved around in different sections of society and he possessed experiences I could not even imagine. This had given him an admirable sensitivity, especially when it came to directing women and children. We spent months living together in schools, public halls and hotels, all the while having conversations and arguments. Beyond the context of the film, this gave me a deeper understanding of the invisible emotional currents coursing through Hindu society.

Gopi and YNK had found a boy named Chandrashekhar for the role of Cheeni. Just as he chose Kumar (Vishnuvardhan) for *Naagarahaavu*, Puttanna Kanagal cast Chandrashekhar as the hero in *Edakallu Guddada Mele*. He did not prove successful as an actor, but still, when the film was being made, he announced, 'There is no director in Kannada as brilliant as Puttanna Kanagal,' and annoyed Karanth.

The owner of Mysore's Premier Studios, M.N. Basavarajaiah extended support to *Vamsha Vriksha* in the form of camera, equipment and crew. The crew did not have experience working outdoors, and this caused problems from time to time. Further, the screenplay was very long, and shooting dragged on much longer than expected. Though Iyer did not show any impatience with the delay, he seemed unhappy with the film while it was being shot. He would take Chandrashekhar and Kumar to one side and grumble: 'The only people I can show this film to will be my wife and children, using a home projector.' His attitude changed completely once he saw the rushes. He began to go around beaming, making small talk with everyone.

The person who disappointed us in the technical department was Sharief. Our hearts sank when we saw all the rushes after completing shooting: there were long bands of shadows on the walls; what should have been out of sight frequently intruded into the edges of the frame; some shots were out of focus. None of this worried Iyer. He raved: 'What texture! His photography has such texture!' S. Ramachandra, who was part of the cinematography team, had an explanation for this: 'Iyer is used to the smooth walls and bare pillars of a studio set. The rough edges of a real house are what he's calling "texture".' This seemed quite accurate.

One day, I was at the studio looking at the rushes when a round-faced, curly-haired man with a moustache as sharp as a sword's edge appeared in front of me in blinding white clothes, joined his palms in greeting, and said in a deep voice: 'This artist renders his heartfelt salutations to the brilliant Girish Karnad, who is engaged in the admirable task of leading Kannada cinema in a new direction.' I was taken aback. I managed to say, 'Forgive me, I didn't place you.' He said, 'They call me Udaykumar.' I recognized him as being a famous actor and stammered some more. 'Is there a shooting going on?' I asked. 'I am playing the lead role in twelve films,' he answered theatrically.

A few weeks later, in Dharwad, I was walking about in Dharwad Hotel when I heard a deep voice call out, 'Hey, Girish!' I turned around and it was Udaykumar. He addressed me casually in the singular, as if we had known each other since we were boys. He said, 'I'm telling you this because you're a Brahmin. In this Kannada film industry of ours, there's no hope for anyone who wears a sacred thread. Careful!' He thrust his hand into his collar and pulled out his sacred thread as if it were a bowstring. 'If they see this, they'll use it to cut your throat,' he rumbled. I don't remember how the meeting ended.

Vamsha Vriksha was edited at Premier Studios. Aruna Raje, a gold medallist at Poona's film institute, came down for editing along with her director husband Vikas Desai. On the way, Aruna broke her leg in a car accident. 'Let us wait for her,' Iyer said. His thinking was that she, being a student of the institute, might have something new or special to bring to the film. Aruna and Vikas were stunned by Iyer's patience. Aruna repeatedly expressed her gratitude to Iyer and acknowledged his artistic vision. She said, 'No one waits like this in the industry. They just change the technicians if there is going to be a delay.'

Basavarajaiah was alarmed when he saw the first cut. Rather than use the musty editing conventions of Kannada cinema, Aruna and Vikas had drawn inspiration from French and Italian new wave cinema. In some places, they had slowed down scenes compared to reality. And in some places, Karanth and I, influenced by *L'Année dernière à Marienbad* and *The Pawnbroker,* had decided to use quick, two-to-three-second flash cuts instead of extended flashback scenes. We were eager to experiment, and Iyer had supported us.

Basavarajaiah called Iyer, Karanth and me for a meeting and told us firmly, 'I don't understand this film at all. If we leave it like this, it won't run for even two days. It must be re-edited thoroughly. Let us show the rushes to accomplished directors like M.R. Vitthal and Puttanna Kanagal, and re-edit under their guidance.' After this was discussed for a while, I said, 'What is the use of involving these senior directors? If the editing has to meet with their approval, the shots will also have to be to their taste. We will have to reshoot the film accordingly, which is not possible now. If we get them to re-edit the existing material, the film will be neither theirs nor ours.' Basavarajaiah concurred. 'That is a valid point,' he said. 'So, I will give up my association with this film. Let Iyer pay me one lakh rupees in return for what I have put into the film, and I will step back.' Iyer accepted the deal, and the meeting ended there. Going by the alacrity with which he agreed with me, it seemed that Basavarajaiah had decided to withdraw from the film even before discussing the matter with us.

Iyer was overjoyed. In those days, the government provided 50,000 rupees to each film as a subsidy. That was anyway going to Basavarajaiah, so if Iyer managed to give him another 50,000, he would be the sole producer of the film. He said, 'Oh, I'll get that 50,000 out of some distributor or the other, don't worry.'

But Basavarajaiah was not done with his games yet. We were in Madras for the film's music composition and sound mixing when there was an outcry from Mysore: 'The picture and dialogue are out of sync in the re-recording print. Your editors don't know their work.' Aruna and Vikas rushed to Mysore, where the treachery of the Premier lab became evident. Even the most inept editor will not have a mismatch of more than a frame or two – a couple of inches – between the picture negative and sound negative. Here, every reel had a mismatch of three or four feet. The lab's head, a Marathi man himself, did his best to avoid Aruna and Vikas.

Anyway, the reels were brought to Madras in their mismatched condition, and the visuals and dialogue joined again in the sound studio. This wasted both time and money, but Iyer did not despair.

Karanth would say of Bhaskar Chandavarkar, 'Anything he composes becomes melodious.' We had used one of Chandrasekhar Kambar's songs as a refrain throughout the film. During those two or three days of recording, Sharada was full of childlike rapture, stopping just short of dancing around the studio.

The owner of Minerva theatre, M. Bhaktavatsala, agreed to distribute the film. Iyer was ecstatic: 'Bhaktavatsala is the president of the Karnataka Film Chamber of Commerce. Basavarajaiah will not go against him easily.' Despite this, Basavarajaiah was not quite finished.

Though Bhakta had agreed to pay an advance of 75,000 rupees to distribute the film, he reduced it to 65,000 at the last minute and upset Iyer. But Bhakta gave the film a grand release without compromising on either publicity or reach. In addition, several journalists at the time – YNK, V.N. Subba Rao, M.B. Singh, Vaikuntharaju, among others – took a personal interest in cinema. *Vamsha Vriksha* received sumptuous coverage in the press.

Accolades rained down on *Vamsha Vriksha* at that year's state awards: best film, best direction, best actor (Venkatarao Talgeri), best actress (Sharada), and awards for editing, story and dialogue.

Though the new actors and actresses came in for praise from both viewers and critics, it became clear that Karanth and I, as a result of our mutual respect, had not directed each other very well. The two of us, experienced actors though we were, ended up being roundly criticized for our performances.

Basavarajaiah was disgruntled by the unexpected success of the film. The one lakh he had asked for to relinquish his role as producer had been given to him when the film was released. But the film he was certain would sink without a trace had done remarkably well at the box office. Then, there was the 50,000 rupees that came with the state award, and any further money that might come in if the film won awards at the national level. Basavarajaiah was not happy to be left out of all this, nor was he the kind of person who would sit by idly in this situation.

When the details of the year's award winners were published in the newspapers, the producer of *Vamsha Vriksha* was listed as Premier Studios. The Film Officer at the time, a man named Palegar, was a close associate of Basavarajaiah, and the two of them had colluded to remove all mention of Iyer's association with the film.

I was astonished at the brazenness of it all. Since I had some experience of contracts from my time at OUP, I thoroughly examined the various agreements between Iyer and Basavarajaiah, and quickly found that even god would be unable to untangle this particular contractual mess. In those days – perhaps even now – applications had to be written to the government at every stage of making a film: to acquire film negative, for outdoor shooting, for receiving subsidies, and so on. It turned out that some of these papers named Iyer as the producer, some named Basavarajaiah, and yet others listed them both. It was abundantly clear that it would be useless to go to court.

Karanth wrote a letter to Basavarajaiah saying, 'You should not have done this.' As I expected, there was no reply. I said, 'As if that rogue will care for your gentle words. There's only one solution to this. All of us award winners must unite and inform the government that we will boycott the ceremony if Iyer is not given the producer's award.' The others agreed.

The chief secretary in the administration, Praxy Fernandes, had a reputation for being an official of exceptional intelligence and integrity. (He had used his position to study official records and write a book about Tipu Sultan and Hyder Ali called *The Tigers of Mysore* that any historian would be proud of.) Fernandes arranged a meeting at which all parties to the dispute were present. Basavarajaiah went on the offensive against Iyer right away by saying, 'I will not bow down to this wretch in a dhoti.'

Bhaktavatsala argued, 'But the credit titles at the start of the film say "Presented by G.V. Iyer",' to which Palegar said, 'Not in the print that was given to me.' I said, 'Then someone has cut that portion. It is not a difficult task to show that this is an unauthorized edit. That title appears over a rocking cradle, and there is bound to be a jump in the shot where the film has been cut. Bring us your print and play it for us.' Bhakta said, 'If you want, I will bring the print from my office and screen it.' Palegar appeared anguished. 'It's not right to level such accusations at a government official,' he said. From the way he was slowly getting off his high horse, it was becoming clear that he had not expected this protest from us. Karanth said firmly, 'It doesn't matter what proof or witnesses are presented. Our stand will not change. We don't want any awards if our condition is not met.' In the end, Praxy Fernandes decided that the producer's award would be shared equally by Iyer and Basavarajaiah.

At the ceremony, Iyer, gaunt and dressed in a white shirt and dhoti without any footwear, was seated next to a round-faced, corpulent Basavarajaiah. As prizewinners, we had decided in advance what to do. When we were called on stage, we ignored Basavarajaiah but shook hands with Iyer and congratulated him. Everyone at the event noticed that we had shunned a prestigious member of the Kannada film world, but this is unlikely to have made much of a difference to either Iyer or Basavarajaiah. As can be inferred from this story told by Iyer about his 'co-producer':

One evening, Iyer and Basavarajaiah were walking down a street near the studio when a woman stopped Basavarajaiah, abused him filthily, took off her slipper and thrashed him for a while, before she left screaming and cursing. Basavarajaiah remained impassive through all this, and when the woman left, he said, 'I sunk her family by grabbing everything they had. Shouldn't I at least let her take it out on me a little bit?'

I don't know how much of this story is true and how much is Iyer's embellishment, but I will say that when Iyer narrated the story, it was not without an element of admiration.

Still, in that year or two, Iyer changed and grew in front of our eyes to an extent I have never witnessed in another human being. He was fifty-four when we made *Vamsha Vriksha*, an age by which most people's development has ended. Iyer seemed to start growing at that age. He realized that he had wasted half a century in petty wrangling, and now, newly awakened, he wanted to make the most of the years he had left. He had spent his childhood in poverty, working in drama companies, and from there he had moved on to cinema in the rough-and-tumble early days of the Kannada film industry. Now, through me and Karanth, he heard of world-renowned directors such as Satyajit Ray, Fellini, Antonioni and others, and grew familiar with their work. He had discussions with YNK, with those who had come from FTII – Bhaskar Chandavarkar, S. Ramachandra, Aruna and Vikas – and learnt from them. His talent found a new creative direction. The same person who had made *Chowkada Deepa* now made *Hamsageethe*, whose screenplay, clearly influenced by Ingmar Bergman, bears witness to Iyer's newly burgeoning talent.

He went on to make *Adi Shankaracharya*, *Madhvacharya* and *Ramanujacharya* with support from the respective mutths, win national awards, and earn social recognition as well as plenty of wealth. When he said he was going to direct *Adi Shankaracharya*, I asked him, 'What is the use of making a film in Sanskrit? Who will watch it?' He said, 'Tell me, Girish, who watches even the Kannada films I make?'

One day in 1975, after Iyer had finished making *Hamsageethe*, he was with Karanth when I burst in excitedly. I had just watched Girish Kasaravalli's *Ghatashraddha*. 'What an extraordinary film Kasaravalli has made!' I said. Iyer sat quietly. Later, Karanth said to me, 'Did you see Iyer's face when you praised that film? He was burning with envy.' I too had noticed it. Iyer's strength lay in being able to convert this envy into creative energy.

Iyer was one of the most shrewd, intelligent, creative and inventive people I have met in my life.

OPEN-AIR THEATRE

Around the time Karanth and I were finishing work on *Vamsha Vriksha*, the writer P. Lankesh said to Karanth, 'Bangalore University is hosting a three-day seminar on drama. Why not have a theatre festival alongside?' He took up the responsibility of organizing it. The interiors of Ravindra Kalakshetra were being renovated at the time, so Karanth decided to have the plays in the open area behind Kalakshetra. When I saw the space, I said, 'The tall pillars here are perfect for Greek plays. Why don't we perform *Oedipus*? It will be good if Lankesh himself translates it into Kannada.' Lankesh agreed.

I came to Bangalore and, along with Karanth, checked into Kamat Lodge at Minerva Circle. In the initial days of making *Vamsha Vriksha*, we had stayed at NMH, but since we were now working in Ravindra Kalakshetra, it was Kamat Lodge that became our headquarters in Bangalore.

Those three weeks went by in a daze. I had not been part of a Kannada play in the thirteen years since I had left Karnatak College. Karanth and Lankesh had decided that the festival would have productions of Chandrasekhar Kambar's *Jokumaraswamy*, Lankesh's *Sankranti* and Sophocles's *Oedipus* (translated by Lankesh). Karanth asked me to play Gowda in *Jokumaraswamy* and Oedipus, two roles that had absolutely nothing in common. The burden of this responsibility left me with no chance of getting even a moment's untroubled sleep. Since Karanth's entire day was spent in conducting rehearsals, I was on my own when it came to interpreting the characters. In any case, Karanth's method had no patience for discussing the outline of the play or considering its overall structure. His method was to dive right in and have the actors moving from day one. If obstacles cropped up along the way, Karanth would find a way to get around them.

I took great delight in saying Kambar's lines, written in the Kannada of North Karnataka. I savoured the rhythm of his sentences, the novelty and charm of his words. I took his guidance to learn this distinctive manner of speech and internalized it. But when it came to the dialogue in *Oedipus*, I had to refer to English versions by Yeats, David Grene and others to edit Lankesh's uneven translation.

By then, Karanth had become well-known for his cinema and theatre work, and so adolescent boys who nursed dreams of becoming actors would come to Ravindra Kalakshetra and flock around us. From the look in these boys' eyes – wonder, reverence, ambition – it was clear to both of us that we had begun to acquire a halo. As we moved about with this group of youths behind us, we occasionally overheard hushed words of admiration. But we behaved as if we had heard nothing.

The theatre festival was extraordinarily successful. The gates were opened only at the last minute before *Jokumaraswamy* was performed. The spectacle of viewers standing in a long line to enter after having bought tickets has perhaps never been seen before or since in the history of amateur theatre in Bangalore. *Jokumaraswamy* did not disappoint anyone. North Karnataka's rugged Kannada took over the Bangalore stage for the first time, and it did so in great style. The production had songs with beautiful melodies (borrowed from the folk play *Sangya Balya*), suggestive dialogue, humour, dance. It was all electrifying.

Dore Oedipus came at the end of the festival and proved a unique and powerful experience for the Bangalore audience. The play's intensity and its remorseless build-up to a tragedy are capable of shaking the strongest viewer. Karanth had invited the Kannada actor Rajkumar, who had been with him in the Gubbi company, to watch the play. Rajkumar said, 'Abba! This torture is unbearable.'

As the play's reputation grew, members of the public without much exposure to theatre came to watch it. This section of the audience, unable to take the intensity of the play, began to titter and laugh to ease their own discomfort. It became difficult for me to tell whether I was acting in a tragedy or a farce. I spoke to Karanth and we stopped further performances. Be it theatre or films, Indian viewers cannot tolerate anything that makes them uncomfortable.

Today, the open-air theatre we performed in has been officially named Samsa Open Air Auditorium. It was B.V. Karanth who identified the potential

As Oedipus in *Dore Oedipus* (1971)

of this space, so it should have been named Babukodi Venkatramana Karanth Open Air Auditorium.

Unfortunately, Lankesh's *Sankranti* was completely overshadowed by the success of the other two plays. Lankesh had undertaken the entire venture so he could triumphantly fly his flag over the Kannada stage. But when the festival ended, it was Chandrasekhar Kambar, considered a minor writer until then, who came to be acknowledged as an important playwright. Karanth established beyond a doubt that he was an extraordinary director. Though I had acted in *Samskara,* I had never been seen on the Kannada stage, and with this festival, I secured for myself a place in the history of Kannada theatre. But *Sankranti* had proved insipid, and Lankesh, who was already known as a playwright, emerged diminished from the event. The seminar at Bangalore University that ran parallel to the festival gave a literary imprimatur to this turning of the tables. The demotion must have been intolerable for an ambitious and sensitive person like Lankesh, and he was not the kind of person to sulk quietly in a corner.

At the time, T.N. Seetaram and L. Krishnappa had started a magazine called *Mukta* to publish commentary on the ongoing theatre revolution in Bangalore. Lankesh wrote an article for it which, under the pretext of showing affection for Karanth, only tried to humiliate him. I found it repulsive. Along with him, Prasanna, Nagesh and other theatre-persons who were resentful of Karanth's newfound success attacked him, and along with him *Hayavadana,* which owed its favourable reception entirely to his direction.

On another front, Lankesh attempted to portray me as YNK's lover. I told Karanth in disgust, 'This person calls himself modern. How can he think it is an abuse to call someone a homosexual? If I were truly gay, I would talk about it openly.' I returned to Dharwad and became entirely indifferent towards Bangalore theatre.

A few days after this issue of *Mukta* was released, Karanth and I were sitting at Kamat Lodge discussing the envy burning all around us. Just then, a writer who had criticized Karanth in it turned up. He sat with us for a while, laughing and chatting as if nothing had happened, and finally, he said to me, 'I need to discuss something privately with Karanth. Could you step out for five minutes?' I said, quite brusquely, 'No, I cannot. This is my room. If there's something you can't say in my presence, then meet Karanth elsewhere.' He left in a huff.

Karanth said, 'I can't break relationships like you. He's not a bad fellow. I hope to gently bring him around to our point of view.' I said, 'Karanth, don't be so naïve. You are no longer just a meshtru, a teacher. You are now an establishment figure.' Karanth looked shocked, as if I had just abused him. 'I am an establishment figure too,' I said. 'No one else in our generation has earned the kind of national recognition we both have. Remember that anyone who comes to you now, comes with the purpose of exploiting you.' Karanth looked bewildered. He said, 'If Lankesh said something like this, I would think it is just his nature. But you are saying this about yourself. I am speechless.' He remained quiet for a while.

As a result of Lankesh's article in *Mukta,* YNK broke off all relations with him. Lankesh's acolyte K. Marulasiddappa once told me that, since then, the *Prajavani* newspaper made it a mission of sorts to disparage Lankesh.

Lankesh did not write plays for a long time after this episode.

KAADU

It must have been in 1969 that G.B. Joshi gave me the manuscript of a new novel called *Kraurya,* by a young writer named Srikrishna Alanahalli, that had come to Manohara Grantha Mala. Though it was a straightforward narration of events occurring in a village in Mandya district, the novel had a special quality to it. In this period, villages were depicted as places in which man lived in the lap of nature and led either an idyllic or a helpless life, as places where, though afflicted by poverty and social inequality, people were fundamentally simple, straightforward and innocent. *Kraurya* offered a departure from this romantic view. It was clearly influenced by Kuvempu's *Kanooru Heggadithi,* and though it lacked the latter's humour and expansiveness, it had a thematic unity and a wonderful philosophical underpinning that were all its own.

A young man named Kencha, from Koppalu village, works in Shivaganga's house in nearby Hosuru. Kencha is accused of adultery, and a panchayat meeting is called in Koppalu. Shivaganga goes to attend the meeting, since Kencha works for him, but a senior member of one village is not expected to attend legal proceedings in another without an explicit invitation. Shivaganga violates etiquette by going there, and as a result, gets into a confrontation with Chandre Gowda of Koppalu. This flares up into enmity between the villages, and escalates to bloodshed. Finally, the police have to step in to control the situation.

Alanahalli poured into the novel his own experiences with village life, powerfully working into it the constantly simmering violence, the hold of blind tradition, and the status of women and children as little more than chattel. I met Alanahalli when rehearsals were on for *Dore Oedipus* during the seminar at Bangalore University. He was naturally pleased when I told him I had resolved to make a film of his book. I suggested the more indicative title of *Kaadu* (meaning 'forest') for the novel rather than the literal *Kraurya* (meaning 'cruelty'). He liked the idea.

Samskara and *Vamsha Vriksha* may not have made enormous amounts of money, but they had comfortably earned back what had been invested in them. More than that, they had both earned lavish recognition and awards at the national level. (Until then, from Kannada cinema, only Puttanna Kanagal had won a National Award – for the screenplay of his film *Gejje Pooje*.) The two films had also ensured that the people associated with them gained respect and recognition in the Kannada cultural world. It was not only the artistic qualities of these films that were responsible for their financial success. As film-makers, we had also been careful with money, avoiding wasteful expenditure and shooting to a well-defined budget – we may have started making films, but we had not given up the discipline of theatre. The talk in Gandhinagar about this new wave of films was that you didn't have to fear for your investment.

And so, G.N. Lakshmipathy and K.N. Narayan – 'L.N. Combines' – asked me to direct a film for them. I said I would do it if the film was *Kaadu*. They both liked the story.

After the success of *Vamsha Vriksha,* Karanth and I had decided that we did not want to become a pair like Laxmikant–Pyarelal or Dorai–Bhagavan. We wanted to remain distinct and grow individually. I said I would direct *Kaadu* alone, and Karanth came on board as art director and music director. But whether it was in Alanahalli or in Kanakapura (places where the film was shot), there were others in addition to Karanth and I who helped shape the film: cinematographer Govind Nihalani, Gopi, T.S. Nagabharana, and the various guests who visited us. We all slept on mattresses laid out side by side, and after a peg of rum at night, everyone contributed to the discussions.

From what Srikrishna had told me about his novel, Koppalu was a Vokkaliga village and Hosuru a Lingayat village. So there was a backdrop of community conflict to the confrontation described in the book. A major weakness of Srikrishna as a writer was that his characters were all black-and-white, lacking nuance and complexity. It was evident that Srikrishna had taken sides while developing the novel: the Vokkaliga Chandre Gowda has a Lingayat mistress Basakka; the Lingayat Shivaganga rapes the Vokkaliga Gowdti; those who do the mischief of setting fodder on fire are from Hosuru, and it is they who start the fight when there is a festival involving both villages. Given this one-sidedness, there would be an uproar if the novel's handling of the communities was transferred as is to film.

I said, 'Let us avoid this complication entirely. Let's show both villages as being Vokkaliga.' Srikrishna looked at me uncomprehendingly. 'Why?' he asked. I knew from experience that if one group wanted to take offence, they would somehow find a way to do so. And it wasn't long before Srikrishna gained that experience too.

Puttanna Kanagal was about to leave for a film festival in the USSR. Srikrishna had been invited as chief guest to an event hosted in honour of Kanagal by 'Minugu Taare' (Twinkling Star) Kalpana. In those days, the Bangalore film world was firmly divided into two camps: the Rajkumar camp and the Kalpana–Puttanna camp. In his enthusiasm to praise Kalpana, Srikrishna said something like, 'Our audience, which starts clapping when they see the hero's slippers on the silver screen, has not acknowledged Kalpana's brilliance.'

In Rajkumar's films it had become a much-loved convention that when the hero appeared on screen for the first time, all that would be seen was a close up of his feet. Then, to the claps and whistles of the audience, the camera would swivel upwards to show his smugly smiling face. Srikrishna's words were interpreted as being insulting to both Rajkumar and his fans, and resulted in an outcry. Some Rajkumar devotees announced that they were boycotting the film *Kaadu* in protest.

I called them to Kamat Lodge and told them that though the novel was written by Srikrishna, boycotting the film would not affect him in any way. It

The *Kaadu* team: Gopi, Srikrishna Alanahalli, Govind Nihalani, Karanth and I

The Okuli scene from *Kaadu*

would only hurt the film's producers, and the prospect of art films in general. They withdrew their boycott, but still, until the film released, we remained apprehensive about protests. Because, it turns out that the first shot of *Kaadu* is a close-up of Chandre Gowda's slippers! His feet enter the shot, wear the slippers and go away.

After this episode, Srikrishna grew more wary of shooting off his mouth in public.

The central scene of the novel is the Okuli festival – a celebration involving a water fight between the men of the two villages. I had never seen such an event, but I felt that if this scene could not be shot powerfully, there was no point in making the film. So, despite the scene appearing towards the end of the film, we began our shooting with it. The Okuli pit at the centre of the village had been covered up years ago. We had it opened up again, and we used all the village's water carts to help us create the spectacle. Govind Nihalani handled the scene with extraordinary skill, and it ended up becoming the film's highlight.

The dialogue Srikrishna wrote for *Kaadu* is perhaps the finest use of language in the history of Kannada cinema. YNK went around saying, 'I have never heard such powerful dialogue in a Kannada film.'

When we were casting, I wanted for the part of Chandre Gowda an actor who was well built and could play a hard-hearted, gruff character. When I couldn't find anyone suitable among Kannada actors, I thought of Amrish Puri, whom I had seen play the lead role in my *Yayati* when Satyadev Dubey staged it in Bombay. I mentioned him to cinematographer Govind Nihalani when we discussed the film, and he too agreed that Amrish Puri's height and personality would work in our favour.

Both Karanth and I felt it would add lustre to the film if our *Vamsha Vriksha* distributor M. Bhaktavatsala's charming wife Prema agreed to do the Gowdti's part. I had intended to broach the subject gently with Bhakta, but one day, we were all having a meal at his house when Karanth blurted out to Prema, 'Will you play the lead role in our film?' She looked startled, then said shyly, in English, 'I have dreamed of this.' Bhakta, too, agreed. But for the time being, we kept this casting choice a secret from journalists, and told them about it only when we invited them to Kanakapura.

Prema came from an affluent, cultured family. If she was to play the Gowdti from a village, we told her, she would have to familiarize herself with the role by sleeping on a mat, and by only sitting on the floor of the Kanakapura house. Not only did she accept this regimen, she also ended up becoming a true aunt to G.V. Shivanand's son Nataraj, who played her nephew Kitti in the film. She had a considerable part to play in his getting the National Award for best child artist.

I didn't know actors from Bangalore as well as Karanth did, so he chose suitable actors for several parts: Sundar Raj for Kencha and Lokesh for Shivaganga. T.S. Nagabharana, who assisted Karanth in art direction, showed signs right from the beginning that he would grow into a significant artist. He was himself a Vokkaliga who grew up in a village, so he constantly suggested details that made the film richer.

With his background in documentary films, Govind Nihalani did a remarkable job of shooting the extended Okuli scene. Throughout the film, his lighting was in the style of European film noir, with contrast being used to cast a pall of inevitable tragedy. Since around eighty per cent of the action took place either indoors or at night, this style's heightened shadow-play gave the film a charm of its own. (Govind had studied at Bangalore's film institute, and was a disciple of V.K. Murthy.) But Govind took forever to adjust his lighting. Even for a close-up, he could take forty-five minutes to compose the shot, and as soon as the shot was finished, he would make some tiny change and go for a retake. This habit of his left nine-year-old Nataraj completely drained. Perhaps any other boy would have collapsed from exhaustion, but Nataraj was from the Gubbi clan, and he had the endurance and discipline of company families. As for Govind, he might have been slow, but he was constantly thinking of new ways to design lighting, and was a role model to us all.

Something strange happened when the film was complete and about to be released. Mysterious posters made an appearance in Basavanagudi and around Central College saying, 'O Kannadigas who look at Rajkumar's chappals and clap, come improve your taste by watching Girish's *Kaadu*, which President Giri has appreciated.' Though we never found out who was behind the mischief, some periodicals suggested it was Lankesh. Maybe it was, but Srikrishna also told me that Lankesh praised the film to him after it released, saying, 'The film is excellent. Let critics say what they want.' Lankesh was a man of such contradictions, fully capable of both actions.

As we were finishing *Kaadu*, I accepted the directorship of FTII in Poona. As a result, I was not in Bangalore when the film was being readied for release and the above incident happened. I came down for the release.

Govind Nihalani saw the film with the audience and asked me, 'Why have you edited it to be so slow? There is such powerful material in the second half, but even then the narrative becomes boring.' I thought he was right. *Kaadu* had been edited by a commercial film editor named P. Bhaktavatsalam, who had good judgement when it came to pacing films. I felt it was me – influenced by the theories of *Vamsha Vriksha* editors Aruna and Vikas – who was responsible for slowing down the film. Producer Narayan said, 'The film would have made a lot of money had it been twenty minutes shorter.'

Among the members of *Kaadu*'s cast, the one who went on to become a big star was Amrish Puri. When I cast him, he had no place in Hindi films. The Telugu film-maker duo Bapu–Ramana visited us at Kanakapura when *Kaadu* was being shot. They were friends of Bhaktavatsalam and were considering a Hindi remake of *Paduvaaralli Pandavaru*. The instant they laid eyes on Amrish they decided to cast him as the cruel zamindar in *Hum Paanch*. Though the film didn't do that well nationwide, it was appreciated in Bombay, and that was enough to make a star of Amrish. He kept rising from there. At the height of his popularity, you could find him glowering at the public from just about every Hindi film poster. Still, he retained his humility and we remained friends. Every time he was in Bangalore, no matter how busy he was, he did not forget to call my wife and enquire, 'Bhabhiji, kaisi hain aap?'

As shooting for *Kaadu* was coming to an end, I had a strange – even supernatural – experience. We had finished shooting the street and interior scenes. All that was left were the night scenes that were to be shot in the forest. But our problem was that there was no forest left around Alanahalli and Kanakapura. As Srikrishna said, 'They've made charcoal of it all and sold it.' We were considering travelling to the producer Narayan's hometown in distant Savandurga to find a forest.

While shooting, we were camped at a house outside Kanakapura. One evening, I went out to attend nature's call at the edge of a nearby stream.

City dwellers like me often take pleasure squatting in the open while visiting villages and remote places without toilets. Especially in the evening, when the day's work is done and a cool breeze is blowing, when the birds are going quiet and nature is gently fading away into the dark. In response, the faculties of imagination and thought combine and wander freely. An idea came to me.

The stream in front of me was large, and it being the month of May, the water had dried up entirely, exposing the stream's bed which was packed with pebbles and rounded stones. It looked like a wide, even path. On either side were huge trees – mango, peepul, and a few others – with open ground beyond. The roots that were usually in the water were now haphazardly exposed. Might it not be possible, while shooting at night, to light up only the fearsome branches and grotesque trunks of the trees (as seen from a child's perspective) to create the illusion of a thick forest?

Govind was always enthused by an opportunity for imaginative lighting design, and he agreed at once. The others were pleased too, since this idea saved us the time, effort and, most importantly, cost of going to Savandurga. Govind identified sections of the stream, some trees and roots, and we cleaned these in preparation for shooting. This limited area became the setting for the scene at the beginning, where the Gowdti and Kitti go to the forest, the scene where the black magician sacrifices a cock to an image of the village deity, and the final scene, where Kitti is crying alone in the forest.

Only one important scene was left: the one where Shivaganga and his companions attack the Gowdti when she returns to the forest with Kitti to look for the black magician. At this time, it began to rain unexpectedly. For four or five consecutive evenings, it would pour down just as we had finished our lighting arrangements and were about to start shooting. The light boys would then have to carry the lighting equipment and run into the house. Lokesh began to insist that he be allowed to leave. Narayan, too, grew annoyed and said, 'Let's try once more. If we can't shoot the scene this time, let's end the schedule here and return after it stops raining.' Our hearts skipped a beat at the thought. It was still May, and if we were to return after it stopped raining, it could be after September.

That morning, a Tamil worker with the film unit said to me, 'The village deity has been appearing in my dreams for three days. You have offered a sacrifice and done a pooja, but you have not done the shanti.' We had placed the image of the deity amidst a large tangle of roots and filmed the scene where the black magician offers a sacrifice. Later, we thought the same arrangement of roots was good for shooting the scene in which Kitti cries in the forest, and the deity's image had been thrown in a pile somewhere.

I have no belief in such rites and rituals. But I was ready to do anything if it meant we could finish shooting that day. We retrieved the image and reinstalled it. Karanth and I did a pooja, broke a coconut, and proffered kumkum water. Then, Gopi, Govind, Karanth and I held one corner each of the image, took it to a well nearby and immersed it.

It did not rain that evening. We were able to finish our shooting without trouble.

10

POONA

The Film and Television Institute of India

PRABHAT STUDIO

I had become a film person overnight with the success of *Samskara,* after which I made *Vamsha Vriksha* and received the National Award for best direction (jointly with B.V. Karanth). In 1972, I was asked to be a member of the selection committee for the direction course at FTII in Poona. The committee was chaired by Mrinal Sen, who had seen *Samskara,* appreciated my performance in it, and sent a long telegram to congratulate me. I found it immensely stimulating to spend those three or four days on the campus with Sen and others. Among the students selected for that year's direction course were Ketan Mehta, Saeed Mirza, Kundan Shah, Vidhu Vinod Chopra and Girish Kasaravalli. There were also several impressive, sophisticated applicants who spoke excellent English, but who went on to achieve nothing. I returned from the institute and embarked on directing *Kaadu.*

In September 1973, I received a letter from Prof. Satish Bahadur, who taught film appreciation at the institute. If I was interested in becoming director of the institute, he had written, the ministry in Delhi would follow up.

I was then thirty-five. It was not only *Samskara* and *Vamsha Vriksha* that had resulted in this offer, but also my experience with administration, gained from working as a manager at OUP. I accepted, without any reservations about my abilities. On 1 January 1974, I took charge as director of the Film and Television Institute of India.

I had asked for a term of three years, but the ministry, for internal reasons, gave me a term of one year, renewable annually. In a way, it was a good thing. I have never in my life broken an agreement, and had I received a term of three years, there is no doubt that I would have served out the entire period. This one-year arrangement felt like a less severe commitment. I remember starting at a salary of 2,700 rupees.

I was the third director of the institute. The founding director, Jagat Murari, had been influential in shaping the administration, the course of instruction and the overall character of the institute. Unfortunately, he was not interested in cinema beyond the commercial Hindi film industry, and as a result, the acting course was fashioned for its consumption. Students of direction found no place in this scheme of things, and developed the perception that Murari was indifferent to their concerns. I have some sympathy for him, since I too realized that keeping all the students happy was no easy task. There were two or three strikes in the institute against Murari, and eventually, the students' opposition to him became so severe that he was transferred to the Directorate of Film Festivals.

After Murari, a man named Dikshit, an official from Akashvani who was close to retirement, became acting director of the institute for two years. There were no strikes during his time because a strike would be pointless. He came to his office at eleven, signed files for an hour or so, and went home for lunch. He would return at four after a nap and watch old Hindi films with his family. He had absolutely no interest in the institute. Apparently, he had suffered a heart attack at some point and was just waiting to retire from service. No one bothered with him.

As a result, the institute's administration was half asleep when I took over as director. I had learnt at OUP to begin work not a minute later than 9.30 a.m. In my first couple of days at FTII, I noticed that no one turned up for work before 10.30. I went personally to every office and reprimanded the staff. From the next day, everyone including the administrative officer began to report for work on time.

I put an end to the free milk being supplied to me by the person who ran the canteen, and I made a rule that when office cars were used for personal reasons – whether by me or my mother – a fee had to be charged by the office. While this would be considered routine in a British office, it created ripples of astonishment in a government organization. Still, it is perhaps because of these measures that, I recall gratefully, I had the support of all the institute's employees until the end.

When I came to Poona, I heard from several people that in my appearance I resembled a young V. Shantaram, who had been one of the founders of Prabhat Studio. Since I had no regard for him either personally or as a film director, the title 'nava Shantaram' (new Shantaram) that I heard applied to me on occasion brought no particular happiness. In contrast, it delighted me to be told that in *Vamsha Vriksha* I looked like Satyajit Ray. The excellent Bengali director Nitin Bose, whom I met in Bangalore, carried this story to Calcutta. I laughed heartily when I heard about Ray's response: he had said, in his deep voice, 'Who is this imposter?'

I felt at home in the institute's campus the moment I set foot there. One of the highlights of my time in Poona was being able to walk around the large campus at night. The relics of Prabhat Studio, whose films such as *Amrit Manthan, Sant Tukaram* and *Ramshastri* the whole country had appreciated, were all around me. I had revelled in watching these films when they had been projected from ragged prints in Sirsi, and as a result, this campus had formed a significant backdrop to my childhood – the main road, this banyan tree and that peepul, the pool, this lane, that hill. In the quiet of the night, I would let go of administrative problems and lose myself in these enchanted surroundings to which I felt I was a rightful heir.

One day, while inspecting various departments, I came to the library and saw there, hidden from sight in a corner, a bust. I asked the library in-charge, Phadke, whose bust it was, and he told me it was V.G. Damle. I was stunned – Damle! He was one of the founders of Prabhat Studio and a towering figure in the history of Indian cinema. Phadke explained that when the studio was functioning, the bust had occupied a prominent place in the yard outside the director's office, but Jagat Murari had felt that individuals should not be given much importance in a government institution, and so had shifted the bust to its current location.

I immediately had the bust moved to my office, where, as long as I was director, it held pride of place opposite my table and attracted the attention of everyone who entered. Among the older employees of the institute were several who had previously worked for the studio. My decision caused them great happiness, and along with them, the newer Marathi employees of the institute. The Damle family's residence was still opposite the institute. When Mrs Damle heard that her late husband's bust had been restored to a place of honour, she came home, met Aayi, and fed me sweets.

Aayi was always thrilled to be in Poona. Some of her happiest childhood years had been spent here, and she had a deep love for Marathi literature and culture. Over and above, she was now the institute director's mother.

FTII had two vehicles: one was a diesel jeep with 'Film and TV Institute of India' emblazoned across it, and the other was a long, blue limousine of foreign make given to us by UNESCO. Institute employees used both vehicles for daily work. When I saw that the expensive foreign car was being used roughly, I instituted a fee for using both vehicles, with a higher charge for the limousine.

For my personal use, I bought a Vespa scooter, but never learned to ride it. My friend, the actor Mohan Agashe, ended up using it for himself, causing Bappa much annoyance and making poor Mohan the target of his snide remarks.

At the end of the year, a large bill for using the institute vehicles landed on my desk. This was puzzling since I had only used the jeep. It turned out that Aayi had been using the limousine whenever she wanted to go somewhere. She told me clearly, 'As the film-institute director's mother, I am ashamed to be seen in that rickety jeep.' And so, it was the director in the jeep and his mother in the limousine!

Another incident in which Aayi figured involved a young man named Sawant, who tended to our bungalow's garden. He was a daily-wage worker, and after a year, he gave me an application asking to be confirmed as a regular employee. I returned the application, telling him, 'There are other daily-wage employees who are senior to you and yet to be confirmed. You will have to wait your turn.' Aayi tried to intercede on his behalf, but I gave her the same answer.

A few days later, Sawant came to my office with pedas. He said shyly, 'Thank you for confirming my appointment.' I was taken aback. I sent for the file, and true enough, it had my signature on it. His application had been placed on my table along with other routine files, and I had signed it without paying attention. I called the administrative officer to investigate how this blunder had occurred. He smiled furtively, as if we both were involved in some secret transaction, and said, 'Aayi saheb asked me. How could I say no?' I flew into a rage and told him, 'This is not a private company, it is a government institution. Rules have to be followed.' He bowed his head and agreed, but when he left he was still looking pleased with himself, as if all my shouting had nothing to do with him. When I asked Aayi, she said, 'Oh, poor fellow Sawant, he's a good boy,' and brushed it off. When Bappa died, two years after I left the institute, Sawant showed his gratitude by coming from Poona unasked. He stayed with us for thirteen days and helped Aayi.

The director's bungalow was right next to the women's hostel on campus. Any illness or discomfort experienced by a student in the hostel was reported to Aayi. Food, medicines, and anything else that might be required was supplied from our house.

INVASION OF THE TV CENTRE

I had not been in the director's chair for even a week, when I was confronted by my first serious problem.

By 1970, it had begun to seem inevitable that the television medium would proliferate in India. Doordarshan, with the support of the United Nations Development Programme (UNDP), started a national television training wing to create a cadre of capable administrators for the medium. It began operations from Mandi House in Delhi, but it soon became clear that such an initiative required infrastructure and a building of its own. Since FTII and Doordarshan both came under the Ministry of Information and

Broadcasting, Doordarshan naturally began to eye the institute's spacious campus in Poona.

It was true that FTII needed a television department, and it was natural for this department's building to come up on the institute's campus. But FTII would teach television just as it taught film – as a creative medium. What Doordarshan needed was a place to train technicians and administrators who would work for it. There was nothing in common between those two types of training, and so Doordarshan's training wing had no reason to be here.

Our overlords in the government had listened to some UNDP adviser who knew nothing about Indian ground realities, and decided that the TV training wing would come up on the institute campus. As the proposal took shape, Mandi House began to realize the problems created by such an arrangement. The main problem was not technical, but human. Those who would be trained to be television administrators were middle-aged, salaried government employees, most of them married. In contrast, the students of the institute were between eighteen and twenty-five, usually just out of college. Fights, drinking, noise, mischief were all naturally part of the lifestyle of students of this age. It was hardly reasonable to expect these two groups to live in the same hostels and share the campus, but this should have been thought of before deciding to house the training wing in FTII's campus.

Within a week of my having taken charge, a committee from the ministry headed by Justice Khosla came to Poona. But rather than Justice Khosla, it seemed to be one of the members, the Doordarshan Director General P.V. Krishnamoorthy, who was leading the committee. As I deliberated with them, it became clear what the committee was for. On the surface, it was to look into how television could be integrated into the institute's curriculum, but the committee's real intention was to divide the FTII campus into two and start a separate institute for television training. I asked PVK angrily, 'Who asked you to come here? If you didn't want to be with us, then why not go anywhere else and start your centre?'

Justice Khosla was sympathetic. He said, 'There is no doubt that this is unfair to you. The TV centre has become the cuckoo that has grown up in your nest.' But it was a waste of time talking to PVK. He spoke with impatience and some imperiousness, as if he was trying to convey that everything had already been decided and they were only here to break the news to us.

I called Delhi the very next day, went there and camped in the government guest house on Kasturba Gandhi Marg. I spoke to my senior officer in the ministry, Additional Secretary Deshraj Singh, who took me to the minister himself, I.K. Gujral. I had already had some contact with him over *Samskara*, but it had not been face to face. He was a soft-spoken man with a goatee, cultured, without the slightest trace of self-importance, and he listened to me carefully. I explained the situation and said, 'I have been appointed by your ministry as director of the Film and Television Institute of India. I cannot have the institute's campus divided into two on my watch. If this plan goes through, I will submit my resignation.'

Gujral was astonished. Apparently, this was the first he was hearing about dividing the FTII campus. He clearly stated, 'No, Girish is right. The television centre has to be part of the institute. The campus cannot be divided.' And so, if the institute campus – and my beloved world of Prabhat Studio – has remained whole to this day, the credit must go to me!

In October the same year, FTII went from being a government institution to an autonomous body. Until then, our expenses were being met directly by the Ministry of Information and Broadcasting. Now we had an annual budget and a governing council to supervise its spending. Hrishikesh Mukherjee was appointed the first chairman of the council. It did not take long for us to realize that 'autonomous' only meant that the government relinquished its responsibility for the institution, not its hold over it.

HISTORY

When the government of India decided to start a film institute, the idea did not receive much support from the industry. Yet, it was unquestionable that there was a dire need for a place where individuals could receive training and specialize in film technology. At the time, the only way to enter the industry as a technician was to become an assistant to someone experienced in the field, slog under him – it was always a he – for several years, pick up what scraps of experience one could, and wait for either the 'boss' or a director to offer an opportunity to display one's ability. This system ensured that old ideas dating back to the infancy of the Indian film industry in the 1920s were handed down unimaginatively from generation to generation, with innovation often squashed as needless uppityness. The only qualification that mattered was the claim that one had been working in the industry for the last ten or twenty or thirty years.

The idea of a film institute found an enthusiastic welcome in Madras, where the government came forward with all kinds of amenities and the requisite financing. But unfortunately for Madras, Prabhat Studio in Poona had gone bankrupt and been shut down. Its property came on the market at the same time. Prabhat had a vast compound with open space which allowed for future growth, three large studio floors, a laboratory, a fully equipped sound studio, cameras and plenty of equipment, not to speak of a host of unemployed technicians who had hands-on experience of film production. It was the perfect set-up, and the financial desperation of the owners had brought the price so low that the government would have been stupid to pass it over. A film archive was also added to the institute, raising the prestige of the enterprise. Enraged at the snub, Madras started its own independent film school, which has been equally productive.

The institute offered six courses – direction, photography, editing, sound, scriptwriting and acting – with ten students in each course except in acting, which had twenty seats. This used to be the standard set of subjects taught in those days in most film schools across the world. But a problem no school had been able to solve was this: how do you evaluate the potential of a candidate who aspired to be a film director? The requirements for that job are so varied, undefinable, and dependent on a person's ability to draw upon inner resources, that no satisfactory syllabus for training a student in direction is possible. Add to this the fact that the interviews for applicants at Poona were held in English, which completely dissociated the candidate from his or her regional literature and culture. It was not uncommon for a candidate who was fluent in English to pick up a few facts and names related to cinema and impress the selectors.

In most cases, it took only a few months of doing the direction course – which lasted three years! – for a typical student to realize that he lacked the aptitude for it. Then there was the grim reality that, even if he somehow slogged through the three years, there was not the remotest prospect of finding employment in the film industry. This reality pushed him deeper and deeper into despair, as he spent more years hanging around under the so-called Wisdom Tree right in front of the director's office, sneering at the local film industry for its vulgarity and 'escapism', and talking grandly of Truffaut, Godard and Fellini.

The other matter that haunted everyone in the 1970s was the enormous international success of Satyajit Ray and the nature of that success. The international reception of Ray's *Pather Panchali* and subsequent films established neo-realism as the only respectable artistic form. The average Hindi film, with its emphasis on romance and song-and-dance routines, was treated with disdain as tasteless fare which pandered to the lowest common denominator in the audience. Satish Bahadur, professor of film appreciation, declared that Ray was the only Indian director worth paying attention to, and he himself was the only critic to truly understand his work. (His successor Chabria went even further, denouncing as decadent any attempt at structure and psychological exploration of character in a film script.)

Graduates of the institute knew the indifference and contempt that awaited them when they sought work in Bombay. Their defensive reaction was to dismiss the industry altogether. The saddest result of this attitude was that, although the institute had as a teacher of music a man as intelligent, vibrant and creative as Bhaskar Chandavarkar, the products of the institute remained completely unresponsive to the extraordinarily rich and innovative music emerging from Bombay at the time, and the imagination with which it was being picturized. Raj Kapoor, Bimal Roy, Guru Dutt and Mehboob Khan were all dismissed as 'commercial'. I was present in a class in which Ritwik Ghatak apologized for having written the script of *Madhumati*.

Ray had been spotted at Venice by the French critic Georges Sadoul. As a result, European and British critics began to be venerated. I remember the immense smugness with which Derek Malcolm recounted that the first question Ray had asked when he arrived at a South East Asian film festival was about where the British critics were lodged. In 1984, I was attending a party thrown by the All India Film Producers' Council at the International Film Festival in Bombay (a pretty shabby affair I must admit). Derek Malcolm and I were standing in a corner, ignored entirely by the hosts, when Derek suddenly burst forth (and I quote him verbatim): 'These pieces of shit! They think they are big because they are big in India. They don't seem to realize that no one in the outside world gives them a shit.' And it suddenly dawned on me that he was rattled by the fact that no one in the Indian cinema scene was bowing and scraping in front of him – as I, for instance, was doing. He was demanding the obsequiousness that we – disciples of Ray – had got him used to.

In the late 1960s, the Film Finance Corporation was started under the leadership of B.K. Karanjia. He did an excellent job of supporting experimental cinema. But the lack of any attempt to create venues to exhibit these products sabotaged the prospects of its growth. In the next few decades, new technologies emerged and the fields of sound, editing and photography became so complex that technicians could not do without proper professional training. Today, the film industry is dominated by technicians trained in the institutes at Poona or Bombay or Bangalore. But the atmosphere in the acting and direction departments is unchanged. The anxieties haunting these two courses remain, creating an atmosphere of perennial despondency, and half a century of history has not supplied the remotest solution to their problems.

THE ACTING COURSE

The first major decision I took after becoming the director of FTII was to scrap the screen test which every applicant to the acting course was expected to take. This was a radical decision for the establishment, since it hit at the very foundation of the philosophy that guided teaching at the institute – that its main purpose was to cater to the needs of the Hindi commercial film industry. The screen test was meant to help the selectors choose those candidates who had a 'cinematic appearance'. And given that, some talent for acting and the ability to dance. The search was for the good-looking and potentially glamorous, for first-class star material. Bombay, the home of Hindi cinema, and other centres of language films, like Madras and Calcutta, were already overflowing with young talent with 'chocolatey' looks. The institute was to make its own choice, train it, shape it and present it on a platter to the film moguls, with no obligation on their part towards the institute. I thought the whole idea farcical.

The change naturally upset Prof. Roshan Taneja, the professor of acting. But even I had not anticipated that this decision of mine would yield such immediate results. Among the aspirants for the acting course that year was a student with strikingly different looks who had already trained at NSD in New Delhi. He was tall, scrawny and bore the marks of his malnourished childhood on his pockmarked face. Had the screen test still been in place, he would have been rejected in the very first round. But the improvisation he presented at the interview showed him to be an exceptionally gifted actor.

The jury I had invited for the selection rejected him outright. Their opinion was that he was undoubtedly a brilliant actor, but his looks disqualified him from working in the film industry. I disagreed. 'His looks are his problem,' I argued. 'Our job is to train him if he has any talent.' Only one other member of the jury, the actor Jairaj, supported my argument. The rest were firm in their opinion that instead of letting him face inevitable humiliation in the industry, we should gently guide him to accept theatre as his métier. For the only time in my professional career, I overruled the jury and admitted the young man to the acting course.

Om Puri went on to justify my faith in his ability by blossoming into one of the major actors of his generation, building an international reputation with films like *Gandhi* and *East is East*. I was very touched when, twenty years later, he received the Filmfare Award for lifetime achievement with the words, 'I would not be standing here today if Girish had not set aside precedent and admitted me to the institute.'

An unintended consequence of Om Puri's admission to FTII was a rare visit by one of the titans of Indian cinema.

Among the applicants to the acting course that year was a young man named Dilip Dhawan. An (inevitably) good-looking young man with bluish eyes and boyish features, his application was supported by letters of recommendation from a dozen movie moguls of Bombay. He was not particularly gifted, and certainly did not stand out amidst that year's batch of candidates. But Taneja, the professor of acting, was eager that we should take due cognizance of the keen and unanimous interest the moguls had taken in the boy's career, and admit him. I refused. There were twenty sanctioned seats in the course – ten for men and ten for women – and they had all been filled, the last one by the unlikely Om Puri. But Taneja continued to be unusually persistent. 'Let us place Dilip in the eleventh place,' he suggested. 'Let's not say we have totally rejected him. Just let him be the first on the waiting list. That would indicate that we have given due attention to their interest in the institute.' C.V. Gopal, the deputy director, warned me: 'Let us either admit the boy or reject him. This waiting list business will open a Pandora's box.' Rather than annoy a senior member of the staff in my very first year, I agreed to the compromise suggested by Taneja and fell into a trap.

We announced a waiting list in which Dilip's name was at the top. The list had been on our notice board for only a couple of days when my weekly meeting with the teaching staff was interrupted by a frantic Dabak, my door attendant. 'Mr Raj Kapoor is here,' he panted. 'He is waiting outside.'

Raj Kapoor owned a farm in Loni, a little outside Poona, but in thirteen years of the institute's existence, he had never once bothered to step into its campus. Members of the staff, startled by this sudden visit, assumed the meeting would be instantly terminated in order to welcome Raj Kapoor, and started gathering their papers. But Raj Kapoor had not bothered to take an appointment, and I saw no reason to interrupt my scheduled programme. I asked Dabak to give Raj Kapoor a chair in the administrative officer's room – since we did not have a proper waiting room for visitors – and proceeded with the meeting. When it ended and the teachers started dispersing, Satish Bahadur whispered to me: 'I hope you realize none of your predecessors would have made Raj Kapoor wait like this.'

Raj Kapoor had barely lowered his hulking self into the chair I had offered when he began to pour out his woes: 'What have you done, Girish-ji? I returned home from Dubai yesterday toh maatam chal raha tha, maatam. There was mourning going on there, wailing and breast-beating.'

Since it was clear why he had come, I went to the nub of the matter: 'The acting course has only ten seats, and Dilip wasn't among the ten best candidates. To select him, I would have had to sacrifice a better candidate.'

Raj Kapoor nodded gravely, indicating that he completely understood my argument. He said, 'If Dilip has no talent at all, then reject him. I won't say a word. But if he is first on the waiting list, surely you could extend your consideration a bit, if only out of respect to the producers who have supported his application? When we have staked our entire lives, our fortunes, on the film industry, shouldn't the institute show some consideration for what we have contributed?' His voice quivered with the pain of humiliation.

I felt like a fool to have disregarded C.V. Gopal's warning that had come from many years of experience with the games played at the institute. At the same time, it was strange to sit there and have an actor of Raj Kapoor's stature spin out his consummate artistry for my sole consumption. After a deferential but firm tug-of-war of this nature, I stated what I knew was the perennial grievance of the institute: 'You producers support the applications of candidates to our institute, and it upsets you when we ignore those recommendations. That is perfectly understandable. But may I point out that in the last thirteen years of the institute's existence, not one of those producers has employed a single graduate of the institute in any capacity in their films? You recommend but do not employ.'

'Girish-ji, you know what an unpredictable tangled web of an industry we work in,' the great film-maker moaned. 'There are so many gifted individuals I would like to give a chance to, but my hands are tied by the heartless pressures of the industry.'

Finally, I said, 'Let just one of these producers promise me that he will give Dilip a significant role in his next production – not an important role, but a role that will register – and I'll admit him to the course.'

Raj Kapoor looked at me for a moment, spread out his arms in a gesture that all at once communicated that he understood my argument, that this is how the world was, that we were both caught in a much larger network of obligations, and that all said and done he knew I was the boss here and he would bear no grudge. He beamed affectionately: 'I have done what I had come to do. Now it is up to you to decide what's appropriate.' He got up to leave.

As I accompanied him to his vehicle, I said, 'It is no small matter to have Raj Kapoor visit the institute. We do need your goodwill, your guidance. We are delighted to have you come here. I shall not – I cannot – say no to you. Please inform Dilip that he has been admitted to the institute.'

Raj Kapoor thanked me and left. Dilip later told me that Raj Kapoor sent for him immediately after this meeting and told him, 'I have got you admitted to the institute. Now don't come to me asking for work.' When Dilip finished his course and joined the industry in Bombay, not one of the producers who had so generously supplied him with recommendations offered him a role. It was his classmate Saeed Mirza's TV serial *Nukkad* that brought him national attention.

I became aware of the invidious position of the acting course within a few months of taking charge at the institute. At a party thrown by the parents of a student of acting, a group of past students of the course met me and pleaded, 'The institute has been churning out close to twenty graduates every year for the last thirteen years. At the moment, there are more than two hundred of us here in Bombay looking for roles. Not one of the major producers has shown any interest in us. The four or five graduates who have entered the industry, like Rehana Sultan and Shatrughan Sinha, are there thanks to a single small-budget film-maker, B.R. Ishara. Most producers sneer at us and make us wait endlessly in their outer rooms. The girls are greeted with a blatant, "There is a party tonight. Be there." We have become unwanted beggars in the industry. Why is the institute adding to our woes by producing twenty more graduates every year?'

Their point was valid. There was no television in those days, and the commercial film industry was the only venue open to these young men and women. To make matters worse, the phenomenal success of Ramesh Sippy's *Sholay* meant that 'multi-starrers' – big-budget films which inflated their image by casting most of the available major actors – flooded the market. A handful of actors – like Amitabh Bachchan, Dharmendra, Hema Malini and Vinod Khanna – cornered all the roles in most of the films. As a first-rate actor like Farida Jalal explained to me while we were working together in a TV serial: 'If a glamorous star like Neetu Singh is reduced to playing supporting roles, what hope did someone like me have? I simply decided to move to Bangalore.'

But even if the solution to the problem was to suspend the acting course for a few years, the decision was not easy to implement. The world outside – particularly the media – was only interested in the institute for the glamour potential of the acting course. When I did succeed in solving the problem to my satisfaction, the media accused me of settling a score with my predecessor, Jagat Murari. Or of punishing the acting department for going on a prolonged strike to force my hand. But I realized on my very first day that the problems of the acting course could not be solved in isolation; I had to tackle the direction course along with it. The two were inextricably linked.

THE STRIKE

There have been so many strikes in the history of FTII that the phenomenon has become something of a joke. But I suspect I am the only director who had to break a strike despite being sympathetic to the cause of the striking students. The educational requirements for applying to the courses made conflict inevitable on the campus. The entrants to the direction course had to have finished their graduation, while it was a sufficient qualification for acting to have finished school. So the former were usually older, and looked upon the latter as immature and illiterate, intent only on looking attractive. The latter looked upon the former as pretentious and incompetent, strutting about with dreams fashioned from the blocks of European cinema. The belief that Jagat Murari was only interested in glory within the Indian commercial film industry, with no concern for the practical problems faced by students, had already led to three strikes against him by the students of direction and driven him out to a job in the ministry. The strike I faced was led by students of acting, and in my heart of hearts, I agreed with them.

These students had genuine grievances. For one, students of direction were required to make a twenty-minute long feature film in their third year, but there was no rule that bound them to use acting students from the institute while making this diploma film. Many of them chose to go outside the institute and cast proficient actors from the Marathi stage, of whom there was no shortage in Poona. The result was that several students of acting left the institute without having a single feature film that showcased their abilities. Further, given the backdrop of mutual contempt between students of acting and direction, the fact that students of direction could choose to cast or ignore fellow acting students led to a lopsided power dynamic. There was always resentment simmering between the two departments, and it was clear that the situation was unfairly weighted against the acting students.

If the students of acting had not protested until then, it was because their eyes were firmly set on the Bombay film industry and they were eager to leave the institute with a certificate as quickly as possible. Besides, a protest would have been of no use – Murari's replacement had taken no interest in the institute during his two years there. I tried to correct the dire situation that had developed. And this resulted in a strike.

The year before I became director, two students had joined FTII after spending three years at NSD: Naseeruddin Shah and Jaspal. They were well versed in the political ways of Delhi, and they had brought its aggression to Poona.

Still, Naseer's temperament was not without an element of self-doubt. One day, he came to my office to see me. 'I have two problems,' he said, looking worried. 'The first is that I am Muslim. The second is that my looks are very ordinary. With these drawbacks, do I have any chance of being successful as an actor?'

I said, 'Look, everyone knows that Dilip Kumar is Muslim. When the audience likes an actor, they don't consider his religion. And when it comes to your features, there is nothing that you can do about them. It's true that you might not become a star, but equally, it is rare for a star to get the opportunity to act. There the good looks themselves become an obstacle. An actor with ordinary features has the possibility of taking on a wide range of roles.' He did not seem particularly reassured, and left with a frown on his face. But he went on to prove my words right.

I had no experience in dealing with students. Only a few days after I joined the institute, I explicitly told the students of acting, 'There is no doubt that injustice is being done to you. I will try to change the current system.' Jaspal and Naseer latched on to my words and began to insist that I act at once.

With the institute having just been declared an autonomous institution, it had convened the first meeting of the governing council. The students of the acting department chose this time to begin a hunger strike. It went on for a week. On the last day of the meeting, the members of the council were gheraoed. Students laid siege to my office, preventing members – including the secretary of the Ministry of Information and Broadcasting Anwar Jamal Kidwai, and the film-makers Hrishikesh Mukherjee and Mrinal Sen – from leaving. They demanded that the institute's rules be changed at once.

No institution can change its rules instantaneously. Nor was it practical to do so: the students who had to direct their diploma films were in their final year, and a last-minute change in rules would likely incite a protest from them. Diploma films would not end up being made that year, and the training of students from other technical disciplines would be compromised. Though this was all evident, Naseer and Jaspal did not relent. Their shouting and sloganeering continued unabated in front of my office. Mrinal Sen said approvingly, 'They both seem to be good actors.'

Since high-ranking government officials had been gheraoed, I was compelled to inform the police. Soon, there was a police unit at FTII's main gate. To invite them in would be to accept that I had failed to control my own students. I went to the gate to talk to the police officials. At this point, Saeed Mirza and a few other students came forward and said, 'Don't let the police enter. We will form a ring around Kidwai and the other officials, and safely escort them out.' I did not take them up on their offer. Had I done so, there was the possibility of violence flaring up between groups of students and making the situation worse.

I had told Kidwai and the others that they should leave by the institute's back gate when I sent them a signal. As the drama at the main gate intensified, I saw that the striking students were all distracted by it. I sent the signal. When word reached me that the officials had sneaked out through the back gate, I announced it to the students and the police. A crisis had been averted – at least for the day.

The larger problem remained, and it can be said that matters came to a head because of one student from the direction department: Girish Kasaravalli. Shooting for that year's diploma films was to begin with Girish. He came to me a few weeks before the shooting dates and said, 'I have finished all my preparation. What is the point in my staying on in Poona and wasting time? B.V. Karanth is about to start shooting for *Chomana Dudi*. I will go work with him and get some experience.' I allowed him to leave. But I warned him, 'Your film is being shot first. If it is delayed, the shooting of every other film will have to be postponed. So don't return late.' Girish agreed and left.

Girish's technical team arrived in Poona as agreed, but he was nowhere to be found. His cinematographer Jahangir came to me, distraught, saying, 'What should I do? My schedule has been turned upside down.'

Naseer and others used the pretext of Girish's absence to give vent to their own grievances: 'This is a good example of the arrogance shown by students of direction. How can you tolerate this?' And regretfully, Girish had not cast a single one of his fellow students in his film. His actors were all from Poona's Kannada theatre world.

At this time, I had to visit Bangalore on official work. When I met Karanth, I told him about Kasaravalli's behaviour. Karanth said, 'You should take action against him as you see fit. I did not call Kasaravalli or ask him to stay. He came on his own, and he stayed as long as he wanted to.' I felt I had no alternative but to penalize Kasaravalli.

I returned to Poona and sent Kasaravalli a show-cause notice asking why action should not be taken against him. His reply arrived after a week: 'I didn't work on Karanth's film at all. I have been ill and confined to bed.' He claimed I was levelling false allegations against him. Attached to his reply was a letter from Karanth attesting that Girish Kasaravalli had nothing to do with his film and had not participated in its shooting. Also attached was a medical certificate.

From time to time, I had heard Karanth's close disciples – Sundar Raj, Nagabharana – saying that he was given to tripping you up when you least expected it. Now, I too had experienced it. The next time I met him in person, I asked why he had behaved like this. He said, 'I don't know anything about it. The cinematographer S. Ramachandra asked me to provide a certificate. I did so.' He shifted the blame on to Ramachandra and looked at me with his usual helpless expression. This ingenuousness that managed to leave others in the lurch would prove costly to him in the future. After all this, when *Chomana Dudi* was released, Kasaravalli was clearly credited in the titles as associate director!

The incident strained my relationship with Karanth. He was later appointed director of NSD. I was on its governing council. When he found himself in a difficult situation because of misbehaving students, rather than go to his aid, I took a dig at him now that the shoe was on the other foot, and laughed when his face fell.

Despite all this, Karanth and I directed *Tabbaliyu Neenade Magane/ Godhuli* together. But it did not prove as rich an experience as co-directing *Vamsha Vriksha*. More issues cropped up between us in the future, related to Karanth's drinking and so on, but the Girish Kasaravalli episode remained a thorn in my side until the end.

Kasaravalli was generally thought of as a cultured person, an excellent student, and someone who was dedicated to cinema. So his transgression astonished everyone, especially the teachers. Still, there is no doubt that in his life after the institute, Girish Kasaravalli has conducted himself with uncommon civility and trustworthiness.

After Girish upset the timetable, Naseer and Jaspal took the opportunity to enter the scene. The entire acting department demanded that they be given roles in that year's diploma films, or they would prevent the films from being shot. I tried to get them to see reason: 'We cannot at the last minute change a system that the students of direction have been assured of for three years. I will arrange independent films for those of you who do not get a part in any of the diploma films.' But Naseer and Jaspal had come through the crucible of Delhi's student politics. Without their lead, the other students would not have brought matters to such an impasse. The strike went on.

The ministry in Delhi gently indicated that I had their backing if I wanted to expel Naseer and Jaspal from the institute for indiscipline. But any course of action that relied on the ministry's support was as good as admitting that I was helpless as the institute's director. Rather than accept defeat like this, it was essential that I bring the strike to an end with my own efforts and re-establish my authority.

But my hands were tied as long as the students were on campus. If I threatened to shut the institute, they might remain on campus and go on a hunger strike. All paths to resolving the matter would then be closed.

In those days, an annual International Film Festival was organized in Delhi during the first week of January. This was just after the institute's December break. I called the students and told them earnestly, 'Go to Delhi for the film festival and come back. We can then deliberate with cool heads about what to do next.' The students agreed. At this time, a landslide outside Lonavala had blocked the train tracks to Bombay. I arranged a bus from FTII to Bombay, from where the students could proceed to Delhi.

Once I was certain that the campus was empty, I called journalists and announced: 'The institute gates will not open until every student of acting accepts every one of my conditions in writing.' Now the acting students were at my mercy.

I knew one thing with certainty: Naseer and Jaspal were actors who were dedicated to theatre, but their fellow students were eager to go to Bombay as soon as possible and make a future for themselves. Their youth was important to them – every month the strike went on served to cut short their career correspondingly. I knew I only had to sit back and wait for them to surrender.

At the time, Ram Gopal Bajaj, my friend from NSD, was working in Delhi with an industrialist named Alok Jain. Bajaj had great regard for Naseer. He was worried that Naseer's future might be ruined amidst the ongoing turmoil, so he went back and forth between me and the acting students in an attempt to resolve the matter. I stood firm, and finally Bajaj brought a letter of surrender from them in which they agreed unconditionally to my stipulations.

I, too, went to Delhi for the film festival. There, I saw Naseer in a performance of Edward Albee's one-act play, *The Zoo Story*, and was reminded of what a fine actor he was. I say 'reminded' because Mrinal Sen and I had seen his rage and fury during the students' siege of the governing council and marvelled at his talent.

FTII reopened. I had won unambiguously. Now, I didn't want any personal enmity to linger. Besides, the students of acting had been justified in protesting against the existing system.

In the meanwhile, Shyam Benegal had asked me to play a role in his film *Nishant*. His first film *Ankur* had been stunningly successful. Shabana Azmi had become a star and Shyam was being universally acclaimed for the film. Now, for his second film, he was looking for a young actor. 'If you know of any talented actor who is not conventionally good-looking like a Hindi-film hero, send him to me,' he said.

The very next day after the institute opened, I sent for Naseer. 'Go meet Shyam Benegal,' I told him. Shyam gave Naseer the role as soon as he met him, and this single act of mine melted away any resentment the acting students might have had against me. Still, there were those, like Ketan Mehta and Jaspal, who accused me of bringing the strike to an end by bribing Naseer with a role in Shyam's film.

In Jaspal's eyes, Naseer had personally betrayed him by accepting my conditions. He came in front of me and beat his chest, saying, 'I am for sale too. Buy me too.' Jaspal seemed to go to pieces in the aftermath of the strike. Later, while playing a small role in Shyam's *Manthan,* he broke down in the middle of shooting. He also began to threaten Naseer. While shooting *Manthan,* Naseer's safety had to be ensured by providing him accommodation far away from Jaspal. Some months later, Jaspal stabbed Naseer with a knife. After he was released from jail, they say he roamed about begging. He eventually died in obscurity.

Naseer went from acting in *Nishant* to *Manthan* to Shyam's other films, and developed into one of our finest actors. It is unlikely that Naseer would have become such a renowned actor without Shyam's support. But of late, I have heard that Naseer has been making disparaging statements about art films.

One of the unfortunate consequences of the strike was that I did not get a chance to study the weaknesses of FTII's courses of study and change them in a way that could benefit everyone. All my time went in addressing the strife on campus. This was the enormous long-term damage that Naseer and Jaspal inflicted on the institute.

Once the institute began functioning again, the professor of direction, Ghosh, came to me and said, 'When the entire institute is in chaos, it is unfair to single out only Girish Kasaravalli for punishment.' I agreed. In any case, I had been more bothered by Karanth's behaviour in the matter than by Girish's. Shooting resumed, and Girish made a film that ended up being judged the best diploma film that year. I called independent directors from Bombay to cast students from our acting course who had not been accommodated in diploma films. Shyam Benegal came and used Naseer in a short film.

Every student of direction was required to submit a screenplay in the examination. Not everyone completed this requirement. For example, Ketan Mehta put in front of us a half-written screenplay, but his abilities were evident even in an incomplete draft, and so the screenwriter Nabendu Ghosh, who was the external examiner, and I gave Ketan full marks.

Girish Kasaravalli, as if the mischief he had already done was not enough, submitted as a feature film screenplay a few sheets of paper from an exercise book on which he had condensed U.R. Ananthamurthy's short story 'Ghatashraddha' and senselessly written 'Scene 1', 'Scene 2' and so on before each paragraph. His attitude seemed to be: 'I'm not interested in writing a screenplay. Do what you want.' Nabendu was perplexed on seeing his submission. 'What should we do?' he asked. 'This is hardly a screenplay. But they say his diploma film is very good?' I said, 'Yes, he is a good student. I don't know why he is behaving like this, but this is an examination. If the screenplay he has submitted is unacceptable, then we must fail him.' Girish Kasaravalli did not get his diploma that year. (I don't know what happened after that.)

Girish went on to direct the feature film *Ghatashraddha*, and it won the Swarna Kamal, the National Award for best feature film. Then, he began to say, 'Girish Karnad and Nabendu Ghosh failed me because my English is poor.' But there was no truth to it. The interview for admission to the institute was conducted in English, and Girish's English was in no way inferior compared to his fellow students. After that, he had studied for three years at the institute – in English. His allegation was ridiculous.

I changed the coursework at FTII from the next year. Until then, direction, cinematography, editing and other technical aspects were taught as if they had no relation to each other. This was a relic from a bygone age. In the modern system being adopted around the world, a student learnt to make a film end to end. It was possible for a single individual to write the screenplay, do the photography, edit and finish the film. The system at the institute changed to one where all students would study a common course for the first two years, and then choose their specialization in their third year. This change had the support of the institute's entire faculty. The only people who didn't have a place in this new system were the young men and women who came with the sole aim of becoming actors. But there was NSD in Delhi, where actors could be trained. I spoke to Alkazi, who was director of NSD at the time, suggesting that their graduates could come to Poona to act in diploma films, and he agreed. The new course of study came into effect in 1975.

ADMINISTRATION

The thinker André Béteille has said that in India we turn our brightest people into administrators, and then, the mode of administration turns them into politicians. While I experienced this first-hand during my time as director of FTII, it is also true that an administrator occasionally has the opportunity to make truly significant contributions to the cultural world. I experienced this too, but over a decade later, when I was appointed chairman of the Sangeet Natak Akademi. Saras was opposed to my taking up the post since she thought it would only amount to a bureaucratic distraction, but I accepted in the hope that I could do something good in the position. And I turned out to be right.

I had finished chairing the first meeting of my governing council, when I was approached by a frail figure, grey-haired and bearded, clad, if I remember correctly, in ochre. He introduced himself as Appukuttan Nair, a name I recognized immediately as that of a scholar of performing arts in Kerala. 'If nothing is done immediately, Kutiyattam will die,' he said, in a voice which immediately grabbed my attention, since it had a note of genuine panic that was very different from the usual wheedling tone of fund-seekers. 'The last guru, Ammannur Madhava Chakyar, is old and extremely depressed. He is afraid he may live to witness the form die. There are no students, and there is no money to pay for the basic facilities needed for teaching or performing.' I was surprised, because my predecessor, Dr V.K. Narayana Menon, was from Kerala and yet, in my discussions with him after I had taken over, he had made no mention of the problem. 'Didn't Dr Menon do anything?' I asked, and got the answer, 'He only had time for Balasaraswati.'

Anyway, thanks to Appukuttan who continued to hound me after the meeting – he was a master 'hounder' – the Akademi formed a committee consisting of Keshav Kothari, the secretary of the Akademi, Bhaskar Chandavarkar, Ashok Ranade, and Dr Kiran Seth of SPIC MACAY. The committee visited Natana Kairali in Irinjalakuda and Margi in Trivandrum to study what could be done, and recommended that these two centres together needed at least five lakh rupees a year to survive. Our financial adviser was, at first, aghast. He told me it was not within the powers of the Akademi to sanction such a large sum, and in any case, no one in Delhi had heard of Kutiyattam. I would have to go to the ministry to have the money sanctioned, and I knew what that meant. Fortunately, I was able to convince the adviser that there was a real crisis: the Chakyar was the last living link in a tradition that went back at least 1,200 years, and he was key to the survival of one of the oldest – if not *the* oldest – continuous performance traditions in the world. If he died, the whole art form would be lost.

Many performing art forms in India have died out in this fashion during the last two centuries, since a performance tradition needs living teachers to hand down the discipline to the next generation. The authenticity of present-day Mohiniyattam, for instance, has been questioned on these very grounds. We managed somehow to get the grant sanctioned, and Appukuttan paid me what I consider the best compliment I have received in my entire life: 'If you had not acted quickly, Kutiyattam would have died out.' It is not often that one is given credit for saving an ancient art form from extinction. If I have any real claim to fame, it is this one.

But that was later. Returning to my time as FTII's director, there is no doubt that my understanding of cinema grew sharper and deeper through watching films and having discussions with teachers, students and technicians. But I was also painfully aware that the burden of administration made it impossible for me to undertake any creative activity or even find the time to read. I knew I did not want to stay on, constantly grappling with students. Just as I was beginning to think of what to do next, the solution to the problem fell into my lap.

THE EMERGENCY

On 5 June 1975, Indira Gandhi declared a state of emergency in India. There was a change in mood across the country, but this was nowhere more pronounced than in government offices, where a silent fear took hold, and it felt like everyone was suddenly speaking in hushed tones.

A few days after the Emergency was declared, I was at Films Division, Bombay, talking to its director Khandpur. I said, jokingly, 'What is this Emergency? Are they going to bug our offices?' Jokes about bugging were common at the time because the American president Nixon had just had his term end unceremoniously over it. Khandpur grew pale when I asked that question. He looked here and there, and said, 'Please, let us not discuss the subject.' This was the first indication I had about the suspicion, betrayal and vicious backbiting that would ensue in government circles as a result of the Emergency. But since I was sitting in Poona, far away from Delhi, the Emergency did not cause me too much trouble.

It did result in my senior officials in Delhi vanishing, though. The minister of Information and Broadcasting, I.K. Gujral, was sent abroad as a diplomat, and in his place came a politician from Raipur named Vidya Charan Shukla. The secretary in the ministry, Kidwai, who always treated me as a friend despite being older and more senior, was replaced by someone named S.M.H. Burney. He was a good man, dedicated to his work, but was undone by becoming embroiled in Emergency politics. Day after day, we would receive reports in Poona of Sanjay Gandhi's atrocities, of the latest orders issued by Indira Gandhi as she tried to become the rashtramata.

Saeed Mirza, one of my best students, met me in my office one day. He was an enthusiastic boy who came from the committed left-wing politics of the Urdu literary world. He seemed frightened. He said, 'I have been working with some movements protesting the Emergency. I have heard that the police have a list with some of our names. What should I do?' I reassured him: 'Give up being an amateur revolutionary for now. Matters are far more serious than what we can see from Poona. I will protect you as long as you are here. If I hear anything from my police friends, I will let you know.' Thankfully, nothing happened to him.

Stories of V.C. Shukla's officious ways reached us in Poona one after the other. He had called all the senior Hindi film producers and threatened them, saying, 'If you fall in line with what the government is saying, all will be well. Or else ... ' Shyam Benegal described to me how they had all listened meekly.

My friend Vinod Doshi, who was managing director of Walchand Hirachand, received a call from Shukla's office. Vinod immediately put the phone on speaker so that his colleagues could hear what the minister had to say. Without any preliminaries, Shukla stated that he was coming to Bombay and wanted to know if Vinod Doshi had made arrangements regarding some girl they had previously spoken about. Vinod realized at once that the minister had wanted to speak not to him, but to the film producer Vinod Doshi. He turned off the speaker, and even as he said, 'Sir, this is the office of Walchand Hirachand,' Shukla's voice vanished from the line.

I, too, received a phone call from Delhi. The broadcast media in the West had been severely critical of Indira Gandhi's authoritarian Emergency, and India's image had been tarnished internationally. This had angered and hurt Shukla (and Indira Gandhi and Sanjay). Now, the government of India wanted to counter that view by making documentaries about the injustices prevalent in Western societies – poverty, the inhuman treatment of black people, and so on. The ministry was calling to seek my advice on who could be entrusted with the making of these films. I was immediately alarmed by this scheme, and said I would go to Delhi and personally express my views on the matter. I left at once. There, the joint secretary S.K. Khanna took me to meet the minister. One of the officials gathered around the minister was the director general of Doordarshan, P.V. Krishnamoorthy.

Shukla's manner radiated arrogance. He was light-skinned, with the sharp, delicate features agreeable to the upper classes. He had a deep voice, and eyes that seemed half-closed in a well-practised show of authority. He spoke in a slow, stately cadence, using the movement of his eyes to underline his words. 'What is it, Girish?' he said. 'You seem to have some objection to our plan.'

I explained my thinking to him in detail. The entire world knew that there was wretched, widespread poverty in India, that there were deep injustices in the way our society treated Dalits, Adivasis and women. If, instead of using our resources to address these concerns, we invested in films pointing out the deficiencies of the West, we were sure to become a laughing stock. And then, who would show these documentaries? Who would see them?

'So, your opinion is that we sit here with our arms folded and not do anything?' Shukla asked sarcastically.

I had spoken to Shyam Benegal in Bombay before leaving for Delhi, and he had given me a suitable idea. Economically advanced Western societies, in the name of progress, had been making indiscriminate use of the earth's natural resources. While the world's poorer countries were struggling for food, water and electricity, affluent Western countries were squandering finite resources such as petrol, coal and water on needless luxuries.

This view is commonly held today, and Western societies have accepted their role in destroying the environment. But in the 1970s, there was not much discussion around the subject. The West behaved imperiously, as if the world's energy resources were meant exclusively for their enjoyment.

If documentary films were made around these subjects, they could find a viewership across Asia, Africa and South America. Further, I said, we could put forth these arguments without looking like we had an inferiority complex.

Shukla stared at me for a while, sucking at his protruding front teeth with his lower lip. 'All right,' he said. 'But who can make these films?' I mentioned four or five names. 'Fine. We will inform them,' he said. With that, our meeting ended.

I had already been considering leaving the job, and the meeting with Shukla helped me make up my mind.

My second year's contract was due to end on 31 December. I wrote to Burney informing him that I did not want to continue for a third year. He phoned asking me to stay on, but there was nothing further that either of us could say. Though word had spread that I might leave, I had not announced it. On New Year's Eve, I was at a party at the house of Jayoo and Nachiket Patwardhan, friends who lived near the institute. That was when I broke the news to them, and to Bhaskar Chandavarkar and his wife Meena.

I relinquished my position the next morning.

Another Kannadiga, N.V.K. Murthy, was appointed director. By then, Shyam Benegal had asked me to play a part in his *Manthan* and I was to leave immediately for Rajkot. Murthy had agreed that my parents could continue to live in the director's bungalow with him until I returned from Rajkot. This was convenient for Murthy, too, since his family was still in Bombay.

I returned to Poona in the second week of March. I stepped out into the garden at four in the morning to say goodbye to my beloved institute's campus and looked up. I can still see the beauty of the constellation Scorpio sprawled across the sky.

FRIENDS

It was not by chance that I spent my last moments as director of FTII in the company of the Patwardhan and Chandavarkar couples. Their affection, intelligence, perceptiveness, humour and wide-ranging interests considerably enlivened my two years in Poona.

I had known Bhaskar since I was sixteen. We were distantly related, even. While making *Vamsha Vriksha*, just as I had asked Sharief and Ramachandra from the institute to do the cinematography, and Aruna–Vikas the editing, I had invited Bhaskar to compose music for the film. While his music for the film was excellent, his true triumph as a composer of film music was with *Ondanondu Kaladalli.* Satyajit Ray saw the film and said, 'Tell Bhaskar his music is brilliant. There is not a single note that is out of place.' But that came later, in 1977, after I had left the institute.

Bhaskar gained renown in the Indian theatre world when he composed the music for Tendulkar's play *Ghashiram Kotwal.* He made use of Maharashtra's tradition of devotional music while depicting skulduggery and intrigue in Poona's eighteenth-century durbar. Rather than simply inserting songs into a play, he made *Ghashiram Kotwal* his own, so much so that Tendulkar never wrote a musical after that.

When I came to Poona, *Ghashiram Kotwal* was mired in controversy. Jabbar Patel had originally directed it for a group called the Progressive Dramatic Association (PDA). After a few shows, there was sharp criticism that the play amounted to character assassination of Nana Phadnavis, an important historical figure in Maharashtra, and the PDA's Bhalbha Kelkar rescinded the sponsorship. The cast of the play, mostly students from the medical college, started a new organization called Theatre Academy to continue performing the play, but they had trouble finding a venue because of the controversy. This was when Mohan Agashe came to me and asked if a couple of performances could be staged at FTII's auditorium. And so, even if it was behind the scenes, I had a role in a play as extraordinary as *Ghashiram Kotwal.* My students, who had been content to stay on campus and had, until then, no exposure to Marathi theatre, were stunned when they watched the production. The play's main song, '*Shri Ganaraya Nartana Kari*', became the institute's Holi song that year.

Karanth saw *Ghashiram Kotwal* in Poona when he came to visit me. He was captivated by the way actors were positioned on stage as screens that could open and close, and even more so by the clever use of devotional music to comment on political violence. He went to Bangalore and used these ideas wholesale in his production *Sattavara Neralu.* But after *Sattavara Neralu* became successful, he never admitted that it was inspired by *Ghashiram Kotwal,* not even in private! But then, Vijay Tendulkar never admitted either that *Ghashiram Kotwal* was inspired by Satyadev Dubey's production of my

Hayavadana. I suppose we could say that this silent indebtedness between Kannada and Marathi had come full circle.

Jayoo and Nachiket Patwardhan were architects by profession and had a highly evolved sense of visual aesthetics which they were keen to use in new ventures. As a result, when Mani Kaul made a film of *Ghashiram Kotwal*, he brought them on board as art directors. Later, they were part of my film *Utsav*, in which they recreated an ancient Indian civilization. To my mind, their work on the project was a triumph of art direction unsurpassed in any other film.

When I spent evenings with these two couples, we might have a serious discussion or a light-hearted conversation or immerse ourselves in poetry, but it all amounted to a creative critique of the culture surrounding us.

Another person entered my life during my second year in Poona. This was Jaya Chakravarthy, Hema Malini's mother. When she sent for me the first time, from a five-star hotel, she said it was only to ask if I was interested in playing the lead role in the film *Swami*, which she was producing. But when repeated invitations followed, I began to suspect she was looking for a groom for her daughter Hema Malini.

In our film industry, it is usually girls between the ages of sixteen and twenty-seven who are cast as heroines. The heroes they are paired with are older men around thirty-five, who are sexually experienced and often married. The process of shooting a film invariably involves spending extended periods in each other's company, travelling together, and staying in distant, beautiful locations. There is singing, dancing and physical contact, and it is hardly surprising that all this can lead to a relationship. And if it isn't the hero, it is an older director. All in all, young women get emotionally involved with married men and find themselves trapped. It becomes difficult for them to find a man involved with films who is as successful as them, and it is often more convenient to look for men who have made a name for themselves outside the industry.

Hema Malini was the most successful star of that era, and the press routinely called her India's most desired woman. Dharmendra was married.

Even if his wife did not object to his relationship with Hema, his own parents and siblings would understandably kick up a fuss if there was any talk of marriage. Because crores of wealth would be at stake. But this might not have been a problem in Hema's case since she was wealthy too.

Eventually, I started being invited to Hema's house for meals. Her two brothers began to meet me. After the spectacular success of *Swami*, Jaya Chakravarthy began work on the film *Ratnadeep* and paired Hema with me in it. One evening, when we were shooting in Khajuraho, Hema asked me to accompany her on a walk and asked the important question. She said, 'The press is saying we are going to get married. How do you feel about the idea?' I said, 'Thanks. Look, I don't give any importance to what the press says. My reason for saying no is that I am engaged to someone in the United States.'

This was a half-truth. While I had already asked Saraswathy to marry me, she had not yet accepted. But even if Saraswathy had not been on the horizon, it was impossible for me to think of marrying Hema. Maybe it is sufficient to give just one reason for this. I had once asked Hema, 'Why didn't you ever act in Tamil films in Madras?' She had said, 'Oh, the people there are so black!' and giggled.

MARRIAGE

On 1 January 1976, I left Poona and came to Bangalore. I checked into the Cauvery Hotel on Cunningham Road, where Saraswathy, who had come from Kodagu was already staying. I asked her, 'Will you marry me?'

It had been ten years since we had first met. But she had been working in the United States, I had been preoccupied in India with all sorts of things, and we had never brought up the subject of marriage. I didn't stop with just the question. I came clean and told her, 'I have absolutely no income. All I have done so far are art films and two years of government service. You have been a doctor in the US. You must have earned quite a lot.' She laughed and said, 'I've spent everything I have earned on travel, on living a life of my own. Beyond my pension, I too have nothing for the future.' We realized just how financially secure our proposed married life was.

'You have made me wait ten years,' she said. There was nothing to do except nod in agreement. 'I need some time to think about marriage. Are you willing to wait until I come to a decision?' she asked. I agreed to that too.

From there, Saraswathy went to Madras and returned to the United States. I went to Rajkot, where Smita Patil and Naseeruddin Shah were waiting to shoot for *Manthan*. The film was a success. The same year, *Swami*, produced by Jaya Chakravarthy, astonished the film world and proved a triumph both at the box office and in the eyes of critics.

Even if I wasn't a star in Hindi cinema, I knew I could be a successful actor at least. The trouble was that I hadn't the slightest interest in acting. What I really wanted with a passion was to be a director like Satyajit Ray. So I turned my back on Bombay. I directed with B.V. Karanth the bilingual film, *Tabbaliyu Neenade Magane/Godhuli*. On my own, I directed *Ondanondu Kaludalli*. But there was no possibility of any sort of stable income from films like these. I began to worry that if I did not somehow manage to save some money, I would be in serious trouble. I once again turned my attention towards Bombay.

I was forty-two. My question to Saraswathy had remained unanswered for four years. A letter from New York arrived with her answer: 'Yes, I will marry you.'

Aayi had been a child widow, and it was because of the Arya Samaj that she had been able to marry again. She wanted me to have an Arya Samaj wedding too. Sarawathy's mother was a Parsi, a fire worshipper, and she too approved of a ceremony conducted without any idols, in front of a sacred fire. We decided on an Arya Samaj wedding.

Perhaps the priest was enthused by Shashi Kapoor and the other well-known figures present, for he showed no signs of finishing with the ceremonies even after the guests had finished eating, and both our eyes were swollen and burning from the smoke. 'Can't you hurry up?' I pleaded with him. He chastened me: 'Do you think we are playing a game here?' And so, fourteen years after we first met and expressed an interest in each other, Saraswathy and I were finally married.

Saras and I with our mothers at our wedding

EPILOGUE

Ardhakathanaka, or Half the Tale

In 1641, a Jain merchant from Agra named Banarasidas wrote *Ardhakathanaka* in Braj Bhasha. It is perhaps the first known autobiography in Indian literature (even if it happens to be written in the third person). In it, Banarasidas records the political, social and religious occurrences of his time, and writes with surprising frankness about his personal life. We learn that he was cheated by a sanyasi who sold him a mantra that was supposed to give him a dinar coin every day. That he fainted and injured his head by falling down the stairs when he heard of emperor Akbar's death; and then, when it looked like lawlessness would take over, that he wore torn clothes and walked around pretending to be a tramp. He admits to contracting a venereal disease from going to prostitutes. And so on.

There's an intriguing reason for his naming the book *Ardhakathanaka*. A Jain belief has the human lifespan as a hundred and ten years, and Banarasidas was half that age when he wrote his autobiography: fifty-five. Had I not been so taken by Bendre's poetry, I could very well have titled this book *Ardhakathanaka*, but for a reason different from Banarasidas's: it covers about half my life. But as it stands, this book gets its Kannada title – *Aadaadta Aayushya* – from a line in one of Bendre's poems: *Nodnodta dinamaana, aadaadta aayushya* (The days go by in the blink of an eye, this lifetime at play). I don't know if there will be a book about the second half of my life, but if there is, perhaps I could call it *Nodnodta Dinamaana*!

At home with Radha (Shalmali), Saras and Raghu

AFTERWORD

When our father and mother married, they each knew five languages, but the only one in common was English. This became a family legend. Ten years later, we would count out these languages on two hands: Konkani, Kannada, Marathi, Hindi, English; then English, Malayalam, Tamil, Gujarati and Kodava takk; with the two 'English' thumbs overlapping. It was a cultural diagram of the household, in which all those languages were heard and spoken, but only one held it all together.

Appa found his way to English through love of its poetry and plays. What struck us later in our lives – as we tried to make the reverse journey, and again while we read *This Life at Play* – is just what a distance he had covered.

He was a child in the 1940s, raised in a world without electricity yet full of cultural transmission. He liked to talk about that during power-cuts at home, in the nineties, and shares it again in this memoir: his nostalgia for 'the many shades of darkness' after every sundown, and for the 'abundance of stories' that emerged in those true nights. It doesn't seem like a coincidence that those two elements of his childhood, the darkness and the storytelling, evoke a theatre hall – the place he loved most through his life.

Even so, his creative journey was linked to the electrification of Indian culture and entertainment. The wind under the wings of his exceptional career was always being the right age, in the right place, when a new industry lit up: modern theatre, then independent cinema, then television.

More than that journey, though, we think of him growing up in a world immersed in old ways, yet reaching the threshold of the 2020s as never less than a progressive, and often a happy radical.

Like others in his generation, his work unearthed and revived what felt modern in traditional sources – strands of egalitarianism and feminism, themes of psychology, sex and taboo. They put all that in languages that regular Indians spoke at home. But Appa seemed ahead of many of his contemporaries, and quite in sync with ours, in how he wrote women: interested in their desires over their desirability; their suppressed power rather than their piteous condition. How he related to actual women – friends and colleagues – was nicely observed by the architect Nina Bopiah, who said, 'He was a man who liked women, I think. As opposed to a man who loved them.'

He was also a man who liked to fight the good fight, as opposed to a man who loved to. His interest in politics never rivalled his devotion to art and language, but in his later years, he did appear at protests as often as promos. He sat with Dalit students to defend eating beef, and with queer folks to demand the decriminalization of their lives. He spoke up for Taslima Nasreen, as well as for M.F. Husain. He would not decline a request from someone like Aruna Roy, even if it meant dragging his family across Freedom Park on a rainy day to encourage a few dozen women sitting in the drizzle to demand a universal pension.

In 2015, Appa stood with Gauri Lankesh in vigil when M.M. Kalburgi was killed; two years later, he stood with others when Gauri Lankesh was killed.

One of the last public events he went to was at the Town Hall in September 2018, on the anniversary of Gauri's assassination. A lot had happened in the preceding months, including the arrest – on bewildering grounds – of a slate of activists and scholars, all summarily denounced as 'Urban Naxals'.

At the time, Appa struggled to walk more than a few metres at once, even with an oxygen machine ('snarled up in cannulas like Laocoön,' he said). On the inside stairs up to the auditorium level, he seemed almost ready to faint, swaying and hanging on to the banister with both hands. But he finished the climb and made his entrance – into a hall packed to the rafters – with a placard around his neck declaring 'Me too Urban Naxal'.

His refusal to compromise with any lumpen politics meant he was frequently at risk of physical attack. In the early 1990s, stones crashed through the windows of our living room in Jayanagar, spraying glass where Radha was doing her homework. In 2018, after Gauri's murder, the police announced that his name was first on a list they recovered from the suspected assassins. By the end, a theme of our parents' lives was the police commissioner's effort to post armed constables at their gate and our parents' effort to get rid of them.

So, for one generation he was a prodigy, for another a heart-throb, for a third, a part of their intellectual upbringing, beamed into homes on *Turning Point*. For even younger Indians, he may be remembered as an anchor against a bleak tide pulling at their country for the past decade. As one Gen-Z reader described him: 'Part of India's intellectual legion, that guards its boundaries of dialogue and peace and narrative.'

Yet that story begins earlier, if not early enough to figure in *This Life at Play*. Like most Indians, he watched with disgust the rath yatra of 1992, the demolition of the Babri Masjid, and the bloodshed that followed. After that, his most personal cause was to stop the poisoning of the well of secular coexistence. On 15 August 1993, he went to Ayodhya. There, he played master of ceremonies for over a hundred artists, including Sitara Devi and Kelucharan Mohapatra, as they joined in a night-long performance of music and dance on the Ram ki Paidi ghats, reclaiming the city from the vandals. He went on fighting communal fires wherever they were lit, as at the shrine of Baba Budangiri, with his fellow travellers in Kannada letters, including U.R. Ananthamurthy.

At the base of his attitude was a simple lack of insecurity: about his standing as an artist, a Kannada writer, an Indian or a Hindu. He knew that none of the men who denounced him could ever match his authority on national culture or heritage, or his record as their steward. He put that unassailable position to use in two ways: to push creative and imaginative boundaries; and to lend courage to others to defy hate and ignorance.

Sanskrit, for instance, deserved to be counted as a sixth finger on our hands. He learnt it from his mother, studied it in college, adapted from and then lectured on Sanskrit drama. One of his favourite boasts (and he did know how to boast) was that he had taken the initiative to save

Kutiyattam, an ancient form of dance-drama that uses Sanskrit. The only book he had ever insisted that we read – putting copies in our hands – was the Mahabharata. Our copies were in English, but of course he had read the original Vyasa.

Yet he held oral traditions and folk styles in equal esteem, and would never subsume them in any idealized, classical legacy springing from the *Natyashastra* or the *Abhinaya Darpana*. He was also never afraid of Western literature or his debt to it: to Auden and Anouilh, but also Agatha Christie and *The Wind in the Willows*.

His life seems to testify on behalf of that progressive era in India: that its outlook never stemmed from weakened roots (as they would now have you believe), but from having roots in abundance. They were deep enough that he could always hold his ground, but he could pull them up enough to move to meet the world.

It is a loss that there won't be a second part to these memoirs, to cover his years in the movies, from *Manthan* to *Kadhalan* and *Ek Tha Tiger*, and his struggle to balance those heady demands with time and space to write. (He did that, memorably, with a Fulbright residency in Chicago, in 1986. From that year, close to scholars like C.M. Naim and mentors like A.K. Ramanujan, emerged his most beautiful play, *Naga-Mandala*.)

It was the first half of his life he needed to narrate, since it happened further from the limelight. After a point, he said, 'it's just one award ceremony after another', and nobody should have to read about that.

We were strangers to his later work in the cinema, perhaps because he often was himself. He never brought it home, the way he did with the stage, and rarely watched the blockbusters he was in. One of the committed routines of his life was keeping a diary (he walked in the early morning, napped in the afternoon, drank whisky in the evenings – and wrote a diary, every day of every year, with a green rollerball Pentel). In his diary, he would record the name of every play he watched, with comments, whether it was *Jerusalem* on London's West End or a company natak revival at Ranga Shankara. On days when he was on film sets, there is sometimes just one word: 'Shooting'. What he liked about being on set, he said, was that all the waiting gave you time to read.

At home, the company he enjoyed most was of writers, translators and theatre folk. Over time, his admiration became focused on scholars and poets – Ramanujan, being both, received the most of it until the end. He never held back his praise for Sheldon Pollock and Romila Thapar, or friends like Gopalkrishna Gandhi and Ramachandra Guha. *This Life at Play* reflects how his regard was greatest for anyone he considered a teacher – whether it was V.K. Gokak or Akira Kurosawa; or Richard Eaton, a historian at the University of Arizona, a man he had never met but to whom he dedicated his final play (along with Krishna Kolhar Kulkarni of Bijapur).

As for his children, he let us become our own people. For some years, we blamed that lenience for the fact that we weren't more literate in Kannada, or learned in the shastras, or at least proper celebrity star kids in Bombay. To the world he could seem, as one message after his death put it, 'like a fruit-laden tree. Always giving. Always growing.' To us it sometimes seemed like being a father, in addition to being a towering intellectual and a celebrity actor, might be one role too many.

As we grew up, and as the pace of his life changed, so did our understanding. In 2012, when Raghu moved back to Bengaluru for a few years, he and Appa discovered they both wanted to write about the city. They actually represented the two halves of the city quite neatly: Appa its genteel and cultured world in Kannada, Raghu its rapid and well-capitalized life in English. They could guide each other across that line, and did.

When Appa finished his play *Boiled Beans on Toast*, he shifted quietly out of his office so his son could borrow it more often. Soon, Appa's laptop was settled in the cluttered little hall where we hung up the washing. Sitting at his desk, Raghu began to write his own book.

Radha got to watch him step into the role of a gracious and welcoming father-in-law (with a whisky always on offer), and later, a sometimes baffled but always caring grandfather. He shared with his grandsons his love of Hindu mythology, delighted them with hand-shadow puppets made over candlelight, and enjoyed their pride each time his recorded voice at Ranga Shankara announced that a show was beginning.

In the two years since his death in June 2019, the greying figure he cut in his last months has retreated – and the strong, smiling, vital person he had been is stepping back up. Here he is, returning from his morning walk, neck perspiring, with the sticky smell of filter coffee from the nearby darshini. Here he is, in his spot on the sofa, hand around a glass, gently bubbling with history, philosophy, folk tale and song – for the benefit of anyone who was ready to listen. Here he is, a large, deep-breathing body in the hushed auditorium, as the lights go down to darkness and stories come to life.

– Raghu and Radha Karnad

TRANSLATOR'S NOTE

Girish Karnad called me in May 2019 to ask if I could assist him in translating his memoirs. He explained that he usually translated his writing himself, and had even started work on the memoirs, but his health did not allow him to give it the time it needed. So, if I agreed to translate the remaining portion of the book, he could edit it for an English readership and prepare it for publication. It was important that this be done quickly because he was ill and did not know how much longer he would live.

Our few phone conversations at the time served as some introduction to how Girish approached his memoirs. I hadn't read the book then, but I remembered it had created some excitement in the Kannada media when it first came out. When I mentioned this to him, he said, sounding quite pleased with himself, 'Yes, that is because I say the things that others don't say.' When I told him that I didn't know if my Kannada was up to the task, he reassured me, explaining that he had made sure to write the book in simple Kannada because he wanted it read as widely as possible.

I had just begun work on the translation when I heard that he had died.

This book might have been considerably different had Girish put it together himself. He had scrawled a note on the front page of the Kannada copy he sent me saying he was considering leaving out around sixty pages but had not reached a decision yet. He didn't say which pages, but I'd guess he was looking at the two chapters around the making of the Kannada films *Samskara*, *Vamsha Vriksha* and *Kaadu*. While many non-Kannada-speaking readers may not have heard of these films, the chapters feel valuable in their own right as detailed and forthright accounts of the film-making process. They also evoke a vigorous cultural milieu born of the jostling of writers, playwrights, theatre-persons, film-makers and journalists, and since these early experiences are bound to have been formative, they feel relevant to the English book. Girish might also have left out portions of the book that explain what is potentially unfamiliar to Kannada readers. Some of these parts may not feel strictly necessary to the English text, but are still interesting because they allow us a window into what Girish thought he had to explain to Kannada readers and how he went about it. An affectionate introduction to the institution of the British pub by Girish Karnad, for instance, is worth retaining simply because it exists.

So, *This Life at Play* comes as a translation of the Kannada book *Aadaadta Aayushya* with only minor deviations. The first three chapters and portions of the fourth and tenth appear in Girish's translation from drafts found on his laptop. They largely stick to the Kannada text but are not always word-to-word translations. The remaining portions of the Kannada book are in my translation, with some editorial inputs from the publisher and Girish's family. At some point, Girish had also started to write, in English, about the second half of his life. Two short episodes from this material have been interpolated in the book: Girish's role in preserving Kutiyattam, a source of great satisfaction to him; and, since it rounds out his experiences with London theatre, the story of the woman who let him have what should have been her ticket to *Guys and Dolls*.

Girish embarked on writing his Kannada memoirs with two chapters that appeared in the literary journal *Desha Kaala*. He then serialized subsequent portions for the newspaper *Prajavani*, and after adding more material, published the book *Aadaadta Aayushya* in 2011. Perhaps these origins show in the English book too, with some parts of his life recounted with longer narrative arcs and some in short, themed sections.

Non-fiction poses its own challenges when it comes to translation. In places I found that a description in Kannada that might be adequate for a reader could still lack sufficient information to be translated with confidence. In the case of fiction, such ambiguities can be worked into a sort of internal consistency, but with non-fiction, there is the external world to reckon with. I tried to consult other sources wherever possible. For example, several descriptions of scenes and settings in the *Samskara* chapter rely on the Kannada text read alongside watching the film and a documentary on its making. This is also the only place in the book I felt it necessary to add some text for the English reader's benefit: a plot summary of the novel *Samskara* (based in part on what Girish has said about the novel elsewhere). There was also the problem of what to do with mis-recollected facts in the Kannada book, given that it is a memoir. ('My memory refuses to adjust to her facts,' Girish writes, about his mother correcting him that there was only one tiger on a road where his childhood memory placed four or five.) This book's editor Rahul Soni and I agreed that we would fact-check objectively verifiable details – when the Second World War started for instance, or who directed the musical *Canterbury Tales* – and ignore the impressionistic, such as a somewhat idiosyncratic recollection of Strindberg's play *Miss Julie.*

Girish's account of his life often uses made-up dialogue to move a story along, a not uncommon device in Indian languages. My first instinct was to convert much of this to reported speech in English, but then I said to myself, 'If a playwright can't tell his story using dialogue, then who can?' and let it be. Other aspects of this book, too, made it feel like a playwright's memoir: it is peopled by clearly drawn characters, whose attributes lead to various situations between them. It is almost as if, as other playwrights have had occasion to observe, the world is a stage on which people must play their parts.

Girish's family – Saras, Radha and Raghu – were involved with this book at every stage, from hunting for files on his laptop to answering my queries to reading drafts and offering suggestions. Our agent, Shruti Debi, adeptly handled the publishing side of the project, allowing me to focus on the translation. Given the material in this book, I consider myself fortunate to have worked on it with the editor Rahul Soni, who is a translator himself and familiar with the Indian cultural context. Gopalkrishna Gandhi, Arshia Sattar, K.M. Chaitanya and Niranjani Iyer were all kind enough to give their comments after reading proof copies. Ramachandra Guha, who years ago nudged Girish to write his Kannada memoirs, made helpful suggestions and gamely tried to track down the English version of an André Béteille quote in the book. I occasionally referred to Uma Kulkarni's Marathi translation of the Kannada book when I wanted another opinion. M.K. Shankar and Muralidhara Khajane both read proof copies and generously made themselves available for long discussions. I am deeply grateful to them all.

– Srinath Perur

Girish Karnad (1938–2019) was a playwright, actor and director. His notable plays include, among others, *Yayati, Tughlaq, Hayavadana, Naga-Mandala* and *The Dreams of Tipu Sultan*. He worked in films and in TV across various languages – Kannada, Hindi, Tamil, Telugu, Malayalam, English and Assamese – and in a number of capacities, including as actor, screenwriter and director. He served as director of the Film and Television Institute of India (1974–75), chairman of the Sangeet Natak Akademi (1988–93), and director of the Nehru Centre, London (2000–3). His work brought him numerous honours, including multiple National Film Awards and Filmfare Awards, the Kalidas Samman, the Sangeet Natak Akademi Award, the Padma Shri, the Padma Bhushan and the Jnanpith Award.

Srinath Perur is the author of *If It's Monday, It Must Be Madurai* (2013) and the translator of Vivek Shanbhag's *Ghachar Ghochar* (2015).